VOLUME 3

BEYOND THE INNOCENCE OF CHILDHOOD:

Helping Children and Adolescents Cope with Death and Bereavement

David W. Adams, M.S.W., C.S.W.
McMaster University
and
Eleanor J. Deveau, R.N., B.Sc.N.
McMaster University

Death, Value and Meaning Series
Series Editor: John D. Morgan

Baywood Publishing Company, Inc.
AMITYVILLE, NEW YORK

Library of Congress Catalog Number: 95-20407
ISBN: 0-89503-130-2 (Cloth)

Library of Congress Cataloging-in-Publication Data

Adams, David Walter, 1942-
    Helping children and adolescents cope with death and bereavement /
David W. Adams and Eleanor J. Deveau.
        p.   cm. - - (Beyond the innocence of childhood ; v. 3)
    Includes bibliographical references and index.
    ISBN 0-89503-130-2 (cloth)
    1. Bereavement in children.   2. Bereavement in adolescence.
3. Grief in children.   4. Grief in adolescence.   5. Children-
-Counseling of.   6. Teenagers- -Counseling of.   I. Deveau, Eleanor
J.   II. Title.   III. Series : Adams, David Walter, 1942-. Beyond the
innocence of childhood ; v. 3.
BF723.D3A33 1995 vol. 3
155.9'37'083 s- -dc20
[155.9'37'083]   95-20407
                                                                              CIP

DEDICATION

To Ellie's brother, **Edward Anthony Gzik,** *who will always be remembered for his encouragement, support, friendship, and profound belief and pride in close family ties.*

Foreword

The confrontation of the concepts of *children* and *death* challenges us. Our basic Western orientation is that we live in a neat predictable world, a universe governed by God for our benefit. However, the fact that children must lose to death those upon whom they rely for physical and emotional support brings this view of the world into question. The question that this volume asks, the third in the *Beyond the Innocence of Childhood* series, is how can bereaved children and adolescents be supported so that they will grow psychologically and spiritually as a result of their experience?

The death attitude system most prevalent in North America today does not provide our children with the tools they need at the time of a death. The dominant philosophy pictured in movies and on television is that life is unremittant joy. The reality is different, and when death occurs, we and children of all ages believe that we have been cheated because life has not fulfilled its promises. We are not taught that each time we say "goodbye," it could very well be the last time.

Children of today are in a radically disjointed perspective. On the one hand they are conscious of violence in the home, on the streets, and in the school, yet they are told that "these are the best years of their lives." They are cautioned about drinking, about AIDS, about drugs, but they are offered little in the way of the emotional, social, and spiritual support that is a necessary basis to resist short-cuts in life. Understanding the normalcy and the reality of death is the first step in acceptance and resolution. This understanding can be rooted in a religious perspective or it can come from literature or art.

It is an honor to be invited to write a foreword to the third volume of Professor David Adams and Mrs. Eleanor Deveau's *Beyond the Innocence of Childhood: Helping Children and Adolescents Cope with Death and Bereavement*. The editors and contributors constitute a "who's who" of teachers, researchers, and clinicians who care for bereaved children and adolescents. There could be no single person or group more qualified to bring together a number of experts than Professor Adams and Mrs. Deveau. I believe that this volume will be most valuable in teaching both the general public and the professional about *effective* methodologies to be used with bereaved children and adolescents.

John D. Morgan, Ph.D.

Acknowledgments

We owe a debt of gratitude to the contributing authors for sharing their time, effort, and expertise in producing the chapters which appear in the three volumes of this book.

We are indebted to Dr. J. D. (Jack) Morgan who provided support and encouragement at each phase of the development of this project and to Stuart Cohen, President of Baywood Publishing Company and his staff for making this publication a reality.

A special thank you is extended to Dr. Phyllis Blumberg, Professor, Family Medicine and Director, Geriatric Educational Development Unit, Educational Centre for Aging and Health, Faculty of Health Sciences, McMaster University, for her encouragement, understanding, and patience. Our appreciation is extended to R. E. (Ted) Capstick, Chair, Board of Trustees, Greater Hamilton Employee Assistance Consortium and Vice President, Human Resources, Chedoke-McMaster Hospitals; Dr. Nick Kates, Past Chair, Department of Psychiatry, Faculty of Health Sciences, McMaster University; and Dr. Michael Stevens, Senior Staff Specialist and Head, Oncology Unit, Royal Alexandra Hospital for Children, Camperdown NSW, Australia, for their encouragement and continuing support.

We wish to thank J. Richard Small, M.S.W., C.S.W. for his suggestions and advice; Trudy Leask for typing parts of the manuscripts and helping to communicate with the authors; and Lois Wyndam and her staff at Chedoke-McMaster Hospital Library for their bibliographical assistance.

Finally, we are most grateful to our spouses, J. Paul Deveau and M. Anne Adams, for their **patience**, advice, and assistance. With continual support, understanding, and encouragement from Paul, Anne, and our children we were able to immerse ourselves in the thousands of pages of manuscripts and complete a challenging, interesting and, at times, monumental task!

vii

Table of Contents

Introduction

The first volume of this series, *Beyond the Innocence of Childhood,* focuses on how children and adolescents acquire a mature understanding of death by addressing the following factors: communication, cognitive development, gender differences, life experiences, and parental perceptions and attitudes concerning death. Another chapter considers children and adolescents' artwork as a medium of expression concerning their understanding of death at different ages.

The second part of Volume 1 moves on to examine many of the influences in today's society that impact on children and adolescents' perceptions and attitudes toward death. Various authors address the following questions: What is the role of the media in popular culture? How does war influence children and adolescents' attitudes toward violence and death? Do young people throw "caution to the wind" in spite of the epidemic of AIDS? How does a culture influence the management of childhood cancer? Do children and adolescents' attendance at funerals, and participation in traditional death rituals, help to facilitate their understanding of death?

The first part of Volume 2 describes strategies which help children and adolescents cope with life-threatening illness and examines the needs of, and interventions required to help, suicidal teens. Individual chapters consider the therapeutic benefits of art, story, music, play, humor and laughter, and pets. Camps for children and teens with cancer or HIV/AIDS provide a different therapeutic option. Another chapter challenges professionals to consider how to help children and adolescents who are suffering with a life-threatening illness.

The second half of Volume 2 concentrates on the needs of dying children and their families. Factors are discussed and guidelines provided for palliative care in the home and hospital. One chapter offers a glimpse into the lives of dying teens while another chapter discusses the value of therapeutic imagery for dying children and adolescents. Should children and adolescents be told that they are dying? This is the critical question asked by the authors who explore truthtelling. Another author challenges caregivers to incorporate spirituality into their care of dying children. A description of the development of the first free-standing pediatric hospice in North

1

America followed by an annotated resource of storytelling and reading materials completes the second Volume.

VOLUME 3

This third and final volume of the *Beyond the Innocence of Childhood* series, takes us into the world of bereaved children and adolescents. Grief is as much an emotional necessity for children and adolescents as it is for adults. However, grief in childhood is very complex and is influenced by age, stage of development, cognitive ability, and any previous experiences with death. Children usually grieve in small amounts and their grief is often expressed through their behavior. If family members are in turmoil, children may feel too insecure to express their own feelings, ask questions, or voice any concerns. Consequently, they may postpone their mourning, not complete their tasks of grieving, and potentially develop serious problems as they mature. Over time, children need to revisit their grief—to unravel, rework, and consolidate their previous experiences with the death of someone close and then incorporate this new understanding of what the death means to them into their present level of cognitive development.

Adolescence is a time of many changes and transitions when teens struggle with parents and society's expectations, and strive for independence and the freedom to make their own choices and decisions. We must acknowledge the fact that the loss of a sibling, parent, or close friend may have profound effects on their developmental needs and their abilities to cope when they feel compromised or overwhelmed. A significant loss may threaten their self-image and generate fears associated with existential concerns about life beyond death.

Parental and family communication and behavior patterns, the amount of emotional support available, the child or adolescent's relationship with the person that died, and the nature of the death all impact on children and adolescents' adjustment to bereavement and their ability to mourn their loss and move on with their lives.

The following chapters stress the importance of providing a stable environment in which children and adolescents are not judged but are given time, space, love, and security that will allow them to work through their grief in their own way.

The nature and degree of children's involvement in the dying process of someone close will influence their grief reactions and impact on their ability to cope during bereavement. According to Therese Rando, considerable controversy exists concerning the meaning and role of anticipatory grief because it is "inappropriately conceptualized, inadequately understood, and often quite poorly facilitated." She examines this complex, multidimensional phenomenon and analyzes the experiences of children who are confronted with a parent who is dying. Rando delineates the difficulties that children encounter as disadvantaged grievers and emphasizes the need to include and involve them during the dying process. She provides treatment strategies and interventions to facilitate the healthy anticipatory grief of children.

Thomas Attig reminds us that respect for bereaved children and adolescents requires the understanding that they are vulnerable because of many limitations including: ability to cope, level of personal development, past experiences with bereavement, existing social circumstances, the relationship with the person who died, and the nature of the death. He emphasizes that death is a "choiceless event" but there are choices in how we respond to and help children cope with bereavement.

David Balk and Nancy Hogan define religion and address its role and value with respect to the severity and duration of adolescent grief and bereavement. They provide a comprehensive review of the literature, present findings from several research studies, and offer fruitful areas for further investigation. Balk and Hogan raise the possibility that bereaved adolescents may develop a deepening personal understanding of the meaning of human existence as a result of their experiences with death.

Siblings identify very closely with each other and often link their fate to one another. When a brother or sister dies, surviving siblings must deal with the loss of someone who has been a friend, playmate, competitor, confidant, and protector. Betty Davies, through a sibling's account of the death of her sister and the findings of several research projects, discusses the long-term effects and implications on adults who experienced the death of a brother or sister during childhood.

In Volume 2, several authors identified therapeutic techniques that provide seriously ill children and adolescents with avenues for the expression of difficult thoughts and feelings. Mary Anderson Miller examines narrative strands as another technique which may renew an understanding of latent bereavement. She suggests that adolescence precipitates a resurgence of grief which may provide opportunities for teens to further accommodate their loss. Recounting life stories may help adolescents re-establish a connection with the deceased, link past and present, and find new ways to examine and manage their grief.

AIDS has pervasive and devastating effects on all family members. Through a personal account, Ruth Rothbart Mayer sensitively describes a father and husband's gradual death from AIDS. Her account of the events leading to his death and the time after provide profound insight into the world of a young child and mother who must cope with the veil of secrecy, guilt, shame, and isolation that AIDS imposes on families.

Suicide in the family plunges children and adolescents into confusion, emotional upheaval, and pain that may last a lifetime. Through interviews with adults who had experienced the suicide of a family member or close friend, Sandra Elder draws out some of the intense feelings and recurrent themes identified by long-term survivors. Information is provided that contrasts differences in the grief process following suicide as opposed to other deaths.

Domestic violence provides another dimension that creates fear, anguish, and turmoil and results in a series of losses for children and adolescents. Barbara Zick describes domestic violence as an increasingly common and vicious cycle of behavior that places children and their protective parent at risk for physical injury and death. She addresses the long-term effects of exposure to such violence on the attitudes and behavior of children and adolescents.

Schools can play a critical role in helping children and adolescents adjust to the death of a friend, classmate, or staff member. Margaret Metzgar emphasizes the need for schools to be prepared for such a death. The theme of her chapter centers on the question: What do we do with the empty desk? She offers guidelines for talking about a death, describes the use of rituals to say goodbye, and discusses the value of commemoration and memorialization.

Support groups for bereaved children and adolescents provide an environment in which they may openly express their feelings of grief, receive support from others who are grieving, and recognize that they are not alone in their thoughts and feelings. The following three chapters address the needs of children from five years through adolescence.

Eileen Ormond and Heather Charbonneau alert us to the reality that "grief is a powerful journey through pain and healing." Their groups for five- to nine-year-old children are organized to follow the lead that the participants provide. A series of group activities enable children to validate their concerns, facilitate the expression of emotions, commemorate the death, and say "goodbye."

Ben Wolfe and Linda Senta reiterate the value of the group process but utilize a different approach to programs for nine- to thirteen-year-old children. The activities within these groups help youngsters use rational thinking and incorporate abstract thought processes that provide social support, validate their losses, and offer ways to express thoughts and feelings. Children work toward closure of their grief during this phase of development in preparation for further grief work during adolescence.

Catherine Johnson closes this section of Volume 3 with an overview of a different approach used in adolescent groups. These groups provide a safe place to express feelings, break down the barriers of denial that are common to adolescence, and facilitate healing and growth. She presents arguments to support the benefits of including participants from both sexes. Unlike other support groups, Johnson uses an open-ended approach and invites teens to bring their friends into the group.

CHAPTER 1

Anticipatory Grief and the Child Mourner*

Therese A. Rando

To the experienced caregiver, the opportunity for relatives to experience anticipatory grief around a loved one's dying is typically a "good news—bad news" event. The good news is the unparalleled potential that the period of anticipatory grief holds for promoting the ultimate postdeath adjustment of the survivor; the bad news is the incomparable poignancy and the conflicting demands of that same period. Most unfortunately, the phenomenon of anticipatory grief usually is inappropriately conceptualized, inadequately understood, and often quite poorly facilitated. As a consequence, all too frequently, the "good news" aspects are not realized sufficiently and the "bad news" parts are overemphasized. When the mourner happens to be a child, the already numerous problems of anticipatory grief tend to escalate. While it is difficult enough to convince adults that children need to mourn a loss that already has transpired, it can become almost impossible to persuade them to permit and encourage healthy mourning in anticipation of a death.

This chapter will attempt to build a bridge between the two areas of anticipatory grief and children—a bridge that is essential given the reality that children are confronted with the dying of family members, regardless of whether adults choose to recognize the fact, legitimize it,

*Some portions of this chapter have been adapted from the author's book, *Loss and Anticipatory Grief* [1, 10] and from the author's article, *Anticipatory Grief: The Term is a Misnomer but the Phenomenon Exists* (see Bibliography).

or help them with it. The chapter begins by examining the experience of anticipatory grief, taking as its basic premise that, while the term itself is a misnomer, the phenomenon definitely exists, and, in fact, incorporates a more complex and multidimensional set of processes than heretofore has been recognized. It then briefly looks at the demands inherent in the terminal illness experience and concludes by specifically addressing concerns pertinent to intervention with a child mourner contending with the dying of a parent.

THE IMPORTANCE OF ANTICIPATORY GRIEF

There is a compelling need to understand and completely appreciate the experience of anticipatory grief—its perspectives, processes, promises, and problems. The primary justification for this lies in the unique ability that anticipatory grief offers as an arena for primary prevention. In the field of bereavement, the focus of intervention is usually on assisting a survivor to cope with an event that already has happened, that is, a *fait accompli*. There is nothing that he/she can do to alter the situation, since the loved one already is deceased. As a result, treatment consists of assisting the individual to pick up the pieces after the fact and to cope with the altered life that remains. In contrast, in the area of anticipatory grief the caregiver has the golden opportunity to use primary prevention strategies and to make therapeutic interventions prior to the death that may facilitate appropriate grief work and mourning, and create a more positive postdeath bereavement for the survivor-to-be. It is well known that the experience of terminal illness—that period of time in which anticipatory grief occurs—has a profound influence on all postdeath bereavement. To the extent that healthy behaviors, interactions, and processes can be promoted during this time, the individual's postdeath mourning can be made relatively better than it would be if the experience lacked the therapeutic benefits of appropriate anticipatory mourning. The time of anticipatory grief offers the individual crucial therapeutic opportunity. Interventions made at this point can prevent the development of problems in mourning; later interventions can attempt only to remedy difficulties that already have occurred [1].

Part of the salutary aspects of anticipatory grief is that it presents the opportunity to minimize or erase the malignant consequences extant in sudden death bereavement which are known to complicate mourning. In sudden death, among other sequelae, the capacity to cope is diminished, the assumptive world is violently shattered, the loss does not make sense; there is no chance to say goodbye and finish unfinished business, profound issues of security and confidence in the world develop, emotional reactions are heightened, symptoms of acute grief and physical and emotional shock persist for a prolonged period of time, and a post-traumatic stress response is often provoked [2]. In optimum amounts of anticipatory grief, there are time and experiences which can obviate all of the aforementioned problems. These can facilitate therapeutic responses in each area; thus not only avoiding harm, but promoting a healthy experience as it pertains to each dimension.

THE CONTROVERSY ABOUT ANTICIPATORY GRIEF

There have been contradictory research findings about the adaptational value and positive effects on the postdeath grief and mourning experience of having some advanced warning and the opportunity to undergo moderate amounts of anticipatory grief prior to a death. There are a number of reasons why the research results have been so inconsistent. Chief among these is the erroneous practice of conceptually confusing forewarning of loss with anticipatory grief [3, 4]. Rando has reviewed the literature and delineated causes for the discrepancies in the writings and research devoted to anticipatory grief [1]. Suffice it to say, the study of the phenomenon has been riddled with invalid premises, confounding variables, a relative lack of precise definition, and frequently poor research designs, with serious methodological weaknesses and use of incomparable subject populations.

Several notable researchers have written that anticipatory grief is an impossibility [5-7]. It is important to realize that these thanatologists are not minimizing the critical value of a period of preparation; they do agree that forewarning of loss allows for certain kinds of anticipatory preparations that can be therapeutic. However, they also believe that anticipatory grief *per se* rarely happens, and they maintain that this is only proper.

Unfortunately, this view of anticipatory grief falls victim to at least three major misconceptions. The first derives from the fallacy that to legitimately be termed "grief," anticipatory grief must resemble postdeath grief in character and substance. The second derives from an overfocus on the ultimate loss of death, with a consequent disregard of, or at the very least an insufficient appreciation of, the other losses inherent in fatal diagnosis and terminal illness. The third major misinterpretation is that anticipatory grief necessarily involves a major decathexis or detachment from the dying individual during the dying process.

Some of the statements made by those who dismiss the concept of anticipatory grief are true. For instance, Silverman [6] and Weiss [7] are correct: A rehearsal is not the real thing. However, just because anticipatory grief is not exactly in character and substance like postdeath grief—which it never could be since the death has not yet transpired and different emotional realities and reactions prevail—does not mean it is not grief. Parkes and Weiss are equally correct: There rarely is the same acceptance and recovery witnessed in anticipatory grief as in postdeath grief [5]. Why should there be? Losses are still in the process of being experienced, so they cannot as yet be accommodated. These differences and the lack of accommodation, obviously precluded by the fact that hope still exists and the final, irreversible separation has not yet occurred, do not mean that grief is not taking place. In point of fact, some losses attendant to the terminal illness already may have been accommodated, even though the ultimate loss of the loved one through death has not been accepted. Additionally, Silverman [6], and Parkes and Weiss [5] are all correct in their shared observation that anticipation of loss frequently increases attachment. Yet, this does not obviate grief either, since anticipatory grief need not mean withdrawal from the dying loved one. Finally, Parkes and Weiss continue to be correct with their assertion that, as a result of omissions or commissions, thoughts, and feelings during the anticipatory grief period, the survivors-to-be are vulnerable to later self-accusation [5]. However, these are realities that are part and parcel of the anticipatory grief experience, illustrating some of its limitations and possible dangers. They are not reasons why anticipatory grief is either extremely rare or impossible. Actually, the term "anticipatory grief" is a misnomer. It is a misnomer, first, because "anticipatory" suggests that one is mourning solely for anticipated, as opposed to past and current, losses. Second, it is a misnomer because "grief" implies (to some) the necessity of (a) similar character and substance to postdeath grief, and (b) complete decathexis from the dying person.

The underlying reason for the significant discrepancies in thought about anticipatory grief essentially boils down to the failure to appreciate sufficiently the complexity of the phenomenon. Anticipatory grief is not a unitary concept that remains unaffected by person, place, time, and experience. Rather, it is multidimensional, defining itself across two perspectives (patient and family), three time foci (past, present, and future), and three classes of influencing variables (psychological, social, and physiological). For the purposes of the remainder of this chapter, the perspective taken is of a family member. Each of the three time foci is addressed below. The reader is referred to Rando for a delineation of each of the sixty-two influencing variables [1].

WHAT ANTICIPATORY GRIEF IS

A full comprehension of anticipatory grief demands an appreciation of the three time foci toward which it is directed during the terminal illness of a loved one. It is an error to conceive of anticipatory grief as exclusively focused on a loved one's ultimate loss through death. Indeed, the terminal illness experience is replete with a number of losses, each demanding its own grief and mourning. Thus, in contrast to the implications inherent in the term "anticipatory," which suggest that it is solely a future loss that is being mourned, there are, in fact, three time intervals toward which anticipatory grief addresses itself: past, present, and future. During the period of anticipatory grief, the grief that is experienced is actually stimulated by losses that have already occurred in the past and those that are currently occurring, as well as those that are yet to come. The following example will illustrate this point. It utilizes a scenario of adult anticipatory grief in order that the reader can more easily identify with the mourner and most effectively comprehend the concept. The discussion presumes a basically healthy relationship between the parties, an open awareness context [8], and open communication about the illness. To the extent that specific circumstances depart from that, extrapolations must be made from what is written here.

Even in the face of an ongoing terminal illness, there are losses— physical and psychosocial—that have already occurred, and which must be mourned. For example, in nursing her husband through his final bout with cancer, it is not uncommon for a wife to grieve for the vibrant and healthy man she has *already lost* to cancer and to mourn their altered relationship, lifestyle, and dreams for the future that will never be realized. It will not be unusual for her to remember the activities they shared when he was well; to recall how, in contrast to his current state, he was strong and independent; to grieve over the fact that so many limitations have been placed on their lives and interfered with their plans; and to mourn for all that has been taken away by the illness. Each of these losses is a *fait accompli*. This is what is meant by anticipatory grief entailing mourning over losses in the past. This past may be recent, as in the case of the altered lifestyle, or more distant, as in the lost opportunities that are regretted in light of the limited time left. These losses are considered past losses notwithstanding the fact that the subject content of the loss may pertain to the future, in terms of the hopes, expectations, dreams, and plans held for it. Whether or not these losses are grieved or even acknowledged is not the issue in this discussion. The issue is that even in the shadow of the ultimate loss of death, there are other losses that have already occurred that *ipso facto* ultimately necessitate grief and mourning.

In addition, this woman experiences conditions which stimulate grief in the present. She witnesses the *ongoing losses* of progressive debilitation, increasing dependence, continual uncertainty, decreasing control, and so forth. A fundamental part of her grief is grief for what is currently being lost and for the future that is being eroded. This is different from grief about what will happen in the future. Rather, it pertains to grief over what is slipping away from her right now, over the sense of having her loved one being taken from her, and over what the increasing awareness of her husband's impending death means at this very moment in time.

This woman also grieves for *losses yet to come*. Not only is her husband's ultimate death grieved, but also the losses that will arise before his death. This may entail grieving in advance for such things as the fact that she and her husband will not be able to take their annual vacation this year or that she knows he will lose his mobility and become bedridden. Such grieving is not limited exclusively to losses that happen prior to the death. It also may focus on those losses that will or might ensue in the future after the death, as a consequence of it: the loneliness, the insecurity, the social discomfort, the assaulted identity, the economic uncertainty, the lifestyle alterations, the fact that he will not be present to walk their daughter down the aisle on her wedding day, and so forth.

It is absolutely critical to recognize that a major component of anticipatory grief is this grieving of the absence of the loved one in the future. Although the true reality of this absence certainly cannot be realized completely until a death has occurred and the person is no longer available for interaction, it is possible to get small, but important, indications of what this will be like through extrapolation of experiences in the present illness that foreshadow the permanent absence in the future. During the illness, experiences such as the wife being forced to attend a social function alone, or the children having to accommodate to their father's absence from their award ceremonies, not only reinforce the present reality, but portend in a small way what the world will be like after the death. This experience of grief does not mean that there is not continued investment in the husband and father in the present—only that there are precursors of the ultimate loss that is drawing closer.

It is from this that one of the major misconceptions about anticipatory grief arises. Too many individuals erroneously believe that if a person is grieving someone's loss in the future this necessarily means that they are starting to separate from him/her in the present. This definitely is not required in anticipatory grief. There does not have to be detachment from the dying patient prior to death. Ideally, any decathexis that occurs in anticipatory grief is not from the loved one in the present. Indeed, there should be continued involvement with the person in the here and now. What detachment takes place should be from the image of that person as a living individual who will be physically present in the mourner's future after the death, a letting go of the ties the mourner has to the future regarding the loved one. Specifically, it entails the mourner starting to relinquish his/her emotional investment in the needs, hopes, feelings, thoughts, wishes, fantasies, dreams, assumptions, beliefs, and expectations regarding a future that would include the dying person as before. In other words, emotional energy gradually starts to be withdrawn or decathected from the notion of the dying person being available for interaction in the future, from the conception of the patient as a person with an earthly life beyond the terminal illness. Another way of looking at it is that the mourner's assumptive world must begin to be revised to incorporate the loved one's ultimate physical absence [2].

Premature detachment from one not yet dead—which has been a major concern of those who detract from anticipatory mourning—is a dramatic example of a component of the process of anticipatory grief that has been misdirected. Certainly, this has happened in far too many cases. Nevertheless, this is not necessary nor inevitable, and when such premature detachment has occurred it signals that healthy anticipatory grief has gone awry. Certainly, some decathexis needs to occur. However, it is not detachment from the actual person that is to be undertaken; but rather from the mourner's aforementioned ties to a long-term future with that person and for that person. The future can be grieved without relinquishing the present. Continued involvement with the dying person, and the goal of maximizing whatever living is possible, is not inconsistent with, nor precluded by, the experience of anticipatory grief.

A critically important task during all of the anticipatory grief experience is to balance the mutually contradictory demands of the process and to cope with the stress that their incongruence generates. There are several sets of competing demands in anticipatory grief. The first pertains to coping with the illness of the loved one and balancing this with paying attention to the ongoing needs of the family, for example, does the family member sit and watch television with the ill loved one or does he/she leave to attend the daughter's school play? The tug-of-war between attending to the needs of the dying and those of the survivors-to-be, which also includes the self, can cause significant stress, anxiety, guilt, depression, exhaustion, and so forth.

A second set of conflicts arises out of the inherently competing demands in the anticipatory grief situation which are occasioned by the discordant tasks of simultaneously holding on and letting go. Depending upon the point in the illness and the circumstances thereof, these pose numerous opposing needs, for example, balancing the loved one's continued need for autonomy with support for his/her increased dependency; struggling with not wanting to do anything to call attention to, or cause more losses for, the loved one with redistributing family roles and responsibilities to compensate for that loved one's decreased capabilities and having someone else function in his/her previous roles.

There are many such dilemmas encountered by the anticipatory griever. This is because essentially the mourner struggles with juggling the three courses of action toward which family members direct themselves when a loved one is dying [9]: 1) anticipatory grief and finishing unfinished business with the dying loved one; 2) accomplishing the first task while supporting the dying person and struggling to find ways to continue to live with him/her as fully as possible until the moment of death, and trying to give him/her as much control as feasible despite the ongoing process of relinquishing personal and familial roles and responsibilities; and 3) starting to reorganize the family in order to maintain its stability following the imbalance fostered by the loved one's illness, to insure the continued survival of other family members, and to commence the change process that must be completed following the death of the loved one—a process which inherently demands grieving for the death of the family unit as it has been known to all of the family members.

By definition, the mourner is pulled in opposing directions. In essence, he/she moves toward the dying patient, as a consequence of directing increased attention, energy, and behavior toward the patient during the illness. This often has the effect of moving the mourner closer to the patient. (The reader will note that this is precisely the point the previously noted researchers cited to prove that anticipatory grief *does not* occur.) At the same time, the status quo is maintained as ongoing involvement with the patient continues, with the mourner striving to preserve some sense of normalcy or continuity. In this regard, the mourner stays the same with the dying patient. Directly coinciding with this, in opposition, the mourner is starting to move away from the dying patient, in terms of beginning to decathect from the image of that patient as someone who will be present in the future, and from the assumptions, beliefs, expectations, hopes, dreams, needs and so forth for that patient and their relationship in the future.

Fortunately, these demands can be responded to in different ways, so that moving toward the patient can occur behaviorally and inter-personally. Moving away—in terms of detachment—can occur intra-psychically and not be evidenced socially through premature detach-ment from the loved one. Clearly, then, anticipatory grief is a conflictual and complex process in a time of significant stress. The following definition encompasses its inherent dimensions:

> Anticipatory grief is the phenomenon encompassing the processes of mourning, coping, interaction, planning, and psychosocial reor-ganization that are stimulated and begun in part in response to the awareness of the impending loss of a loved one and the recognition of associated losses in the past, present, and future . . . The truly therapeutic experience of anticipatory grief mandates a delicate balance among the mutually conflicting demands of simultaneously holding onto, letting go of, and drawing closer to the dying patient [1, p. 24].

It must be remembered that anticipatory grief takes time to unfold and develop. It is a process, not an all-or-nothing thing. It is a phenomenon influenced by a host of variables that must always be taken into consideration. In reviewing the processes of anticipatory grief delineated below, the reader will need to be particularly aware of three of these situational factors which especially impact on the antici-patory grief experienced at any given point in time. In order to appre-ciate it, one must know, among other things: 1) at what point the patient and family are in the illness trajectory; 2) the amount of time since the diagnosis; and 3) the circumstances that have transpired since the diagnosis, including the dying person's attitude and approach to life. It would be grossly inappropriate to compare the anticipatory grief of a newly diagnosed person to that of one who has been in complete remission for fourteen months or to the anticipatory grief of one who is on his/her deathbed. Therefore, caregivers must retain a perspective on anticipatory grief that affords them sufficient realiza-tion of the impacts of the illness changes and fluctuations over time and how these influence the anticipatory grief experience and the ability to cope with it.

Specifically, anticipatory grief entails three categories of inter-related processes that facilitate one another. Ideally, anticipatory grief that is therapeutic in nature prompts appropriate engagement in each of these three sets of processes. These processes, and their inherent subprocesses, are listed below. It is important to recognize that they overlap and are not mutually exclusive. Most of them incorporate a number of specific components, which unfortunately cannot be delineated here due to space constraints but which are referred to in the subsequent section on specific interventions with the child in anticipatory grief. The reader is urged to consult the original resource for complete delineation of the anticipatory grief processes [1], and for how specifically to facilitate the mourner's ability to cope with them [10].

THE THREE INTERRELATED PROCESSES OF ANTICIPATORY GRIEF

1. Individual Intrapsychic Processes

In the individual intrapsychic realm, the family member experiences four interrelated subprocesses of anticipatory mourning:

1. Awareness of, and gradual accommodation to, the threat (4 components)
2. Affective processes (6 components)
3. Cognitive processes (8 components)
4. Planning for the future (3 components).

2. Interactional Processes with the Dying Patient

Anticipatory grief engenders numerous interpersonal processes involving the dying patient. This is quite critical to the concept, and invalidates the belief that anticipatory grief must necessarily lead to premature detachment from the patient, cause the relationship with him/her to deteriorate, or predispose the survivor to guilt after the death. In point of fact, all of the subprocesses here imply continued involvement with the dying patient, with some actually serving to intensify the attachment and improve the relationship. There are three subprocesses:

1. Directing attention, energy, and behavior toward the dying patient (7 components)
2. Resolution of the personal relationship with the dying patient (5 components)
3. Helping the dying patient (11 components).

3. Familial and Social Processes

Anticipatory grief stimulates a series of familial and social processes. These illustrate that the patient's dying takes place in a social context which itself is affected by the loss (6 components).

In conclusion, anticipatory grief is a complex, multidimensional set of processes that may be called forth during the terminal illness of a loved one. It entails grief and mourning not only over future losses, but also over past and present losses. Contrary to popular misconception, the phenomenon *does not* have to eventuate in premature detachment from the dying loved one and, in fact, has the potential for, and capability of, supporting and stimulating continuing involvement with him/her.

EXPERIENCE OF A FAMILY MEMBER
DURING THE TERMINAL ILLNESS
OF A LOVED ONE

As noted earlier, anticipatory grief transpires during the terminal illness of a loved one. Therefore, in order to appreciate fully the experience of anticipatory grief, one must understand the context within which it takes place. In many families when a loved one is dying, so too, are the other family members. While their "dying" is not of a permanent, irreversible, physical sense like that of the loved one, it does constitute the process leading to the permanent and irreversible death of psychosocial aspects of themselves, their lives, their family, and their world. Consequently, the mourning of family members is not solely for the terminally ill loved one, but also for themselves and their families. This leaves them in the position of coping with multiple losses simultaneously, a situation that in other instances would be clearly viewed as comprising bereavement overload [11], but that in this case is construed as merely part and parcel of the anticipatory grief experience.

The onerous and depleting experience of family members, when a loved one is terminally ill, is well-documented in the thanatological literature [e.g., 9-10, 12-15]. Suffice it to say, the time is often one of heightened emotionality, competing demands, intense chaos, and inordinate stress. Often through an uncertain up-and-down course, family members are expected to adapt to a patient who may feel fine one day and quite ill the next. Already present confusion is magnified by situations in the terminal illness that breed inconsistency, resentment, and ambivalence. There is a disturbing lack of norms, and often an absence of clearly specified expectations and responsibilities. Multi-leveled depletion frequently is routine. As observed by Rando [10], a number of problems result specifically from the chronic nature of most of today's terminal illnesses. All of these combine with the family's witnessing of their loved one's progressive debilitation without power to stem its inevitable course; the difficulty of adapting to a loved one who, though slowly dying, may go on living for an extended period of time (i.e., an extended "living-dying interval" [16]); and the demands for major readaptations and investments of self, time, and finances. Together these contribute to the psychological conflicts, emotional exhaustion, physical debilitation, social isolation, and family discord so routinely reported by those whose loved one is dying.

As previously discussed, family members must strike a delicate balance among competing needs in the individual, interpersonal, and family spheres, i.e., they must deal with their own personal anticipatory grief; they must cope with and respond to the terminal illness of the loved one; and they must continue to take care of the family unit and reorganize it in order that it can maintain stability after the death to insure the continued survival of its members. To do so, they must regularly manage clashing responsibilities, discordant roles, antagonistic tasks, and intense emotions, including guilt, sorrow, depression, anger and hostility, and anxiety. The reader is referred to Rando [10] for a detailed discussion of the above and specific therapeutic strategies and interventions.

Caregiver intervention with the family of a dying patient will demand support of their adaptive functioning. The three areas of focus for intervention are: 1) communication and awareness contexts; 2) the anticipatory grief and unfinished business of the family; and 3) clinical therapy intervention and clinical education and advocacy. Again, the reader is referred to Rando for treatment strategies and interventions in each area [10].

THE CHILD AS AN ANTICIPATORY MOURNER: STRATEGIES FOR INTERVENTION

With the phenomenon of anticipatory grief explicated above and a very brief portrait of the terminal illness context within which it occurs, the remainder of this chapter focuses on the child as an anticipatory mourner. The reader is referred to other chapters in this volume that provide fundamental information and speak directly to the issues, developmental capacities, concerns, influencing factors, and intervention needs of bereaved children. The subsequent material builds on that provided in these chapters and will not be repeated here. Such lack of repetition should in no way be construed as indicating absence of applicability of that information to the child who is anticipatorily grieving the loss of a loved one. All of that information necessarily must be incorporated into, and taken inherently to undergird, all comments made here.

It must be kept in mind that the child contending with anticipatory grief, no less than the child in postdeath grief, is disadvantaged as a mourner. This varies by age and circumstance, but, as observed for a young child, the following disadvantages do apply (adapted from Rando [17]). The reader can extrapolate from this with regard to an older child:

- If a loss happens in adulthood, that adult at least has matured and developed already; if it happens in childhood, it can interfere with normal development,
- The child is immature in his/her conception of death,
- The child tends to take things literally and concretely, and has difficulty with abstract concepts,
- The child tends to engage in magical thinking,
- The child tends not to have the words to identify and describe feelings, thoughts, or memories, which are so important in coping with loss,
- The child's ability to remember a loved one in that person's absence may be inadequate,
- The child lacks the cognitive and affective capabilities to comprehend and tolerate ambivalence, a capacity which is significantly important in mourning,
- The child is dependent upon adults and has little control over his life and world; is more limited in what he can do and when he can do it; is more impacted by familial instability and inconsistency; is more vulnerable to inappropriate role reassignments; is more trapped in his psychosocial and physical environment; and has less access to resources which are not immediately available,
- The child often does not have the developmental experiences that can tell her that her pain will subside and life will go on,
- The child does not have the capacity to tolerate pain or anxiety intensely over time as an adult can,
- The child must be certain that his physical and emotional needs are going to be met before he can give in to his grief,
- Parents and other caretaking adults tend not to appreciate the importance of the child's play as a means of coping and communication,
- The child can suffer the negative effects of an adult's attempts at protecting her from death, painful feelings, and the grief of others,
- The child is not perceived as a "legitimate" mourner, and is often socially disenfranchised in her grief.

Any intervention with children in anticipatory grief must take into consideration the particular disadvantages existing in a given situation and specifically tailor interventions to address these. In addition to sustaining some or all of these disadvantages, bereaved children often experience particular trains of thought after the death of a loved one which are associated with feelings of sadness, rage, fear, shame, and guilt. According to Krupnick and Solomon, three questions, whether directly expressed or not, typically come to mind for most children contending with the death of a parent [18]. These are also applicable to the child contending with anticipatory grief, and should be assumed to be on the mind of the child during the terminal illness of a loved one: "Did I make this happen?", "Will the same thing happen to me?" and "Who is going to take care of me now (or if something happens to my surviving parent)?" Krupnick and Solomon assert that adults should not only answer such questions, but should take the time to hear how the children understand the answers, given that miscommunications and misunderstandings can lead to intensified worry or anger.

It can readily be seen how children's status as disadvantaged mourners; and their propensity to struggle with the aforementioned questions, all add to the stress of the anticipatory grief experience. This, of course, compromises children in general. Indeed, the psychosocial adjustment of children with a terminally ill parent has been found to be adversely affected, which, in turn, can adversely affect their anticipatory grief. Siegel, Mesagno, Karus, Christ, Banks, and Moynihan found that children with a terminally ill parent showed higher levels of depressive symptomatology, anxiety, and both internalizing and externalizing behavior problems, than did a comparison group of community children [19]. A significantly higher proportion of them evidenced diminished self-esteem and deficits in social competence. As a group, they experienced problems in multiple domains— with some scoring within clinical ranges—and had fewer resources to help them adjust to the imminent death of their parent.

In her unparalleled work, *When A Parent Is Very Sick*, Eda LeShan vividly dissects the experience of the child whose parent is quite sick or terminally ill and offers coping strategies to support her contention that children need not be as helpless as they may believe [20]. The caregiver seeking to intervene with the child in anticipatory grief would be wise to investigate this little gem of a book, which, although written specifically for the child, explicates the situation for adults and implies to caregivers those interventions mandated for the most therapeutic response. LeShan observes that a number of changes and discoveries during the parent's illness may be particularly difficult for the child to absorb and these will need to be addressed by the caregiver with the child. Among these are the startling realization that parents not only get sick, but that they are not in control—a frightening concept for the child who is dependent upon them. Also, stress-related and illness-related alterations in the parents' ways of relating to the child, and to one another, can be especially disturbing to that child. New feelings and concerns occasioned in the child by the experience of the terminally ill parent bring their own distress and, in some cases, their own conflicts. These demand intervention by concerned adults and include, among others: the child's shock and numbness; fear; long-term anxiety; worry over developing the same disease; guilt; anger; helplessness; resurrected memories of how he/she felt when hurt or sick, and attribution of such feelings to the ill parent; and heightened concern about the family's finances and survival issues.

As with adults who are in the situation of coping with the terminal illness of a beloved family member, the social changes that occur place significant stress on children in anticipatory grief. Changes in the child's own relationship with other family members, peers, and adults; embarrassment about the ill parent; discomfort with diminished parental involvement and/or the over-involvement of others; resentment over increased demands; and anger over not being included and/or provided proper information, all affect the child and influence not only the child's personal emotional reactions, but also his/her interpersonal and social relationships. These will benefit from the caregiver's provision to the parents and other caretaking adults of a) psychoeducational information pertaining to the necessity of appropriate inclusion of the child, and b) intervention geared in a family systems perspective to assist the adults in making appropriate role reassignments and reaching optimum family homeostasis when possible.

Again, as with adults, children must be encouraged to do what they can, that is, to take appropriate action and to participate meaningfully to a reasonable extent in assisting the loved one and the family during the course of the illness. This concept is consistent with the notion of action and empowerment being imperative after victimization of any sort. Having a loved one who is terminally ill *ipso facto* is victimizing to both patient and family members if one accepts Webster's Ninth New Collegiate Dictionary definition of victim as "one that is acted on and usually adversely affected by a force or agent . . . one that is injured, destroyed, or sacrificed under any of various conditions." Optimum amounts of involvement and participation in the care of the terminally ill loved one have long been recognized clinically to be associated with more positive adjustment, and have been demonstrated empirically to be associated with greater satisfaction with the patient's treatment, optimum amounts of anticipatory grief, and better postdeath adjustment [21].

CREATION OF A TREATMENT PACKAGE FOR THE CHILD CONTENDING WITH ANTICIPATORY GRIEF

In dealing with a child in anticipatory grief, it is quite helpful for the caregiver to conceive of intervention in terms of the creation of a treatment package. The purpose is to identify those specific issues and influencing factors which are salient in a particular child's situation and then to design interventions appropriate to them, incorporating them together with relevant generic interventions into one "package."

While space constraints do not permit a full discussion of all elements of the treatment package, the following outline of treatment areas should be useful to the caregiver planning intervention with a child in anticipatory grief:

1. Generic interventions with children
2. Generic loss and grief interventions
3. Interventions with bereaved children
4. Interventions with children with a terminally ill parent
5. Interventions for elements of the three classes of influencing factors applicable in a particular child's situation:
   - Generic factors
   - Factors inhibiting children's grief
   - Factors influencing the anticipatory grief experience (including sets of factors characteristic of the individual mourner and what is to be lost; the specific illness and type of death; the patient's knowledge and response; the family system and its members' knowledge and response; and general socioeconomic and environmental factors)
6. Interventions for anticipatory grief:
   - Interventions for communication and awareness contexts
   - Clinical therapy intervention and clinical education and advocacy
   - Specific component processes interventions
   - Interventions in specific emotional reactions:
     — guilt
     — sorrow and depression
     — anger and hostility

— ambivalence

— anxiety

7. Interventions for any complications in the mourning processes.

Perspective

It can be seen that generating a full-spectrum intervention package for the child in anticipatory grief is a complex process which requires the application of a number of generic and specific intervention strategies and techniques. Yet, lest the reader become overwhelmed, it is important to recognize that much of what has been outlined above is automatically taken into consideration by any effective, experienced caregiver. Interventions for any bereaved individual cannot occur within a vacuum and must never fail to take into consideration the entire context. The child in anticipatory grief is a child first and foremost. Second, the child is a mourner, and third, he/she is a bereaved child. Fourth, the child belongs to a family system with a terminally ill member. Fifth, the child will be influenced by a host of factors which combine to make this a totally unique and idiosyncratic experience which must be appreciated in any treatment interventions. Sixth, only some children who are anticipatory grievers will have complications sufficient to warrant intervention for complicated mourning. The outline helps caregivers keep this perspective in mind in terms of, first, approaching the child and, secondly, choosing the appropriate interventions, including the type and aims of support offered.

Always, it must be remembered that this is a child whose whole world has been dramatically altered, and who—depending upon developmental age, prevailing illness, and family-related circumstances—is totally dependent upon that world which is now so chaotic. The relative helplessness of the child in the craziness of the entire experience must be borne in mind. Despite this, however, the basic position of the caregiver must be to have the child appropriately included in, and given suitable information about, the parent's illness (see below). This stance must be the departing point for all caregiver actions. Caregivers must keep in mind the adverse consequences for the child should this posture be relinquished, and must remind themselves of these whenever abandonment of the posture is considered. The "What's the alternative?" question addressed below may have to be posed and re-posed numerous times.

One of the important considerations for caregivers to keep in mind is that, as with adults, previous losses, griefs, vulnerabilities, and experiences may have been revived by the parent's terminal illness and may be prompting their own stress and grief reactions. As always, developmental losses and issues also prevail. Caregivers should remember that, while in the midst of dealing with a parent's terminal illness, a child frequently is contending with other unrelated losses. For this reason, the child's reactions cannot automatically be assumed to pertain to the parent's illness or impending loss. Old issues along with current ones which have nothing to do with anticipatory grief (e.g., losing one's position on the school basketball team), may elicit the reactions that are manifested. Sensitive inquiry with the child will help the caregiver to ascertain the source of the reactions and this information can direct the required interventions. Even children in anticipatory grief have ongoing life concerns that co-mingle with those pertinent to the loved one's illness and death. These must not be overlooked, especially with a developing child for whom such neglect can compromise future development.

SPECIFIC INTERVENTIONS WITH THE CHILD IN THE THREE INTERRELATED PROCESSES OF ANTICIPATORY GRIEF

There are many aspects of intervention with a child confronting the terminal illness of a parent. Given the limits of this chapter, and in order to sharpen its focus, this section is devoted to examining interventions applicable to the child contending with the three interrelated processes of anticipatory grief as identified above. Much of the material here is adapted from Rando's discussion of understanding and facilitating anticipatory grief in the loved ones of the dying [10]. In addition, the reader is referred to Van Dexter for a review of strategies and intervention techniques for promoting healthy anticipatory grief in the classroom [22]. This is an important resource given that school is the child's workplace, as well as a significant environment for exposure to adults who have the potential to be especially helpful during the time of a parent's illness. Finally, as used below, the term "caregiver" refers both to concerned adults in the child's life, as well as to professionals.

1. Individual Intrapsychic Processes

In these four subprocesses, the anticipatory griever becomes increasingly aware of the threat of the loved one's impending death and copes with the reactions generated by this awareness. Inherently, this involves affective processes dealing with the emotional responses that are stimulated, as well as cognitive processes pertaining to changing one's sense of self and his/her assumptive world, attempting to crystallize memories for the future, bargaining for a reprieve, and contemplating one's own death. These processes interface with those involved in planning for a future that is an uncomfortable but natural outgrowth of the increasing recognition that future losses will occur and the griever must be prepared to deal with them. When the anticipatory mourner is a child, the natural tendency for adults to protect him/her from a painful situation often undercuts the ability of the child to therapeutically engage in these processes. All the previously delineated disadvantages do obtain for the child mourner, typically, a lack of information, immature cognitive and affective capacities, minimal control, and the negative effects of adults' attempts at protecting the child from the situation and the pain it brings. These are particularly potent in compromising the child's anticipatory grief in these individual intrapsychic processes.

Ideally, children begin to come to an *awareness and gradual accommodation to the threat* of the parent's death by receiving clearly understandable, developmentally appropriate warnings. In order to promote adequate preparation, information is imparted which will provide children with as much understanding as possible concerning the implications of the parent's illness. This does not mean that children's hope is taken away, or that a self-fulfilling prophecy is established. It simply means acting with the recognition that, unless the reality is clearly presented to children, they cannot prepare or cope effectively. Adults must be supportive, yet at the same time as specific as possible, in informing children about what to expect. Then, they must ask the child what has been understood in order to check comprehension. Caregivers should be prepared to deliver impactful information more than once, since the emotional defenses of children, like those of adults, can preclude their taking it all in at one time. They experience significant confusion. Therefore, adults should ask for questions from children and give adequate time for response. Children must be informed explicitly that it is acceptable and healthy to continue to ask questions as they occur to them.

The development of progressively deepening awareness of the seriousness of the illness and its implications comes through the dawning realization that certain hopes about recovery or stabilization are not being actualized. Over time, there is a gradual absorbing and coming to terms with the reality of the situation. This is not unlike what happens to the sudden death mourner, where the deprivation of the loved one and the unfulfilled needs for him/her gradually teach the mourner that the loved one is truly dead and that the mourner must make changes to accommodate to this fact. In this situation, the experiences and consequences of the terminal illness are what teach the anticipatory mourner that the loved one actually will die. A cognitive learning process occurs. For example, as the loved one gradually weakens and treatments no longer bring lengthy remissions or as the medication becomes less effective, the mourner is taught, by what happens during the illness and by the frustrations of the desire to see the loved one improve, that he/she is really dying. The reality of this is simply too much to take in at once because it so severely violates both one's assumptive world and all the conditioning one has had about the loved one being alive and part of one's world. Consequently, the mourner can only absorb the reality and start to make the necessary adjustments after painfully learning through numerous terminal illness experiences that the loved one is being lost.

It is for this reason that it is imperative for adults not to shield children too much from the realities of the parent's illness. For instance, if children lack the appreciation that the parent's abilities are waning, or if they are not permitted to see that more medication is signaling another relapse, children will not be confronted with the need to gradually revise their assumptive world to incorporate the increasingly apparent reality of the parent's illness, or to contend with the other demands of anticipatory grief. While this is precisely what protective adults may want, it can harm children. As with adults; children who have insufficient "education" from the illness to "teach" them about the illness and its implications will not become aware of, nor gradually able to accommodate to, the parent's impending death. As a result, the experiences necessary to help children contend with the reality of the situation are compromised, along with their coping abilities. As always, the child's developmental age, the prevailing illness, and family-related circumstances must be taken into consideration here, but the child must be provided with these opportunities to an appropriate extent.

In many situations it can be helpful to encourage some repetitious recollection of events leading up to the illness and the parent's current condition in order to assist children to adapt gradually to the shock of the losses that are being encountered. In addition to looking at the past to see how it lead to the present, the process of anticipatory grief also involves looking to the future. One aspect of this is rehearsing the ultimate death and its consequences, with attempts to adjust in part. The mourner starts to become partially socialized into the bereaved role through this time of anticipatory bereavement [23]. Of course, all of these must be counterbalanced with enjoyment of the continued relationship that remains.

The terminal illness of a parent engenders a host of *affective processes* in the child. These stem from the impact of the grief over past, present, and future losses—along with unrelated losses that have been revived in the current situation—as well as from the enormous stress of the parent's terminal illness. The knowledge of the threat of the parent's death and potential loss intensifies the myriad emotions present in the child. The parent's remissions and relapses may create shifts in the type and intensity of emotions experienced. The child may attempt to modulate or suppress negative feelings in order to eliminate potential stress. This can be harmful in contributing to psychological, behavioral, social, or physical symptomatology. Suppressed feelings can later erupt in inappropriate ways and increase any resentment that exists, at times undermining family cooperation. It is helpful for caregivers to anticipate with the child the emotional reactions that may be experienced, to normalize them when they are encountered, and to suggest ways for the child to appropriately process, express, and cope with these feelings.

In addition to the major anticipatory grief emotions of guilt, sorrow and depression, anger and hostility, ambivalence, and anxiety, children, no differently than adults, can be expected to experience and have to cope with a host of other emotional reactions and cognitive impacts (e.g., disbelief, confusion, rumination, impaired concentration). As well, children must contend with altered perceptions (e.g., feelings of unreality or depersonalization, feeling as if something is about to happen) and the consequences of their defenses and/or attempts at coping (e.g., numbness, protest, regression, search for meaning), along with the sequelae of any of the myriad behavioral, social, or physical responses to loss (see Rando [2] for a complete delineation). Intervention must be geared toward assisting children in understanding and coping with all of these reactions.

Caregivers will have to identify the child's idiosyncratic fears, concerns, and needs in the specific situation, as well as those that are ongoing. Especially because of any affective immaturity that may exist (although adults require this too), caregivers must be certain to give sufficient support in the experiencing of affect and provide assistance in processing it. Specifically, they must help children pace and dose themselves to exposure to the affect; break it down into small and manageable pieces; feel it; identify, label, differentiate, and trace it; accept it; and find some form of expression for it. Caregivers must be mindful of the particular developmental tendencies which can interfere with children's appropriate processing of affect and take these into consideration in their interventions (e.g., the developmental tendency for children five to eight years old to deny feelings). It is critical to structure situations so that children receive adequate respites from the emotional reactions and stress of the parent's terminal illness as well as opportunities for replenishment. It is always mandatory for caregivers to keep in mind that children's dependency on adults makes them uniquely vulnerable to adults' reactions and that this will stir their own emotional reactions.

Children in anticipatory grief also experience and cope with the separation anxiety and fear elicited by the threat of the parent's permanent loss. As noted earlier, they must begin to gradually detach from the image of the parent in the postdeath future, to whatever extent this is possible, without jeopardizing current involvement. As well, they must begin to revise the assumptive world in light of the parent's illness and impending death. This assumes that children are developmentally old enough to recognize their separateness from the dying parent and can learn to tolerate the awareness that the parent will die while they continue to exist. As with any anticipatory mourner, the child needs to maintain some confidence in the face of the profound threat of the loved one's loss. This often includes mastery operations such as information seeking and participation in the parent's care (see below), as well as strategies for maintenance of emotional and interpersonal equilibrium and affirmation of life and its meaning [24].

Cognitive processes also are stimulated in children by the parent's terminal illness. As with any stressful event, the threatened loss of the parent causes children to be hyper-alert and to scan the environment for potential cues related to the stress. This tendency is magnified significantly when children are fearful that they are not being kept informed about what is going on, and so maintain a hypervigilant stance lest something occur about which they have not been apprised. For this reason, it is important for parents and other caregivers to promise children that they will be kept informed about what is going on. They must keep this promise so that children can let down their guard and be secure in the knowledge that information will not be withheld, and know that worry is unnecessary unless they are given something specific to worry about.

The threatened loss of the parent, and any accompanying anxiety about being excluded from things, strikes at the child's security, sense of self, perception of the world, and personal and social functioning in the world. As losses and changes accumulate, and as the child becomes increasingly preoccupied with the impending loss of the parent, the child starts to recognize that the world is now different, and—depending again on developmental age, the prevailing illness, and family-related circumstances—he/she must begin to adapt to that new reality. This recognition is accompanied by a host of emotional reactions, resistances, and ultimately, if there is sufficient time and experience, changes in identity and the assumptive world. The child starts to accommodate to the gradual transformations stimulated by the increasing awareness of the impending loss of the parent. The child moves from a "we" to an "I" in terms of the interactive relationship with the dying parent and starts to revise the assumptive world to incorporate the future loss of the parent.

Because it is important for all family members to construct a composite image of the loved one that can endure after the death, it can be quite helpful for caregivers to encourage the child's review of the past in order to crystallize memories to keep after the death. This "life review" [25] is beneficial to the dying person as well as to family members. Such a review puts the person's life in perspective and may help him/her to integrate it. The process itself may contribute to meaningful interaction between the dying loved one and the family member (see below), and can assist in that member's developing a view of the loved one that is perhaps more balanced than previously, with a more longitudinal dimension. Many times it affords insight into the loved one that heretofore had been lacking. When that family member is a child, such a review can concretize memories, operationalize the relationship, anchor the parent in the child's life history, provide important biographical information, convey the significance and meaning of the parent-child relationship, and provide information to the child which subsequently can be drawn upon for future values clarification, decision-making, and assumptive world revision.

Other cognitive processes occur during the terminal illness of the parent. One may think about one's own death as one watches the parent dying. Caregivers will need to be mindful about providing children with opportunities to process the emotional reactions and vulnerabilities that can arise. There may be bargaining with God or fate for a reprieve for the parent, or for a different illness experience. Though false hopes should not be supported, it is best if caregivers do not interfere with this process unless it is either distinctly unhealthy for the child or interferes with the appropriate treatment or medical care required by the patient. Taking away any person's—not just a child's—hope that bargaining will work is not in the purview of the caregiver. Indeed, it is learning that bargaining attempts ultimately fail that contributes to helping the family member come to grips with the reality of the impending loss. The magical thinking of childhood, which can come to the fore in this situation, must be understood by the caregiver and dealt with most sensitively. The caregiver must walk a delicate line between permitting children to bargain and have hope and providing appropriate clarification of magical thinking. Magical thinking always must be challenged if, left unchecked or uncorrected, it would predispose children to experiences, expectations, or beliefs that were harmful to them during the illness or after the death of the parent.

During the terminal illness, many family members implicitly and without conscious knowledge—although some do explicitly—develop a philosophy of how to cope with the dying loved one's remaining time. Some do as much as possible in an attempt to create memories with the dying person from which they can later receive sustenance, while others prefer to take a more laissez-faire approach and not get caught up in a whirlwind. Though the dying parent should be given primary consideration since it is his/her remaining life that is being debated, caregivers can ask both patient and family members how they wish to spend the time left. Children should be asked specifically whether there is anything special that they would like to do with their parent, and caregivers should talk with them about developing a perspective on how to approach the time that is available. This can be done in a positive, "let's-do-what-we-can-while-we-can-do-it," or "make-the-most-out-of-what-is-available" approach. (See section below on finishing unfinished business with the dying loved one.)

All family members, including children, need to make sense out of their experiences. When a parent is very sick, children will have the need to be able to put the parent's suffering and death into some cognitive framework and/or a philosophical or religious context. While younger children certainly lack the ability to comprehend abstract concepts, and actually can be confused by them, even a relatively young child can benefit from being provided with a context, an explanation, a rationale for the experience that will lend it some meaning or afford it some explication. Operating in a vacuum, the parent's terminal illness is even more anxiety provoking. Children do not have to be comforted per se by the explanation, it just has to be offered to clarify what is happening. While nothing will make it okay for the parent to be so sick, at least there is a reason for that sickness, e.g. "Your mother was given some bad blood during an operation six years ago. That is how she caught the AIDS virus which makes her so sick now. People never knew this could happen and so they didn't take the precautions they do now. It was a very bad mistake."

Additional cognitive processes in the child that can be expected at this time—and that may require caregiver support—include: heightened preoccupation with, and concern for, the terminally ill parent; striving through all the senses to take in the parent in order to emblazon perceptions in the mind and senses for the purpose of constructing a mental and sensory composite image of the parent to endure after the death; attending carefully to the present in order to crystallize memories to keep after the death; and struggling with whether what one did or did not do contributed to the illness or could potentially forestall or prevent the death. Regarding the latter, caregivers again must be aware of, and work to correct, any magical thinking that exists.

When awareness of the threat has been recognized, and the feelings and thoughts associated with it are being processed, *planning for the future* is a natural outgrowth. This may involve considering what the future will be like without the loved one and experiencing associated reactions to it; anticipating and planning for future losses and changes, both before and after the death; and anticipating and planning for practical and social considerations that need to be addressed both prior to and after the death. Being able to plan assumes that one has some understanding of what the future will bring in terms of how it will entail changes and losses to come.

Children need some indication of what to expect, but, like adults, this information must be given at the proper time and in proper amounts so as to be therapeutic in enabling appropriate decision-making, minimizing surprises, reducing anxiety, enhancing a sense of control, maintaining appropriate defense, encouraging optimum participation with the loved one, and facilitating healthy family readjustment and homeostasis. As implied earlier, telling children what to expect in their parent's illness should not be done in a manner that will bombard, overwhelm, or frighten them. The goal always is to help stimulate appropriate present actions and future planning (e.g., help children appreciate the importance of spending time with the parent now since future debilitation will impair the parent's ability to be able to be as responsive as he/she can be now).

Because it is often uncomfortable for family members to consider a future without the loved one, it is imperative that caregivers normalize this process and inform these individuals that such consideration is a natural part of accommodating to the undesired, but inevitable, loss. When the dying person can be a part of that process, for example, in discussing child care arrangements for the years following the death, it can render him/her some control. Such involvement can decrease family members' guilt over contemplation of the future without the loved one, minimize any sense of betrayal that may occur when making major changes after the death, and increase opportunities for family members to benefit from the patient's input, guidance, and preferences. It is always crucial that such planning and discussion occur at the appropriate time in the illness. When broached prematurely, it can isolate the dying person and/or create premature detachment.

2. Interactional Processes with the Dying Patient

In these processes, the mourner actively continues to be involved with the dying loved one. This involvement is necessary, not only to continue to support the dying patient and to insure that there is not premature detachment, but also to provide the time and opportunities for the mourner to care for the loved one and to resolve the mutual relationship—actions that are therapeutic for postdeath grief adjustment. Although some theorists have construed anticipatory grief and continued involvement as seemingly opposite processes, this is quite untrue. Indeed, it is by preparing for the ultimate loss of their loved one through anticipatory grief that family members can become aware of unfinished business remaining with the dying person. It is only by interacting with that dying person that family members will be able to finish that unfinished business—a crucial part of anticipatory grief. In this regard, anticipatory grief facilitates both the identification of unfinished business and the development of ways to achieve closure.

Obviously, the circumstances of the parent's illness, the prevailing family situation, and the child's developmental age have a bearing—as they always do—on the degree to which the child is included in, and involved with, the parent's illness. The only issue open for debate should be the degree or extent of the child's inclusion and involvement. Children will be better prepared and more able to cope when, like adults, they have the appropriate opportunities, information, experiences, and planning afforded to them. They must not be deprived of these experiences if healthy anticipatory grief and accommodation to the loss are to occur. Interaction and involvement with the dying parent iiiiis an inherent and mandatory aspect of this anticipatory grief. Children must be appropriately involved in, and informed about, the parent's illness even if it hurts adults to witness the pain that the children experience. Adults must keep in mind that children will be hurt even more—both before and after the death—if appropriate inclusion and information is denied. That is the basic premise all caregivers must assume when working in any capacity with children whose parents are dying.

During a loved one's terminal illness, it is normal for family members to find themselves *directing attention, energy, and behavior toward the dying patient.* Unfortunately, when the anticipatory mourner is a child, adults, in their desire to spare the youngster from pain and sadness, often discourage the child's actions in these regards. All too often the child's desires to do this are not legitimized, and he/she is pushed to remain engaged, as before, in outside activities, when attention quite normally switches to focus on the ill parent. This does not mean that the child will, or should, relinquish all interest in other than family-oriented matters, but only that when the child's redirected focus on the parent appears it must be understood, legitimized when appropriate, and perceived as a therapeutic process which ultimately can serve the best interests of the child (if permitted to facilitate healthy anticipatory grief). The main issue for the family is to promote whatever communication, interaction, control, living, and meaning remains available to the dying person. Children, no less than adults, need to be helped to do this with their loved one. Withdrawal from the dying parent not only accentuates that parent's losses, but deprives children of the therapeutic benefits of participating in the parent's care, ministering to the parent's needs, helping the family cope with the stress, and, very importantly, reaping the rewards that still can remain in a redefined relationship with the parent.

Children will need assistance in figuring out precisely how to relate to the dying parent who, in many cases, is becoming increasingly different from the person he/she was before. Physical changes (e.g., severe weight loss, strange odors), psychological changes (e.g., personality or temperament alterations), changes in the well parent (e.g., decreased patience), and changes in family life and routine (e.g., no longer eating together around the dining room table) all must be explained to children. Children's appropriate reactions to these changes must be normalized and help provided to process them. Caregivers also will need to help children determine what must be modified (e.g., Dad cannot play ball with them any more, but he can watch a football game on television with them), what can stay the same (e.g., Dad will still want to kiss them goodnight before bedtime), and what must be relinquished (e.g., Dad cannot attend church with them any more). Redefining the relationship with the ill parent, and consequently with the rest of the family since everyone else is affected, is a major task, and one which inherently brings with it a number of secondary losses [9].

As noted earlier in this chapter, anticipatory grief comes with mutually conflicting demands and great stress generated by their incongruence. Adults have significant difficulty trying to balance these conflicting demands of simultaneously moving toward the patient (in terms of directing attention, energy, and behavior toward him/her), staying the same with the patient (in terms of remaining involved with him/her) and attempting to preserve some normalcy or continuity, and moving away from the patient (in terms of detaching from the image of that person being present in the future). Fortunately, the competing demands can be met in different realms simultaneously, as one can move closer or remain the same behaviorally and interpersonally, and can start to move away intrapsychically. Unfortunately, this typically requires quite complex realizations, discerning intellectual and emotional analysis, the capacity to maintain contrary conceptualizations in the mind, and the ability to hold on in a concrete realm while relinquishing in an abstract one. All of this is particularly difficult for children given their immature cognitive and affective capabilities. Much caregiver support is required for accomplishment of this if as much of it as is possible can occur given the child's developmental age, the illness, and family-related circumstances.

Since the complicating issues of anticipatory grief create such enormous stress for the family members, they will need to be educated about such stress and assisted in understanding and managing it. Caregivers must encourage family members to participate to an optimum level in the care of the loved one, yet also to take appropriate respites from that involvement in order that, when they are with the loved one, they can focus themselves toward him/her. Such things as normal resentment, ambivalence, frustration, and guilt should be anticipated with the family and explained as part of the normal process of living with a dying individual. Needs for replenishment must be legitimized and taken into consideration by the family and caregivers. These actions can help minimize or liberate family members from guilt, anxiety, anger, and other negative responses that can interfere with their relating to the dying person and ultimately adversely affect postdeath adjustment.

Children must be included in all of this, although their involvement must be tailored to their individual developmental levels. Their magical thinking can be particularly problematic when it holds them responsible for the parent's illness and death because they had these normal emotional reactions to the illness experience. This type of thinking always must be challenged and appropriate information supplied. Parenthetically, caregivers must realize that the supplanting of magical thinking in children is not necessarily a one-time intervention. Over time they will have to gently query children to ascertain what their comprehension is and determine whether any type of magical thinking exists—no matter how latent—which needs to be corrected.

Sometimes, children must do or witness things that are uncomfortable but necessary for the parent's treatment, e.g., accompanying the parent for dreaded chemotherapy or attending a mother-son dance with an aunt. In such instances, caregivers can help by talking with children about the purpose of the activity and encouraging them to express their feelings and concerns.

One of the most important aspects of anticipatory grief is that it allows time for *resolution of the personal relationship with the dying patient.* The most critical aspect of this is finishing unfinished business with the dying loved one. Children need to achieve closure as much as adults. Addressing psychosocial issues that have never been addressed, or have not been reconciled with the parent, can involve many behaviors. Besides expressing feelings and resolving past conflicts, these actions might include, among others: saying goodbye; explaining past omissions or commissions; articulating important messages; informing the parent of the meaningfulness of the relationship; providing pieces of feedback that are significant; stating promises and intentions for the future; manifesting or ceasing behaviors in accordance with the parent's preferences, values, needs, or desires; recollecting the mutual relationship and shared memories from common experiences; and planning for the future in such a manner that the actions undertaken will not be perceived as betrayals after the death of the parent.

Often it can be helpful for caregivers to ask family members to identify what they think might make them feel uncomfortable, incomplete, or guilty six months after the death. If these are issues that can be addressed presently, they should be encouraged to pay attention to them now in order to reduce any lack of closure, guilt, or anxiety that could arise after the death because of unfinished business. Where time is limited, some children may have to be confronted since unfinished business will only complicate their grief after the death of their parent. In some situations caregivers actually may have to prompt children to talk with the dying parent by saying such things as, "Mom is very sick now and we only have a limited amount of time left with her. It is important that you say or do the things you need to with Mom in order that you will not be left with regrets later on." Of course, this must be modified according to the developmental age of the child and the circumstances. Ultimately, their desires must be respected, but the deleterious consequences of leaving unfinished business must be pointed out to children, just as they are to adults.

The key issue is that children must be helped to identify what is important and feasible for them to say and do in order to have the least amount of unfinished emotional business with that parent remaining after the parent's death. The words or actions must be appropriate to their developmental level and meaningful for them—not merely a rehash of what they think others might expect them to say or do. While this process needs to be encouraged for some children, many undertake it naturally on their own. Almost all children need the permission, support, and legitimization to finish their own unfinished business, along with caring adults who can help them cope with their reactions to the process. In some situations children may avoid completing unfinished business with the parent in order to deny, forestall, or escape contending with the impending loss of that parent. Caregivers will have to sensitively intervene to promote the importance of undertaking such actions (for the parent as well as the child). The ability of the family to withstand open and honest communication always must be taken into consideration when prompting children to be open and disclosive to the dying parent.

Two very painful, although very important, aspects of anticipatory grief are saying goodbye to the loved one at the appropriate time and giving him/her permission to die. Saying goodbye to the parent can be done both verbally and non-verbally through symbolic or concrete actions. It assumes that the child recognizes that the parent is dying, and involves acknowledging that leave taking is occurring. Different words or actions will be meaningful for different people in saying goodbye, for example, "I love you, Mom. You will always be in my heart; I will never forget I am your daughter, whether you are here or not. I will never—I could never—forget you. Don't forget me either, wherever you go, wherever you are."

Permission to die is essentially what family members convey to the dying loved one, making it acceptable at the proper time for him/her to let go. Thus they refrain from attempting to keep the person alive through guilt, responsibility, or unfinished business. It does not mean that the family is unmoved by the fact that the loved one is dying. Rather, it signifies that, despite their wishes to the contrary, they love the patient enough to recognize that death is inevitable. Therefore, they do not act in ways that will meet their needs to have the loved one stay at the expense of the dying person's need to let go. They can permit the transition. Sometimes just making a verbal or nonverbal statement that acknowledges that the loved one is dying gives that person the message that the family members understand and reluctantly accept what is happening.

Children are very powerful here because it is for them that many terminally ill parents struggle to hang on. The goal is not for caregivers to push children to say that it is okay for their parent to die, because no matter how much anticipatory grief has been experienced it is not "okay." Instead, the goal is to bring them to whatever point they can attain in their developmental stage to understand that the parent's illness is irreversible, and has so injured the parent's health that the parent's life cannot go on, despite all wishes to the contrary and any treatment or attempts at fighting the illness the parent may have undertaken to remain alive for them. Resignation, not in the sense of defeat, but acceptance of the inevitable reality becomes the stance, and recognition that this inevitability brings a time to let go is conveyed in some fashion to the parent. The younger the child the more difficult this task is because of the impediments posed by immature cognitive and affective capacities. Nevertheless, explicit recognition to the parent of something as basic as the parent's continual exhaustion can be a precursor for what, in an older child, would be more specific permission to die.

Throughout the period of anticipatory grief, family members ideally work on *helping the dying patient* cope with his/her own anticipatory grief, deal with the specific fears and concerns that confront him/her, and achieve a sense of closure that can provide the loved one with the feeling of peace and the ability to let go at the appropriate time. This entails facilitating an appropriate death [26] by tending to the last wishes of the loved one, determining and meeting his/her needs, and assuming necessary body and ego functions. Most importantly, it involves providing the psychosocial support, acceptance, and intrafamilial awareness context necessary for the patient to communicate about and cope with all aspects of the illness and impending death, including all the consequent feelings, thoughts, fears, concerns, and needs (see Rando [9] for a complete discussion). Children, even though their capabilities and abilities may be limited, can help their dying parent if adults can assist them to translate these behaviors to their own developmental levels. For instance, even young children can help by straightening pillows, sharing their day, hugging their parent, asking how the parent feels, inquiring if he/she wants to talk, listening to the parent's stories from the past, or undertaking little errands.

One of the ways family members can help dying loved ones maintain control and self-determination is by asking how the dying person wishes to be remembered and then attempting to bring this to fruition. Enabling the writing of a will and, if desired, the preplanning of funeral rituals and other postdeath activities can be other ways that family members can assist the patient. Children can be included here and can benefit, as do adults, by talking about how to effect their loved one's desires. A potential problem, for which caregivers must remain continually on the alert, is when the parent places unhealthy expectations on the child regarding the child's postdeath functioning. For instance, telling the child that he/she expects the child not to cry after the death would not be therapeutic for the child and caregiver intervention would be warranted.

The key here is to act consistently in order to assure the child's rightful and legitimate role as a family member in the entire process. If this perspective is maintained, while always acting in accordance with an appreciation of the child's developmental capacities and the prevailing illness and family-related circumstances, then the child has potential access to an optimum anticipatory grief experience.

3. Familial and Social Processes

Anticipatory grief stimulates a series of familial and social processes which underscore how the dying of the loved one takes place in a social context, which itself is affected by ongoing and potential losses. The impacts in the familial and social domains have reverberations for all the individual family members involved, especially children.

Like all other systems, the family system will have to struggle to achieve homeostatic balance after there has been a change. This occurs not only after a death, but after a family member's ability to fulfill previously assigned roles and responsibilities is altered by illness. Consequently, this will necessitate the reassignment of roles and responsibilities to other family members and the adoption of ways to cope with the stress that the illness, its demands, and any anticipatory grief engenders. A prime way in which caregivers can be helpful to families contending with a terminal illness is to educate and promote healthy and appropriate reassignments within the family.

There are four ways in which children are frequently harmed by what transpires in the homeostatic process: 1) They may be given inappropriate roles (e.g., the eight-year-old daughter is expected to be the "little mother" and run the household) or responsibilities (e.g., the ten-year-old is asked to forego all playtime and to babysit his infant brother); 2) they may feel guilty or anxious when other adults are called upon to fulfill the role that the ill parent can no longer assume (e.g., the child's uncle takes him to the father-son baseball game and he knows his father feels badly that he could not go himself); 3) they may not be given the rights that they should have (e.g., they are excluded from knowledge, information, and experiences pertaining to the parent's illness that they require in order to cope); and 4) they are most vulnerable to the intrafamilial changes that occur due to a lack of maturity and self-sufficiency (e.g., the child whose parent has a long-term disabilitating illness suffers from the consequences of the interruption of her normal care and interaction patterns that are necessary for her growth and security). Caregivers can advocate for the appropriate handling of children in all four areas, and can provide parents with the proper psychoeducational information to achieve this.

The terminal illness of a family member usually demands that the rest of the family negotiate extrafamilial relationships. Some of these will involve establishing relationships with health caregivers and learning to navigate the health care system. Others will involve struggling to contend with social relationships that are severely stressed by the family disruption, lack of energy, and redirected focus occasioned by the illness. Children, as well as adults, will need to learn how to ask questions, how to be assertive, and how to express constructive anger and discontent in ways that will not jeopardize future relationships or, in the case of health caregivers, the care of the dying loved one. Information about social avoidance and the anxiety others have around those whose loved ones are dying can be most helpful. It is also important for children, as well as adults, to have normalized for them the resentment that they may experience over the good fortune of friends or over feelings that others cannot understand their plight. Support groups can be especially useful in these situations.

Children must be encouraged to identify people to whom they can address their concerns. This may be very difficult because of their relatively limited access to resources outside of their immediate environment, and because of the demands and stress experienced by those in that immediate environment, for example, their parents. Nevertheless, caregivers must try to help children find even just a few adults who can address their concerns and answer their questions.

Not only must children and other family members learn how to communicate and work with the dying person and extrafamilial friends and caregivers, they also must learn to communicate and work with one another. Given that the family is in flux and that there has had to be role and responsibility reassignments, and given that everyone is contending with significant distress around the illness and impending loss of the person, family members will need all available information, support, and intervention in order to facilitate whatever levels are possible for open communication, cooperation, compromise, and respect. All family members will need to be educated about the importance of including children and warned of the malignant results when protection leads to exclusion.

IN THE FINAL ANALYSIS

In the final analysis, there are four central points that must be kept in mind when addressing anticipatory grief and the child mourner.

The first point pertains to Fulton's conclusion that the wise management of grief in children (as well as adults) revolves around two major factors: 1) the encouragement and facilitation of the normal mourning processes and 2) the prevention of delayed and/or distorted grief responses, i.e., complicated mourning [27]. All caregiver actions must be based on the premise of acting in concert with this conclusion.

The second point concerns the importance of the provision of information about, and the enabling of inclusion in, the parent's terminal illness. Repeatedly, clinical experience and empirical evidence (e.g., Rosenheim and Reicher's study revealing less anxiety in children

informed of the terminal nature of their parent's illness [28]) underscore the necessity of both these courses of action for the best possible
adjustment. Children and adults require both medical and psychoeducational information about the illness and its myriad effects on the
parties involved. The content of medical information can range
anywhere from being apprised of what can be expected in an illness to
how the illness brings changes to people, impacts on how they function,
influences how they perceive themselves, and directs them when they
have good or bad times. It can involve teaching families about medical
treatments, how to deal with institutions involved in the care of their
loved one, and how to identify and secure material, financial, and social
assistance. Psychoeducational information should be provided about
loss and grief in general, family systems and how they adapt to change,
and the needs and concerns of terminally ill individuals. Adults—even
the dying parent—must be educated about the importance of appropriately including children, and the severe consequences of exclusion.
It will be useful for caregivers to help adults understand what is and is
not appropriate, and to give them guidelines for how to determine this.
Caregivers should make themselves familiar with books, tapes, and
other resources, including support groups, which are designed specifically to meet the informational and support needs of the child contending with the dying of a parent. They should encourage children to ask
all of their questions and help them locate the appropriate resources to
address their concerns. Caregivers may find it especially useful to read
the specifics about a prevention program for families with a dying
parent. The program, designed to enable parents to foster their
children's necessary grief work and adjustment, has been reported by
Siegel, Mesagno, and Christ [29].

The third point refers to the "What's the alternative?" question
which must be applied when considering a child's exposure to painful
aspects of life, i.e., loss and death. Caregivers must ask this question of
themselves when confronted with the normal desire to protect a child
from what are construed to be traumatic circumstances. When these
circumstances involve the child's contending with elements of anticipatory or postdeath grief, often specifically entailing the child's involvement with a seriously ill parent or participation in funeral rituals,
the caregiver must ask him/herself, "What's the alternative?" to the
child being included in this situation. If the alternative is worse,
then the caregiver must choose to appropriately (based on developmental age and the prevailing circumstances) include that child and
work to minimize whatever distress there is from that inclusion.
Almost all thanatologists and child therapists share the belief that,

while it certainly is a most painful and anxiety-provoking situation to watch a beloved parent fall ill and die, it is even more painful and anxiety-provoking not to be included in the process. Posing this aforementioned question can help caregivers by providing the rationale for working with children in difficult circumstances when the desire to protect them must be challenged by recalling the deleterious effects of doing so.

The fourth point emphasizes that while it is imperative to recognize the importance of appropriate inclusion of the child in the illness of the parent and the critical need for therapeutic facilitation of, and support for, his/her anticipatory grief, it is equally as important to keep in mind that the child is first, and foremost, a child. There must not be an over-focus on the child as a family member of a dying individual to the disregard of his/her status as a child. Certainly, the illness of a parent forces many children to grow up in ways faster than adults would like. As well, children definitely will experience distress and sustain some scars from the experience. All of this is unavoidable, even though the sequelae are better for children than if they were not permitted to experience healthy anticipatory grief. Nevertheless, the perspective of the child still being a child must be maintained notwithstanding the need to include him/her in experiences that usually would be reserved for adults. This must translate into caregiver actions to create as much security as possible in the midst of the chaos; provide respites; pace exposure to painful situations; create structured and unstructured opportunities to vent emotions, discharge anxiety, receive support, and engage in relaxing and replenishing activities; place into children's lives things which are symbolic of life (e.g., plants, music, companion animals); and assist in maintaining appropriate hope and remembering, even when that hope dwindles, that life can and does go on albeit changed. These actions are appropriate for all family members of the terminally ill, not just children, but they are especially crucial for children because of their previously delineated disadvantages as mourners.

SUMMARY

This chapter has examined the complex, multidimensional phenomenon of anticipatory grief and analyzed the experience of children anticipating the death of a parent. Treatment strategies and interventions have been offered to facilitate healthy anticipatory grief in children, who typically contend with a host of disadvantages because of their psychosocial status.

REFERENCES

1. T. A. Rando, A Comprehensive Analysis of Anticipatory Grief: Perspectives, Processes, Promises, and Problems, in *Loss and Anticipatory Grief*, T. A. Rando, (ed.), Lexington Books, Lexington, Massachusetts, 1986.
2. T. A. Rando, *Treatment of Complicated Mourning*, Research Press, Champaign, Illinois, 1993.
3. R. Fulton and D. Gottesman, Anticipatory Grief: A Psychosocial Concept Reconsidered, *British Journal of Psychiatry, 137*, pp. 45-54, 1980.
4. K. Siegel and L. Weinstein, Anticipatory Grief Reconsidered, *Journal of Psychosocial Oncology, 1*, pp. 61-73, 1983.
5. C. M. Parkes and R. S. Weiss, *Recovery from Bereavement*, Basic Books, New York, 1983.
6. P. Silverman, Anticipatory Grief from the Perspective of Widowhood, in *Anticipatory Grief*, B. Schoenberg, A. Carr, A. Kutscher, D. Peretz, and I. Goldberg, (eds.), Columbia University Press, New York, 1974.
7. R. Weiss, Is It Possible to Prepare for Trauma?, *Journal of Palliative Care*, 4:1&2, pp. 74-76, 1988.
8. B. Glaser and A. Strauss, *Awareness of Dying*, Aldine, Chicago, Illinois, 1965.
9. T. A. Rando, *Grief, Dying, and Death: Clinical Interventions for Caregivers*, Research Press, Champaign, Illinois, 1984.
10. T. A. Rando, Understanding and Facilitating Anticipatory Grief in the Loved Ones of the Dying, in *Loss and Anticipatory Grief*, T. A. Rando (ed.), Lexington Books, Lexington, Massachusetts, 1986.
11. R. J. Kastenbaum, Death and Bereavement in Later Life, in *Death and Bereavement*, A. H. Kutscher (ed.), Charles C. Thomas, Springfield, Illinois, 1969.
12. D. Barton, The Family of the Dying Person, in *Dying and Death: A Clinical Guide for Caregivers*, D. Barton (ed.), Williams and Wilkins, Baltimore, Maryland, 1977.
13. K. J. Doka, *Living with Life-Threatening Illness: A Guide for Patients, their Families, and Caregivers*, Lexington Books, Lexington, Massachusetts, 1993.
14. M. Humphrey, Effects of Anticipatory Grief for the Patient, Family Member, and Caregiver, in *Loss and Anticipatory Grief*, T. A. Rando (ed.), Lexington Books, Lexington, Massachusetts, 1986.
15. E. J. Rosen, *Families Facing Death: Family Dynamics of Terminal Illness*, Lexington Books, Lexington, Massachusetts, 1990.
16. E. M. Pattison (ed.), *The Experience of Dying*, Prentice-Hall, Englewood Cliffs, New Jersey, 1977.
17. T. A. Rando, *How to Go on Living When Someone You Love Dies*, Bantam Books, New York, 1991.
18. J. L. Krupnick and F. Solomon, Death of a Parent or Sibling During Childhood, in *The Psychology of Separation and Loss*, J. Bloom-Feshbach, S. Bloom-Feshbach and Associates (eds.), Jossey-Bass Publishers, San Francisco, California, 1987.

19. K. Siegel, F. Mesagno, D. Karus, G. Christ, K. Banks, and R. Moynihan, Psychosocial Adjustment of Children with a Terminally Ill Parent, *Journal of the American Academy of Child and Adolescent Psychiatry, 31*, pp. 327-333, 1992.
20. E. LeShan, *When a Parent is Very Sick*, Little, Brown and Company (Joy Street Books), Boston, Massachusetts, 1986.
21. T. A. Rando, An Investigation of Grief and Adaptation in Parents whose Children have Died from Cancer, *Journal of Pediatric Psychology, 8*:1, pp. 3-20, 1983.
22. J. D. Van Dexter, Anticipatory Grief: Strategies for the Classroom, in *Loss and Anticipatory Grief*, T. A. Rando (ed.), Lexington Books, Lexington, Massachusetts, 1986.
23. I. Gerber, Anticipatory Bereavement, in *Anticipatory Grief*, B. Schoenberg, A. Carr, A. Kutscher, D. Peretz, and I. Goldberg (eds.), Columbia University Press, New York, 1974.
24. E. H. Futterman and I. Hoffman, Crisis and Adaptation in the Families of Fatally Ill Children, in *The Child in His Family: The Impact of Disease and Death*, Vol. 2, E. J. Anthony and C. Koupernik (eds.), John Wiley & Sons, New York, 1973.
25. R. N. Butler, The Life Review: An Interpretation of Reminiscence in the Aged, *Psychiatry, 26*, pp. 65-76, 1963.
26. A. D. Weisman, *On Dying and Denying: A Psychiatric Study of Terminality*, Behavioral Publications, New York, 1972.
27. R. Fulton, On the Dying of Death, in *Explaining Death to Children*, E. Grollman (ed.), Beacon Press, Boston, Massachusetts, 1967.
28. E. Rosenheim and R. Reicher, Informing Children about a Parent's Terminal Illness, *Journal of Child Psychology and Psychiatry, 26*, pp. 995-998, 1985.
29. K. Siegel, F. P. Mesagno, and G. Christ, A Prevention Program for Bereaved Children, *American Journal of Orthopsychiatry, 60*:2, pp. 168-175, 1990.

BIBLIOGRAPHY

Rando, T. A., Anticipatory Grief: The Term is a Misnomer but the Phenomenon Exists, in *Journal of Palliative Care,4*:1&2, pp. 70-73, 1988.

CHAPTER 2

Respecting Bereaved Children and Adolescents

Thomas W. Attig

INTRODUCTION

This chapter defines what is required to provide respect for bereaved children and adolescents by introducing the concept of respect for persons and then concentrating upon special features of respect for bereaved children and adolescents. It begins with discussion of how children and adolescents thrive in action, experience, and connection. It then considers how that thriving is vulnerable as children and adolescents experience bereavement. It ends with discussion of respectful response to bereaved children and adolescents in their vulnerability.

Respect for any thing requires understanding of 1) its distinctive character and how it thrives and 2) how its thriving is limited, threatened, or vulnerable. However, merely understanding these things does not suffice. Respect also requires that these understandings shape action 3) at least not to exacerbate the vulnerability or interfere with the thriving and 4) optimally, to actively support the thriving.

Respect for an individual person requires an understanding of not only how persons in general thrive or are vulnerable, but also the particulars of the life of the individual. Respect minimally requires that one not exacerbate his or her distinctive vulnerabilities or interfere with his or her unique pattern of thriving and, optimally, that one actively support his or her thriving.

The present chapter uses this concept of respect for persons to define what respect for bereaved children and adolescents requires.[1] The first section, Understanding How Children and Adolescents Thrive, characterizes children and adolescents as experiencing and acting persons who learn to be at home in the worlds of their experience. They care about many things, and within their distinctive patterns of caring develop self-identities and thrive as unique individuals. As they come to care about others, they become vulnerable to potentially life-transforming bereavement. The central section, Understanding Vulnerabilities of Children and Adolescents, examines that vulnerability. Individual vulnerabilities derive from 1) limits in their coping capacities, their background experiences, and their personal development; 2) the social circumstances within which they grieve; 3) the nature of the relationship with the deceased and the impacts of particular losses upon life pattern, self-identity, and thriving; and 4) the nature of the death itself as they experience it. The concluding section, Acting on the Understandings of Thriving and Vulnerability, identifies actions required in order to respect bereaved children and adolescents including minimally, not exacerbating their vulnerability or interfering with their coping and, optimally, actively supporting their coping and thriving. The former behaviors threaten or compromise, whereas the latter contribute to their relearning their worlds and establishing new patterns of thriving within them.

UNDERSTANDING HOW CHILDREN AND ADOLESCENTS THRIVE

Respecting children and adolescents requires reaching an understanding of how each individual has established, or is in the process of establishing, a life pattern in which he or she thrives. It requires learning what he or she finds interesting, enjoyable, satisfying, fulfilling, rewarding, or meaningful, and learning how each individual makes satisfying or sustaining connections in the world.

Realizing Achievement Values

Adults thrive as they realize what Victor Frankl calls achievement values [1]. That is, they find meaning in **doing** things as they pursue purposes they deem worthy; contribute to their families, friends or

---

[1] This chapter draws heavily upon the author's work in a book tentatively entitled, *Grieving: Relearning the World*, forthcoming from Oxford University Press, especially Chapter 3, Respecting the Bereaved.

broader communities; create, use their talents, accomplish or achieve; and thereby make a difference while they are here. Respecting them requires learning about how such activities give meaning to their lives.

The range of ways that children and adolescents experience themselves as achieving, contributing, and making important differences through what they do may vary from the range for adults, but it is broad and richly varied. Moreover, much of childhood and adolescence is a process of developing into, and learning to be, a fully functioning adult. This learning and development brings great satisfaction and feelings of accomplishment. The very young spend much of their time at play. Play not only brings pleasure, but it often imitates adult behavior, supports learning of new skills, satisfies curiosities, promotes social development, and provides experiences of accomplishment. As children mature, their play takes on different and often more complex forms. Children and adolescents alike make contributions at home through actions such as taking care of themselves and their bodies, taking responsibility for their places and possessions, doing chores, helping with siblings, caring for pets, and helping parents and older siblings with projects. In school they acquire physical abilities; learn new skills in reading, writing, and calculating; expand their understanding of the worlds around them; and acquire intellectual abilities. They develop social skills and learn new roles in cooperative activities; engage in creative activities in music, art, dance, and theater; and engage in competitions, including sports. Many take lessons to enhance their skills and abilities to enjoy a broad spectrum of physical, social, spiritual, or creative activities. Many join youth groups, such as girl or boy scout troops, church groups, and 4-H and other clubs, where they engage in still other activities, learn new skills, find identity, and sense they are contributing. Some children and many adolescents work outside of the home, some as volunteers and others for wages. Respecting children and adolescents requires learning about the activities that fill their days, what it is that they like to do, and how, in doing them, they find satisfaction, fulfillment, purpose, a sense of contribution, or feelings of accomplishment.

Realizing Experiential Values

Adults thrive as they realize what Frankl calls experiential values [1]. That is, they find meaning in **experiencing** things deemed valuable as they look within themselves, interact with others (especially in love relationships), dwell in the surrounding natural environment, or commune with the divine. Either at the time of the experiences or upon reflection, they perceive that the experiences contribute to the worth and meaning of their lives. They are grateful for knowing the experience, fulfilled in it or satisfied by it. To respect them requires learning how these and other experiences help them to believe their lives are worthwhile.

The range of ways in which children and adolescents perceive themselves as fulfilled, satisfied, or living meaningfully through what they experience may again vary from the range for adults, but it, too, is broad and richly varied. Children and adolescents constantly acquire new experiences and appreciate what they offer. Much youthful excitement and enthusiasm come from experiencing the unprecedented and discovering the satisfactions of diverse experiences. Respecting children and adolescents requires learning how they find satisfaction and meaning in play, games, sports, performance, laughter, the senses, the imagination, personal growth, learning, responsibility, choices, recognition, reward, physical closeness, affection, generosity, acceptance, forgiveness, friendship, stories, shared moments, celebrations, music, drama, parks, beaches, walks, bike rides, nature's wonders, perseverance, reverence, prayer, divine grace, and forgiveness. Children and adolescents find their individuality in their own life experiences and thrive in combinations of those experiences that they perceive as contributing to the value and meaning of their lives.

Meaning through Connection

Adults find some activities and experiences especially meaningful when they perceive themselves as **connected to something transcendent,** something greater than themselves. They perceive these experiences as trans-personally significant or contributing something of lasting value. Other experiences are valued when they realize connectedness to friends, family, the community, a tradition, a cause, nature, God, the future after they have gone, or an afterlife. Through such connections in action and experience, adults sense that they live in the service of a higher purpose, have a reason to live, leave the world a better place for having been here, and through this, acquire their personal identities [2].

Over time, children and adolescents learn to establish and value such connections. They do so primarily in their connections with their parents and families, then with friends and peers, and later, with the larger community, nature, God, the future after they are gone, or an afterlife. This learning occurs as concepts of these things become available to them, and as they experience and engage in the activities that ground their sense of connection.

UNDERSTANDING THE VULNERABILITIES
OF CHILDREN AND ADOLESCENTS

Respecting bereaved children and adolescents requires understanding how each experiences, and copes with, his or her vulnerability to loss. Most fundamentally, bereaved children and adolescents are vulnerable to the potentially far-reaching impacts of loss upon their life patterns. They experience the pain of the loss as the expected pattern of caring for and about, and thriving in relationship to, the deceased is halted abruptly. Spending time and effort in grieving disrupts and distorts other expected patterns of caring and thriving in the broader context of their lives. Their development and thriving as unique individuals is in crisis, and how they grieve decisively influences their future thriving and who they become. As they grieve, they learn to live in the absence of the one who has died.

Some factors may interfere with, hinder, compromise, undermine, inhibit, or even stifle effective coping. These factors frustrate their attempts to establish a transformed pattern of caring and thriving, regain momentum in their personal development, and again live meaningfully. Among these are: 1) limitations in their own coping capacities and background experiences; and complications from their past or present stage of personal development; 2) possible adverse affects or interferences that derive from the social circumstances within which they grieve; 3) complications that derive from unhappy features of their relationships with the deceased; and 4) complications deriving from the especially challenging nature of some deaths. Respecting bereaved children and adolescents requires understanding any or all of these personal vulnerabilities.

Vulnerabilities that Derive from Something about the Grieving Child or Adolescent

Limitations of their own coping capacities and background experiences with loss and grieving define perhaps the most significant and distinctive vulnerabilities for children and adolescents. Limitations in any of the dimensions in which persons cope, i.e., the psychological/emotional, behavioral, physical, social, and intellectual/spiritual, hinder or compromise success in grieving. Lack of experience with loss, or a history of ineffective coping with loss, has similar effects. Children and adolescents are also vulnerable developmentally in ways that adults typically are not. Because they are caught by bereavement in early stages of personal development, children and adolescents are vulnerable to revisiting of their losses when they reach new stages of personal development. Ineffective grieving early in life can disrupt development or complicate its further progress.

Vulnerabilities for children and adolescents include the following limitations of their coping capacities.

1. Consider first, vulnerability due to **emotional and psychological limitations**. Some young people are simply less prepared than others for the psychological and emotional challenges of dealing with loss. Some are less able to identify their own emotional responses to loss. Unprecedented feelings frighten and leave them at a loss as to what to do or say. They lack the vocabulary to express what they are feeling. Some express their emotions non-verbally but may be misunderstood as they do so. Some imagine wrongly that they are responsible for the death, e.g., because they wished the person dead. Many come to bereavement with fragile and unstable self-confidence, self-esteem, and self-identities. As they reach or exceed tolerance limits, the impact of bereavement may overwhelm them, induce psychological numbness, or drive them to use immature psychological defense mechanisms to protect themselves. They may simply cease coping emotionally or psychologically. This shutdown, in turn, may undermine effective coping in other dimensions.

2. Bereaved children and adolescents are vulnerable in the **limitations of their abilities to cope behaviorally**. Grieving requires effort as well as time. Some young people are more passive by disposition. Some feel helpless and need to learn that they have choices in response to choiceless events. Children and adolescents often lack models for appropriate coping behavior during the mourning period and for putting together new life patterns. Regressive behavior is common. Many expected desires, motivations, dispositions, behaviors, habits, and day-to-day hopes and expectations are no longer viable in a world where the deceased no longer exists. If they cope by persisting as if the deceased were still alive, they retreat in fantasy, no longer living in the present but in the past. Some are less flexible or adaptable than others in adjusting desires to the new reality. Some are less able to establish a new pattern of day-to-day living where they fill time in different ways and expend effort in alternative experiences and activities.

3. Bereaved children and adolescents have **physical limitations**. Dependence makes them more likely to be anxious about the basic necessities of life: food, shelter, and love. As social beings, children and adolescents require bonding for survival. Death often breaks significant bonds just when children are first establishing, testing, and/or learning to value and trust them. Consequently, they are vulnerable to heightened separation anxiety and feelings of insecurity, distrust,

abandonment, and alienation. The breaking of bonds and the attendant feelings take a physical toll. The more extensive the array of challenges to be met in grieving, the more likely it is to become an enervating and exhausting ordeal. The physically fragile, the ill, and the physically disabled are at greater risk for physical complication in their grieving. Even those who are older and more responsible for meeting their own physical needs neglect them in times of crisis. Loss of good health can compromise bereaved children and adolescents in other dimensions of their coping.

4. Bereaved children and adolescents are also vulnerable in their **limited capacities to cope socially**. Some children are blind to their own needs or to the potential comfort, consolation, and support that others can provide. Some are inhibited in reaching out for support because of lack of ability to explain what troubles them or to state what they need or hope for in response from others. Others are shy or fear showing their vulnerability or being rejected or treated insensitively. Some believe that it is inappropriate to ask for help or do not know how to ask. Some fear adding to the burdens of others who are grieving themselves. Some decline to accept support when it is offered. Some put off helpers as they are seen as too demanding, volatile, complaining, or ungrateful. Some hold views that only certain persons should provide support, e.g., close family or friends. They neither seek nor accept support from others, including clergy, teachers, mental health professionals, and support groups. Some withdraw precipitously from nearly all social interaction out of fear of being hurt again. Many are ignorant of the possibilities and potential benefits of participation in family, community, and ritual responses to death.

5. Bereaved children and adolescents are vulnerable in their **intellectual and spiritual limitations**. They lack the support that settled answers provide. Their disorientation is greater to the extent that they do not understand what the realities of death and loss entail. Some do not understand the concrete realities of illness, death itself, funeral and visitation practices, disposition of the body, and mourning customs. Some lack abilities to give voice to the questions they have. Some find it difficult to obtain comprehensible and satisfactory answers to the questions they do raise. They are vulnerable to misinformation provided in response to questions and information that feeds their fantasies rather than aids their understanding of reality. What they overhear or misunderstand in adult conversation often confuses them. They are often ignorant of the impacts of bereavement and what the grieving process involves and disturbed by doubts about whether what they experience and do is normal or acceptable. They typically lack mature beliefs about such things as the meanings of life, death,

and suffering. Some realize for the first time that they, too, can die, e.g., when a sibling or peer dies. They often lack experience in spiritual practices such as prayer, contemplation, and meditation that can bring consolation, forgiveness, and peace.

6. Bereaved children and adolescents are vulnerable to **limitations in their coping capacities deriving from their personal histories with loss.** Past loss and grieving shadow present bereavement. Some children simply lack experience with grieving altogether. The unprecedented experience surprises and catches them unprepared to deal with challenges they perceive to be unlike any they have faced before. Some failed to grieve past losses effectively or were actively discouraged as they tried to do so. Some buried or inhibited their own grieving or developed ineffective grieving patterns. Some are in the midst of unresolved grieving when another loss occurs. Few break with unhappy precedent in their coping pattern without self-conscious effort or the guidance and encouragement of others.

7. Although adults, too, may lack well developed coping capacities, children and adolescents are **vulnerable in their personal development** in at least two distinctive ways. First, when they are bereaved in early stages of their personal development, they are destined to replay and regrieve losses at later stages of their development. Later events in their lives may trigger renewed grieving, especially holidays, birthdays, and major turning points such as school entrance, advancement in school, graduations, the onset of puberty, first dates, important successes and failures, career selection, marriage, and births of their own children. Revisiting the losses of their childhood and adolescence, such as the death of a parent, grandparent, sibling or friend, may present new challenges to understand reality without the deceased, and to define how they want to be and go on without him or her. Revisiting losses may include fresh emotion, behavioral disorientation, renewed longing for the deceased, new social complications, and new questions about the significance of the loss and the meaning of life without the deceased. Functional and effective coping with the loss early in life may not be maintained in the face of new developmental needs.

Second, ineffective grieving early in life can disrupt or complicate development. Regression is common, especially among younger children, in any or all dimensions of personal development. Missed opportunities to learn about expression of emotion can reverberate for years and even decades. Children and adolescents can suffer serious setbacks in the emergence of self-confidence, self-esteem, and self-identity. Missed opportunities to learn that there are many ways to respond to what happens in life, to choose and give direction to one's own life after loss, can retard behavioral development and reinforce tendencies toward helplessness and passivity. Disruption of processes of building and learning to trust bonds with others can induce severe and long-lasting separation anxiety and compromise the quality of personal bonding far into the future. Missed opportunities to learn to ask for and receive support from others, offering and giving it or participating in family and community responses to death, can inhibit social development and set unfortunate patterns for years to come. Missed opportunities to learn through asking questions and receiving honest, orienting, and age-appropriate answers can stifle intellectual development and undermine appreciation of the orienting power of the mind. Missed opportunities to introduce children and adolescents to spiritual traditions and practices in accessible ways and to do so in such a way as to promote their own explorations can undermine their spiritual development and inhibit growth in appreciation of means to peace, consolation, and discernment of the possible meanings of life, death, and suffering in general, in their own case, and that of the deceased.

Vulnerability that Derives from the Social Circumstances of Bereavement

Children and adolescents do not grieve in isolation. They grieve in social contexts where they live with family, friends, peers, and within cultural settings and surrounding communities. In interaction with others they develop their identities, take on roles, accumulate histories of loss, and see others as models for dealing with loss. They, like adults, are vulnerable to such things as inadequate support and poor modeling. Unwelcome expectations of others, unhelpful mourning practices, confining or inflexible cultural norms, intolerance and spiritual inflexibility, and binding gender expectations add to their burdens. They often experience estrangement, alienation, unavailability, and other forms of social distance from persons from whom they most desire or need support. School, church, or work continue to make demands upon them and some receive censure from others for failure to fulfill their functions. They often receive bad advice and counsel about grief, and some are affected by inadequate, unavailable, or inaccessible support from social service and mental health agencies, religious organizations, or support groups.

Children and adolescents are especially vulnerable to the inadequacies of response of others to their grieving in several distinctive respects.

1. The **mistaken belief that children do not grieve** leads some to dismiss the significance of their loss experiences altogether. The worlds of their experience change as profoundly as those of adults. The loss of presence of the deceased is experienced by them in potentially every corner of their worlds. They are challenged by the objects and places left behind (inside and outside the home), events and special occasions, and relationships with fellow survivors within and outside the family. They also struggle to find ways to continue to care about the deceased in his or her absence. They, too, feel less "at home" in the world, less safe and secure, less confident of the meaning of everyday life, and less assured that the greater scheme of things makes sense when taken together. They experience major disruptions in the pattern of their daily lives, the unfolding of their life stories, and their patterns of connection in the world. They struggle emotionally and psychologically, behaviorally, physically and biologically, socially, intellectually and spiritually to come to terms with what has happened and its impact upon them. To fail to acknowledge this by treating children as if they do not grieve, is to leave them to deal with major changes in the world and themselves in a terrible isolation.

2. Closely related to the view that children do not grieve, and perhaps an extension of it, is a **myth of childhood innocence**. Yes, children and adolescents are often inexperienced and naive about a wide range of phenomena. Yes, much of their experience is new and fresh. However, not all experience in childhood and adolescence is sweet, innocent, and positive. Difficult things happen in their lives as well. When they do, some of the innocence is shattered. It does no good to try to preserve their innocence when death touches them personally. By virtue of the events themselves, they are no longer innocent. To pretend that they are untouched by the events, and to treat children and adolescents as islands of innocence, is to enter an adult fantasy that perhaps meets a perverse adult need but neither comprehends the experience of children or adolescents nor meets their needs. Rather, the pretense promotes denial, avoidance, or fantasy about reality in children or adolescents and leaves them isolated from the support they need in the face of unprecedented and all too harsh new realities in their lives.

3. Children and adolescents are vulnerable to the **dismissal of the significance of their losses**. Others may simply not appreciate the intensity of children's or adolescents' caring or the importance of attachment to grandparents, siblings, friends, public figures (e.g., rock, movie or sports stars), or pets. Even when the intensity or importance are expressed openly, they may be discounted, ridiculed, or otherwise

trivialized. The remoteness of childhood and adolescent experiences from those of some adults makes such dismissal more likely.

4. Children and adolescents are vulnerable to the **neglect of their needs** as they grieve. Fellow survivors, including parents, siblings, other family members, or friends, who might be expected to be supportive, may be so caught up in their own grief that they overlook the needs of children or adolescents. While it may be too difficult for significant others to give when they themselves are so needy, unintentional neglect results when children and adolescents are forgotten, as they are all too frequently. This neglect is intensified when children are shunted away or dismissed with no suggestions for alternative sources of help and support. In the broader social context, communities can fail to recognize the needs of grieving children and adolescents, expect their needs to be met within nuclear families sometimes stretched to their limits by shared bereavement, and neglect to provide needed professional and volunteer services for children or adolescents.

5. Children and adolescents are vulnerable to **others' intolerance of their grieving**. Some adults find it extremely difficult to be in the presence of children or adolescents who are hurting. It pains them too much, and it may remind them of painful times in their own youth. It does not fit with their ideas of the order of things. Feelings of helplessness, of not knowing what to do or say, of inadequacy in wanting to make things better, or to fulfill unrealistic expectations of themselves as parents may lead them to avoid grieving children and adolescents.

6. Children and adolescents are vulnerable to **abuses of power and authority**. Dependent, perceived as lacking maturity, and in subordinate positions, they are especially vulnerable to others' efforts to control them in ways that deny them opportunity to grieve at all or to grieve on their own terms. Others may restrict their expressions, censure their behaviors, limit their choices, foreclose their opportunities to interact with others and participate in family and community responses to death, and discourage or stifle their attempts to orient themselves to reality and find answers to questions. Especially destructive are demands that young persons take on inappropriate roles for their age, e.g., as "the man (or woman) of the house." Often efforts to control are well intentioned and in the name of "what is best for them." Such paternalism adds to feelings of helplessness and powerlessness just when children and adolescents most need to sense that they have some choice in responding to life's challenges and giving direction to their lives.

7. Finally, children and adolescents are especially **vulnerable to peer pressures and insensitive responses**. Young children often face not only unwelcome curiosity about their experiences of loss but

also taunts and ridicule. So much of child and adolescent self-esteem, self-confidence, and self-identity derive from finding their places among their peers. As they seek independence from their parents, they come to rely more heavily upon peers for support, and peers may not be up to offering the support they need or seek. Not knowing what to do or say, peers may withdraw, avoid them, deal with them abruptly, make hurtful remarks, offer precious little comfort, or make them feel uncomfortably different or strange. Bereavement often sets young persons apart from their peers just when a sense of belonging matters so much. Pressures to conform are immense. As they approach and enter adolescent years, they become increasingly vulnerable to expectations of others that they conform to group norms and gender stereotypes. Learning to be a young man or young woman is a central part of identity formation. Boys may find it difficult to show feelings or express needs that are thought to be incompatible with male independence or macho toughness. Girls may be uncomfortable in allowing boys to see them upset or crying, or they may too readily care for others while neglecting their own needs.

Vulnerability Deriving from the Nature of the Relationship with the Deceased

Distinctive features of relationships with the deceased make bereaved children and adolescents uniquely vulnerable.

1. The **tapestries of their lives require more or less reweaving** depending upon such things as the duration and degree of intimacy with the deceased. The more the connection to the deceased is interwoven in the tapestry of their lives, the greater the vulnerability to having to reweave the fabric. Until they reweave new life patterns, their thriving remains diminished. They must reconstruct daily routines once built upon perceptions and expectations that the deceased would be present. They must absorb major disruptions in the unfolding of their life stories, find and define new ways of going on, and redefine hopes and expectations for the future. They must establish new patterns of connection in the world that allow for give and take that supports their sense of meaning and purpose in living. Respecting bereaved children and adolescents requires understanding the peculiarities and detailed contours of the reweaving required.

2. In some instances, **lingering unfinished business and concerns associated with ambivalence, anger, guilt, or dependence** in relationships with the deceased challenge them. Bereaved children and adolescents are vulnerable to complications in their grieving

that derive from especially challenging or stressful aspects of their relationships with the deceased. Typically, they are troubled by lost opportunities to complete unfinished business. Most commonly, they long to share anticipated experiences, realize hopes and aspirations for accomplishing something together, utter unspoken words of love and affection, and say goodbyes.

Unfortunately, not all relationships are uncomplicatedly loving. Some difficulties in grieving derive from hurtful or dysfunctional aspects of relationships with the deceased such as unresolved anger, ambivalence, guilt, or dependence. Negative ties are as binding as positive ties. Often they bind more firmly. Loosening such bonds is often profoundly complicated and the intervention of trained professionals often a near necessity. Survivors' negative feelings persist. Inability to express or resolve them in interaction with the deceased frustrates them. Some feel guilt about harboring those negative feelings and leaving them unresolved. Negative treatment and possibly abuse by the deceased continue to adversely affect survivor's self-esteem, self-confidence, and functioning in relationships with others. Some resent persistent destructive consequences of the relationship upon their current life pattern. Some cannot forgive to an extent that allows them to return to meaningful living as survivors.

Sometimes bereaved children or adolescents feel guilty toward the deceased for having mistreated or in some way failed them. In some cases, the responsibility is imagined rather than real, but the feelings are not imagined and must be dealt with. In some cases, the responsibility is real and death closes the usual avenues toward reconciliation, forgiveness, or compensation. When bereaved children or adolescents perceive themselves as in any way responsible for the death, guilt can be excruciating. Tragically, at times, they are responsible, though rarely entirely so.

Negative bonding with the deceased can complicate and prolong fruitless longing for the return of the deceased. The desire is not exclusively loving and affectionate. Resentment, frustration, and bitterness likely prevail. They can bind strongly. The unfinished business challenges survivors profoundly. They struggle even to recognize or acknowledge these negative elements in their relationships with the deceased. Even when they do so, they often cannot effectively express or come to terms with them. Moreover, strong family and social pressures often reinforce reluctance to acknowledge, express, and come to terms with the negative bonding. Unless bereaved children and adolescents do so, the hopeless longing for the deceased will persist.

Vulnerability that Derives from the Nature or Circumstances of the Death Itself

The distinctive character of some deaths complicates bereavement. Sudden and unexpected deaths heighten surprise, intensify shock and numbness, startle children and adolescents into realizing how the relationship with the deceased was taken for granted, and leave more business unfinished. It is difficult to take in the reality of the loss. Violent, mutilating, or random deaths bring shock, horror, and trauma that interfere in usual grieving processes. Witnessing such deaths exacerbates these interference factors and often adds the effects of post-traumatic stress syndrome (e.g., hypervigilance, hypersensitivity to stimuli, nightmares, and fixating visions) to the challenges of normal grieving [3, pp. 61-66]. Deaths perceived as preventable or caused by human actions or neglect frequently distract from normal grieving as survivors preoccupy themselves with those responsible and adjust to a world they perceive as threatening, menacing, and untrustworthy. Deaths of siblings or peers provoke often frightening realization of personal mortality. Suicidal deaths of peers or stars can prompt copycat behaviors and are especially challenging as they are sudden and usually unexpected, often violent and mutilating, involve human action, and draw much public attention, especially among peers. When survivors, in retrospect, sense that they could have done something to intervene but did not, guilt can be nearly overwhelming. Deaths of parents, or others on whom children or adolescents depend, bring anxieties about survival needs and what might happen to others who provide for them.

ACTING ON THE UNDERSTANDINGS OF THRIVING AND VULNERABILITY

Thus far, discussion of respecting bereaved children and adolescents focused upon understanding how they 1) thrive in experiences, actions, and connections within individual life patterns and 2) are vulnerable both to the disruption of those life patterns that loss entails and to factors that compromise, hinder, interfere with, or even undermine effective coping with loss. Together these elements comprise the necessary conditions of respect for bereaved children and adolescents. Bereaved children and adolescents must be understood in their distinctive capacities to thrive and in their particular vulnerabilities and limitations.

Respecting bereaved children and adolescents, however, requires more than understanding their thriving and vulnerability. Respect requires that this understanding inform interaction with them. First, and minimally, respect requires restraint in action to avoid exacerbating vulnerability or interfering with coping. Doing either undercuts their autonomy as they give direction to their own lives and seek again to thrive and find life meaningful and purposeful. To fail to respect autonomy compounds deprivation, delays progress in grieving, and postpones returning to thriving in viable, transformed life patterns.

Optimally, respect for bereaved children and adolescents requires more than mere non-interference; it requires actions that acknowledge them as community members, promote community with them, and thereby contribute to their thriving. Non-interference in their lives does not suffice to sustain community with them, for their capacities to thrive and find satisfaction, meaning, and purpose in life are severely compromised. These capacities can be sustained in most cases only through maintenance of bonds with and active support from others. Grieving revives both 1) appreciation of the possibility for continued satisfaction, meaning, and purpose in living and 2) motivation to resume such living despite the loss. Constructive support and active helping preserve community membership, facilitate grieving, enable a return to thriving, and contribute to reestablishing viable life patterns.

Helpers should recognize the potentially far-reaching impacts of loss on present life and future development of bereaved children and adolescents. Helpers can support them by letting them know that they understand that grieving takes much time and energy. They can offer patience, flexibility, and forgiveness in their expectations of them at home, at school, or in other roles and relationships. They can encourage them to seek advice and support from the sources that children and adolescents think will be most helpful. They can offer their own presence and provide reassurance of continuing affection, care and concern, and empathy. They can make themselves available to listen actively, offer constructive advice when asked, and provide comfort and support as requested or accepted. They can acknowledge the legitimacy of their grieving and discourage others from dismissing or trivializing it, or abandoning them when they most need community support. They can help them to understand grieving as an active coping process and encourage them to resist passivity and helplessness. They can encourage them to actively engage in grieving at their own pace and in their own ways.

Helpers can attune themselves to the individual and distinctive contours of the individual child's or adolescent's experience and the ways the relationship with the deceased was woven into his or her life pattern and recognize and respond sensitively to the points of greatest vulnerability. They can support and encourage them as children and adolescents address their unique tasks in coming to terms with objects and places, events and special occasions, relationships with others, aspects of their daily routines, changes in the unfolding of their life stories, and hopes and aspirations for the future.

Helpers can recognize children's and adolescents' developmental disadvantages in emotional and psychological, behavioral, physical and biological, social, and intellectual and spiritual coping skills and adjust their supportive responses to take these disadvantages into account. They can interact with them in age-appropriate ways, provide good modeling of effective coping, and support development of coping abilities in all dimensions.

Emotionally and psychologically, helpers can assist children in developing vocabularies to identify and express their emotions or support them in alternative expressions through touch, physical expression, play, art, and music. They can provide their presence, offer abiding love and affection, and welcome children's and adolescents' presence and contributions to family and community life to reinforce self-esteem. They can bolster self-confidence by encouraging and supporting them as they find things to do and say in response to what happened to them. They can help them cope with changing personal identities by providing support as they puzzle over who they are now that the one they loved has died, return to familiar roles and ways of doing things, or try new roles and unfamiliar ways of doing things.

Behaviorally, helpers can support children and adolescents as they discover what remains viable in their patterns of living or adopt new patterns. They can help them to identify alternatives, gather information about and evaluate options, choose from among them, enact the choices, and evaluate the results of their choices. As they do so, they help to develop the skills children and adolescents require for choice and autonomy.

Physically and biologically, helpers can help children and adolescents by insuring that their physical needs for food, rest, and shelter are met. They can encourage them to take good care of themselves and keep a watchful eye for deterioration in their health. They can reinforce personal bonds with them through, e.g., simple presence, touch, comfort, and reassurance of their worth. And they can encourage others to offer the same rather than to compound feelings of separation and abandonment. They can also help them to see that bonds with the deceased need not be thought of as completely severed by helping them find ways of continuing to care about what the deceased cared about and by sharing memories and otherwise treasuring the stories of the lives now ended.

Socially, they can help children and adolescents by welcoming their presence in family and community responses to death and helping them find ways of participating. They can help them as they reshape patterns of interacting with others, including family, friends, peers, or others in the wider community. They can offer to be with them in especially challenging social circumstances; help them anticipate and rehearse conversations and other interactions; offer to intercede with others; help them with new relationships; and encourage and support them as they seek help from individuals, support groups, or professionals.

Intellectually, helpers can provide honest and age appropriate answers to questions that enable children and adolescents to understand the realities of life, death, suffering, bereavement, and grieving. They can appreciate that children especially need concrete explanation, orient themselves best with their senses (i.e., seeing, hearing, and touching for themselves), and are usually ill-prepared to deal with abstractions save in very beginning ways. They can help them to develop greater self-awareness and reflective abilities as they seek to understand themselves in bereavement.

Spiritually, they can help children and adolescents to recover old, and discover new, goals and purposes in day-to-day life and hopes and aspirations for the future. They can begin to introduce abstract theological or religious concepts provided the children are clear about the concrete realities of what has transpired. They can support them as they seek security, peace, consolation, and a return to feeling "at home" in the world, despite human limitation and vulnerability and the mystery that pervades the human condition.

Helpers can anticipate and normalize revisiting loss as children and adolescents come to later stages in their development. As they regrieve their losses, they can again provide comfort, reassurance, and support as they meet new challenges and cope in all of the dimensions outlined above.

Helpers can resist temptations to control or protect bereaved children and adolescents. Instead of intervening paternalistically, they can recognize that it is "best" for children and adolescents to be supported in finding and defining their own ways of coming to terms with loss and returning to thriving within their own lives, since, after all, no one can do this for them.

Constructive helping such as is outlined here can help children and adolescents avoid the pitfalls of ineffective grieving, its effects on their personal development, and its potentially long-lasting and detrimental legacies in later life. In all of these ways helpers can demonstrate respect for bereaved children and adolescents and affirm community with them.

REFERENCES

1. V. Frankl, *Man's Search for Meaning, An Introduction to Logotherapy* (3rd Edition), Touchstone Books, New York, 1984.
2. R. Lifton, *Broken Connections: On Death and the Continuity of Life,* Basic Books, New York, 1983.
3. K. C. Peterson, M. E. Prout, and R. A. Schwarz, *Post Traumatic Stress Disorder: A Clinician's Guide*, Plenum Press, New York, 1991.

CHAPTER 3

Religion, Spirituality, and Bereaved Adolescents*

David E. Balk and Nancy S. Hogan

ADOLESCENT BEREAVEMENT RESEARCH SINCE THE 1980s

At one time it was accurate and fashionable to note the paucity of research attention paid to adolescent bereavement. However, during the 1980s a body of scholarship began to emerge. Though adolescent bereavement has not yet captured the mainstream interests of adolescence research, we can no longer begin by saying investigators have paid scant attention to adolescent grief.

Adolescent sibling bereavement has been the topic most investigated [1-20]. Researchers have given some attention to adolescent parental bereavement [21-26]. Surprisingly, little attention has focused on adolescent grief at the death of a friend. One exception is an in-depth case study of high school students' reactions to the death of a peer from cancer [27]. In another study the researcher used a psychodynamic model to examine adolescent bereavement over the sudden death of a peer and offered vignettes depicting adolescent coping [28]. Given the incidence of adolescent deaths due to accidents, homicides, and suicides, one would expect greater research interest in bereavement over a friend's death.

*Preparation of this chapter was made possible by grants to David Balk from the Prevention Research Branch of the National Institute of Mental Health (MH 45044) and from the William T. Grant Foundation; and by a grant to Nancy Hogan from the Institute for the Study of Culture and Nursing of the University of Miami School of Nursing.

Investigators of adolescent grief over a sibling, parent, or friend's death, have studied several familiar variables. Topics frequently explored have been emotional responses, relations with peers, relations with family members, academics, self-concept, and physical health. An overview of these topics is provided in the introductory article to a special issue of *Journal of Adolescent Research* devoted to death and adolescent bereavement [4]. Fleming and Adolph provided a model for understanding the developmental issues involved when adolescents are bereaved [29].

Some researchers have looked at adolescents' reactions to their terminal illness. This research builds on the understanding that adolescents comprehend what death means, but as Charles Corr (personal communication, February 12, 1990) noted, "The issue for adolescents is not so much the capacity to understand death, but the significance of that understanding for them, that is, the way in which it bears meaning for them."

The major themes, to date, in research literature about dying adolescents concern: 1) the emotional devastation the knowledge elicits, 2) the intensity of adolescents' desire to know about their disease and their prognosis, 3) the efforts adolescents employ to retain privacy, dignity, and control, and 4) the struggle adolescents engage in to make sense out of dying off-time and young [30-33].

A ROAD LESS TRAVELLED IN THE ADOLESCENT BEREAVEMENT LITERATURE

Two topics that researchers have investigated sparingly is the place of religion, and the development of spirituality in the life of a bereaved adolescent. The topic of religion in adult responses to death has received research attention [34-38]. In his famous article on the symptomatology and management of acute grief, Lindemann acknowledged the leading role religious agencies played affording the bereaved solace and helping them counteract guilt [39]. More recently some attention has been given to spirituality and bereavement [40-45].

We know that Freud, who was an atheist, considered religion an illusion, but then we know that some mainline Christian theologians also condemned religion [46]. A generation of Protestant theologians, between World War I and the end of World War II, considered religion hypocrisy and "cheap grace," an effort to manipulate God rather than to believe in God. Primary advocates of this view of religion were Karl Barth, Dietrich Bonhoeffer, Rudolf Bultmann, and Paul Tillich [47-50].

Typically, theologians have made sharp distinctions between religion and spirituality. One of the distinctions refers to the judgment that religion is an escape from faith. We recognize that this insight about some religious practices has validity, but we refuse to make a drastic judgment that all religious practices or religious beliefs are illusory or are merely efforts to manipulate. Religion depends on culture. It is the attempt to give organized, cultural form to experiences of the sacred. Christianity, alone, has a seemingly endless variety of cultural expressions of religious belief about Jesus. A variety of cultural expressions of encounters with the sacred is also true for Judaism. We suspect such variety is true for any organized religion.

Religion provides rituals, symbols, stories, and acts such as prayer, whereby the believer expresses worship and perhaps experiences the presence of God. Some of these symbols and stories deal with death and the meaning of life.

Spirituality transcends religion. Some religious believers are not spiritual, and some spiritual persons reject religious beliefs. Spirituality is known primarily as the human capability to experience wonder and awe; for some persons, the experience of wonder and awe is a revelation of the holy.

Spirituality is a manifestation of the human species' effort to make meaning. In some persons their spirituality finds expression in an organized religion; in others, organized religion holds no meaning, but a relationship with that which is more than themselves does hold meaning. Spirituality is the development of this relationship.

One form spirituality takes is to reflect upon what it means to be human. We understand spirituality to be a matter of an unfolding consciousness of the meaning of existence.

In this chapter we look at the places religion and spirituality occupy in adolescent bereavement research. First, we consider religion as a means of coping with death and bereavement. Second, we examine the possible changes in understanding the meaning of existence that death and bereavement can elicit during adolescence.

RELIGION AS A MEANS OF COPING

Contemporary models of coping with life crises are decidedly cognitive in nature. The model developed by Rudolf H. Moos is an excellent example [51, 52].

The Moos Model of Coping with Life Crises

Moos presents five sets of adaptive tasks and three domains of coping skills. The adaptive tasks are to:

1. Establish the meaning and understand the personal significance of the event;
2. Confront reality and respond to the situational requirements;
3. Sustain interpersonal relations;
4. Maintain emotional balance;
5. Preserve a satisfactory self-image and maintain a sense of self-efficacy.

The three domains of coping skills are:

1. Appraisal-focused coping (logical analysis and mental preparation, cognitive redefinition, and cognitive avoidance or denial);
2. Problem-focused coping (seeking information and support, taking action, and identifying alternatives);
3. Emotion-focused coping (affective regulation, emotional discharge, and resigned acceptance).

Three factors influence cognitive appraisal of a crisis: background and personal factors (e.g., religious beliefs), event-related factors (e.g., the extent to which the event is anticipated), and environmental factors (e.g., the support received from members of one's church, synagogue, or mosque). Cognitive appraisal triggers coping skills as well as the adaptive tasks. The determinants of crisis outcome are a product of the interaction of these aspects, moderated by cognitive appraisal.

Religion enters the Moos model at several points. One point is the place of religion in one's background and personal factors. For instance, does the adolescent consider religious interpretations of human existence to be meaningful? Religion can also be part of the person's environment, as noted in the type of support provided by one's fellow believers. The Amish have been depicted as excellent examples of environmental support following a death [53].

Religion also enters the Moos model in the adaptive tasks and the coping skills. One of the adaptive tasks is to establish the meaning and understand the personal significance of the event. Not uncommonly, bereaved persons, for whom religion is meaningful, will turn to their religious beliefs as a means to make sense of the death of their loved one.

The effort to make sense of a death exemplifies the human species' drive to find meaning. One issue to ponder is how religious belief enables some bereaved people to find meaning, whereas for others, their religious belief becomes a mockery. Lewis was quite clear that God had abandoned him in the acute stages of his grief [54]. One excellent scriptural investigation of this theme can be found in Leon-Dufour's *Life and Death in the New Testament* [55].

Religion can also be seen as a coping skill in any of the three domains that Moos identifies: appraisal-focused, problem-focused, and emotion-focused coping. Other researchers have noted, for example, the role religion plays in emotion-focused coping [35, 38].

Moos emphasizes that the outcome of a life crisis influences further experiences. This emphasis is, of course, in line with the conclusions made in the crisis intervention literature about the influences life crises exert on development [39, 56-60].

The Pargament Model of Coping

Kenneth Pargament has been studying explicitly the role religion plays in human coping [61-63]. He has synthesized a model quite congruent with the approach taken by Moos.

Pargament's model emphasizes that personal appraisal of events is key to determining a person's response. Thus, his model's focus on personal attributions emphasizes the cognitive aspects of coping. He accents that coping also requires action in his discussions of the coping behaviors found in problem-focused and emotion-focused coping.

Religion is a significant component that Pargament identifies in coping responses. He shows that religion can affect personal attributions of an event, can offer an active means of responding to an event such as through prayer and trust in a benevolent God, and can lead to various outcomes including a different understanding of the meaning of human existence [62].

The Leighton Model of Coping

A third model, explaining human responses to critical life events, was formulated in the 1950s when Alexander Leighton studied the development of psychiatric disorders [64-66]. This remarkable study, long overlooked, introduced some concepts of particular value for our focus on religion and adolescent bereavement. These concepts are 1) the life arc, 2) the cross-section of the moment, and 3) essential human sentiments.

The life arc was Leighton's effort to conceptualize personality as a holistic, dynamic phenomenon that extends from birth through growth and maturity to decline and death. Leighton clearly antedated the emergence of life-span human development theory and its emphasis on change over time during one's life.

Within all life arcs there will be critical life events. Many of these events are anticipated, such as graduation from high school or the birth of a baby. Other events are not anticipated. One such unanticipated event during adolescence could be the death of a parent in a car accident.

Leighton called these anticipated and unanticipated life events *"the cross-section of the moment,"* and stated clearly that each possesses duration, or "temporal thickness" [65, p. 24]. This temporal thickness links one's present and previous life experiences and extends into the future as a matter of personal anticipation of outcomes.

In our example of an adolescent faced with the death of a parent, the accumulation of the adolescent's coping with earlier life events provides some repertoire to manage this unexpected and exceptional trauma. The adolescent's imagination provides some anticipation of life without the parent who has died.

Leighton also asserted that basic to all human personality development is the continual effort to achieve the following ten *essential human sentiments:*

1. to possess physical security
2. to achieve sexual satisfaction
3. to express hostility
4. to express love
5. to secure love
6. to secure recognition
7. to express creativity
8. to be oriented in terms of one's place in society
9. to secure and maintain membership in a human group
10. to belong to a moral order [65].

Changes over the life arc produce changes in the quality of the essential human sentiments. As an example, one of the essential human sentiments is to secure recognition. The quality and meaningfulness of that sentiment will differ dramatically for a five-year-old girl who receives a gold star for a kindergarten painting and the same person at age thirty-five who is recognized as the outstanding young business executive in her community. Apprehension over physical security differs dramatically for a thirteen-year-old girl whose father has died and for a thirty-six-year-old wife and mother whose husband has died.

Bereavement assaults each of the essential human sentiments. Regaining fulfillment of the sentiments could provide a measure of healing from grief. The role of religion in such healing may be seen, at least, in relation to the sentiment of belonging to a moral order. Given the common expression of anger toward God during grief, the link to expressing hostility is also apparent. It seems likely that there will also be connections between religion and the other sentiments.

The Role of Imagination and of Hope

Leighton mentions the central role of the human capacity to antici-pate the future, while dealing with a cross-section of the moment. Anticipations of the future play a central role in grief. For each of the authors of this chapter, bereaved adolescents and adults have affirmed that they knew they were beginning to regain wholeness when they felt hopeful about their futures.

Lynch noted the remarkable restorative powers that hope provides to humans coping with distress [67]. In a very similar vein, Frankl made openness to the future the singular aspect promoting healthy psychological functioning [68].

Hope fills two roles in coping. It provides evidence of recovery, and it is a means to achieve recovery. Hope is an imaginative response whereby humans transcend the cross-section of the moment and, in the vision of some writers, share in a spiritual experience [67, 69-70].

EMPIRICAL DATA ABOUT RELIGION AS A MEANS OF COPING WITH ADOLESCENT BEREAVEMENT

There is evidence to indicate that religion plays a part in the coping of some bereaved adolescents. In some cases this evidence may be part of background and personal factors [52]; or it may involve attributions of, and responses to, an event [62]. In other cases, religion discloses as a striving for essential human sentiments which are disrupted by a traumatic cross-section of the moment [65], or it is an expression of hope [67].

Bereaved High School Students

Ross Gray's study of adolescents grieving a parent's death noted that religion differentiated depression responses measured by the Beck Depression Inventory (BDI) [22-24]. The BDI is a 21-item self-report instrument measuring cognitive features of depression; the higher the BDI overall score, the greater the indication of depression. The instru-ment has very good psychometric properties. Adolescents with religious beliefs had significantly lower BDI scores than bereaved adolescents without such beliefs.

The majority of the 144 bereaved adolescents studied by Hogan believed that "faith had become more important to them" and that it helped them cope with their grief [13]. However, only 30 percent indi-cated that a priest, rabbi or minister had helped them with their grief.

Thirty-one percent revealed that they blamed God for the death some of the time and 24 percent declared that they no longer trusted God.

Balk noted that many adolescents, bereaved over the death of a sibling, found religion became increasingly important in their lives [1, 71]. However, this turn to religion occurred after considerable anger was directed toward God and after there was significant questioning of God's place in human existence.

Cluster analysis and discriminant analysis techniques [71] identified that adolescents bereaved over a sibling's death differed in their perceptions of the value of religion in their lives. For instance, the religious youth remembered they felt confused and more convinced after the death that their grief feelings would never abate, whereas the non-religious bereaved adolescents remembered feeling more numb, depressed, and fearful. On average two to three years after the death of their siblings, proportionally more of the religious youth reported that their grief feelings had subsided, and more of the non-religious youth reported feeling depressed and confused about the death.

Balk cautioned against deciding that religious sentiments give adolescents an edge in coping with bereavement [71]. Trust in God before the death may elicit a great sense of betrayal and open the adolescent to feeling cynical about existence. "Faced with not only the apparent but the brutal sense of having been abandoned by God, the believer has a considerable task not only to work through grief but to reconstruct a religious world-view that is honest to the fact that a loved one has died" [71, p. 14].

Bereaved College Students

LaGrand studied how college students in the State of New York coped with separation and loss [72, 73]. The students had experienced a variety of losses, among them the end of friendships, the end of love relationships, and the death of someone loved. Nearly 30 percent of the students reported grief over a death. LaGrand reported that some students turned to religious beliefs to build acceptance of the death of someone they loved. He noted that women, more than men, found religion provided support in their grief [72-73].

Floerchinger noted that college personnel increasingly are aware that bereavement is prevalent in college student populations. She noted that for some bereaved college students, religion provided "a very logical source of strength, hope, and comfort" [74, p. 152]. She also warned that college counselors, who are uncomfortable with religious beliefs and values, could be ineffective or harmful to bereaved students who consider religion important.

On five separate occasions, Balk surveyed college undergraduates enrolled in an introductory course on human development [75-77]. The survey covered topics related to death and grief. The figures remained stable from one data gathering period to the next.

Of the 1,639 students available to respond to the survey, 994 completed the instrument (a response rate of 60.6%). Respondents were primarily female (79%), twenty years old on average, and predominantly Caucasian (94%). The majority (58.6%) were members of a Protestant denomination, 31.6 percent were Catholic, and the remaining 9.8 percent were Jewish or Muslim, or said they were agnostic.

A large percentage of the 994 respondents (82%) reported that a family member, usually a grandparent, had died. Sixty percent indicated that a friend had died. Slightly more than half (50.2%) had experienced the deaths of a family member and a friend. The average time since the death in the family was 4.4 years, but for 23 percent the death had occurred in the past twelve months. The average time since the death of a friend was 2.5 years, but for 27 percent the friend had died in the past twelve months. In themselves, these figures reveal a startling phenomenon about the incidence and prevalence of death and bereavement in the lives of these college students.

Over half of the students (52.5%) said they were moderately religious, and 10 percent said they were very religious. Less than 6 percent said they were not at all religious. Sixty-three percent ($n = 626$) said religion had played a significant role in the development of their attitudes toward death, and less than 4 percent said it had played no role at all. Over 43 percent strongly believed in a life after death, and another 26 percent said they tended to believe in a life after death. Approximately 8 percent said they doubted there was life after death.

Students were grouped according to whether or not they had experienced a death. Chi square analyses indicated that neither bereaved nor non-bereaved students were more religious than the other; neither group said religion had played a more significant role in forming their attitudes to death; and neither group had different beliefs about a life after death.

Balk followed up these surveys with an investigation of the value of social support for bereaved college students [78, 79]. The Prevention Research Branch of the National Institute of Mental Health (NIMH) provided a great portion of the funding (MH 45044), and the William T. Grant Foundation also provided some funds. Hereafter, we will refer to this investigation as the NIMH study.

A total of 110 bereaved students entered the NIMH study. The majority of the students were female (80%), over half (52%) were twenty-one years of age or younger, and the great majority (95%) were

Caucasian. Most students (52%) were Protestant, 28 percent were Catholic, and the remaining 21 percent of the students either indicated membership in another religion or indicated no religious affiliation. Forty-eight percent had lost an immediate family member, 26 percent lost another relative such as a grandparent, and 26 percent lost a friend. It had been an average of nearly two years since the death, but 63 percent of the students were in their first year of bereavement.

The majority said that recovery was proving to be more difficult and taking longer than they had anticipated, and they felt sadder than they had expected. In contrast, many said their non-grieving friends expected recovery would be easier, involve less sadness, and take less time.

One of the instruments used in the NIMH study was the Grant Foundation Bereavement Inventory (GFBI). This instrument, developed by members of the Research Consortium on Adolescent Bereavement sponsored by the William T. Grant Foundation, is still exploratory. The GFBI assesses bereavement on several dimensions, and participants are asked to respond to items in terms of how they had reacted in the past month. Nearly all of the items are scaled from 1 to 5 ("Never" to "Almost all the time"), or scaled from 1 to 4 ("Not at all" to "Very much"). Dimensions investigated in the GFBI included reminiscing about the deceased, reunion fantasies, disbelief about the death, identification with the deceased, feelings of disloyalty to the deceased, recovery from bereavement, and coping practices. Examples of an item for each dimension are provided in Table 1.

Table 1. Dimensions Measured on the Grant Foundation
Bereavement Inventory: Sample Items

GFBI Dimension	Sample Item
	How often during the past month have you . . .
Reminiscing	—Talked about him/her with other people?
Reunion	— Had dreams about him/her?
Disbelief	— Found yourself doing things or acting as if he/she has not died?
Identification	— Thought of yourself as being like him/her?
Disloyalty	— Stopped yourself from having a good time?
Recovery	— Felt it is okay to go on with your life even though he/she is dead?
Coping practices	— Kept your grief personal and private?

Alpha coefficients calculated on the 110 students' responses to the GFBI dimensions averaged .79. The lowest alpha coefficients were .56 for the Disloyalty dimension and .72 for the Recovery dimension. The highest coefficients were .94 for Reminiscing and .90 for Disbelief. The remaining coefficients were .78 and above.

The GFBI asks participants how helpful religious practices have been. Choices include helpful, distressing, both helpful and distressing, and neither. Nearly half (49%) of the students said religion had been helpful to them, 4.5 percent said it had been distressing, 12 percent said it had been both helpful and distressing, and 34.5 percent said religion had been neither helpful nor distressing.

Multivariate analysis of variance (MANOVA) was used to test students' responses to the GFBI. Students' perceptions about the helpfulness of religion were used as the independent grouping variable. The students who said religion had been distressing were grouped with the students who said it had been both distressing and helpful. Thus, for the MANOVA test students' perceptions were placed into one of three groups: 1) helpful, 2) distressing, and 3) not helpful. The Wilks Lambda Criterion indicated a significant MANOVA effect ($p = .008$). Follow-up univariate F tests revealed that the extent of helpfulness of religion differentiated responses to six of the seven GFBI dimensions, as indicated below in Table 2.

Students for whom religion had not been helpful spent significantly less time, than the other students, remembering the person who had died, and significantly less time engaged in thoughts of being reunited with that person. They were much more likely to feel bothered by coping practices (such as keeping grief personal and private, working

Table 2. Univariate F-Tests on Grant Foundation Bereavement
Inventory Dimensions and Helpfulness of Religion

GFBI Dimension	F Ratio[a]	Significance of F
Reminiscing	6.31	.003
Reunion	6.32	.003
Disbelief	5.95	.004
Identification	3.35	.039
Disloyalty	1.67	.193
Recovery	4.59	.012
Coping practices	7.54	.001

[a]$F(2,106)$

through grief by oneself, not thinking about the death, and keeping busy).

Students for whom religion was distressing spent significantly more time 1) finding the death difficult to believe, and 2) comparing themselves to the person who had died. Unlike students for whom religion was not helpful, they spent significantly more time feeling different than their friends, feeling uncomfortable around their friends, and concerned that something bad was going to happen.

CHANGES IN UNDERSTANDING HUMAN EXISTENCE

We have looked at religion as a coping response. Now we will discuss changes in understanding human existence as a manifestation of spirituality.

A thesis in crisis intervention literature proposes that a crisis represents a dangerous opportunity [51, 56-58]. The notion suggests that coping with a crisis can lead to beneficial developments, whereas failure to resolve the crisis will almost surely lead to harm. In this section of our chapter, we focus on the aspect of crisis as an opportunity, and look to changes in understanding human existence as an indicator of the development of this opportunity.

Using Leighton's concepts of "the life arc" and "the cross-section of the moment" to consider the developmental aspects of a life crisis, one can see that dealing with bereavement affords adolescents a "dangerous opportunity" to transform their reasoning about reality [65]. First, we know that adolescent development includes qualitative changes in reasoning; second, models of coping accentuate that life crises offer paradoxical opportunities for development; and third, empirical findings support the assertion that life crises can produce growth. In Leighton's model, coping with the death of someone will extend into an adolescent's future, altering his/her anticipations about life, and providing new data to assess later cross-sections of the moment.

Researchers, who have studied adolescents faced with tragedy, have emphasized their resiliency and their ability to profit from life crises. Offer noticed that adolescents in families facing serious life circumstances, such as a death or severe illness, used the event as a means to mature [80]. Not uncommonly, adolescents indicated that coping with a sibling's death had made them more mature than unaffected peers [1, 11, 12].

Developmental models posit that changes in adolescent cognition make a transformation in consciousness about reality possible.

These models cover identity formation, moral reasoning, and faith consciousness.

Identity Formation

Marcia argued that an essential part of adolescent identity development involved making a personal decision about religion; Marcia acknowledged that not all of an individual's decisions reflected a personal commitment but rather revealed conformity to the values held by others, usually parents [81]. Marcia's research was an explicit effort to study Erikson's ideas about the formation of identity [82-84].

Moral Reasoning

Kohlberg maintained that the development of more mature reasoning about morality occurs during adolescence [85]. He based much of his work on the model of cognitive development produced by Piaget [86, 87]. With Gilligan, Kohlberg posited that adolescents become moral philosophers in their contemplation of existence [88]. Austin and Mack have extended this notion, that the adolescent acts as a moral philosopher, to death studies [89].

The Development of Faith Consciousness

The main theorist to deal with religious understanding as a developmental process is James Fowler [90-92]. He refers to the development of religious understanding as the unfolding of a quest for meaning; the product of this quest is a growth in faith consciousness. He recognizes that this quest is open to all human beings, whether they espouse or reject explicit religious beliefs and practices. Albert Camus, the French essayist, writer of literature and avowed atheist, represents a supreme example of the quest for meaning and of a growth in faith consciousness.

How can this assertion regarding Camus not simply be dismissed as the arrogance of an atheist? The answer lies in what Fowler understood about faith. Fowler wrote that faith is what gives meaning "to the multiple forces and relations that make up our lives" [91, p. 4]. Faith enables individuals to see themselves "in relation to others against a background of shared meaning and purpose" [91, p. 4].

Fowler argued that faith consciousness develops in a sequence of stages dependent on the development of cognitive operations. Thus, his view is wedded to Piaget's stage theory of cognitive development [86].

A transformation in faith consciousness is possible in late adolescents (18 to 22 years old) as long as two other developments also occur.

One, the person must have been faced with the need to examine, evaluate, and reconstitute his/her already formed values and beliefs. Two, the person must act autonomously on those re-examined values and beliefs [92].

EMPIRICAL DATA ABOUT CHANGES IN UNDERSTANDING THE MEANING OF EXISTENCE

Is there any empirical evidence to support the belief that a new faith consciousness occurs in the lives of bereaved adolescents? We maintain that a singular sign of this development has been available for years. We are referring to the growing evidence that an ongoing attachment to the person who died marks the lives of bereaved adolescents and signifies a change in their understanding of human existence.

Accepted views of bereavement recovery, based on the notion of letting go of the deceased, have influenced bereavement researchers to interpret signs of ongoing attachment as pathology. Freud said grief work involved detaching libido investment bit-by-bit from the inner representation of the deceased [93]. Bowlby argued that grief resolution occurred because the bereaved detached from the loved one who had died and made new attachments in the world [94]. Both anecdotal and research evidence indicates that bereaved persons do 1) reinvest in the social world, but 2) maintain an ongoing attachment to the inner representation of their dead loved ones.

The call to reformulate an acceptable understanding of grief resolution has been present at least since the magnificent overview of bereavement published by the National Academy of Sciences [95]. We contend that efforts to reformulate what it means to resolve grief form the cutting edge of bereavement research today.

The main theoretical architects of the "ongoing attachment" vision of grief resolution are Hogan [96, 97], Klass [42-44], and Stroebe and associates [98]. Hints of this "ongoing attachment" view are provided in Lindemann [39]. He noted that religious agencies offered comfort to bereaved individuals by supporting their wish for abiding interaction with the deceased. While Lindemann insisted that grievers began to heal when they allowed themselves to feel the distress of their grief, he also noted that they needed "to find an acceptable formulation of (their) future relationship to the deceased" [39, p. 75].

Hogan observed that bereaved parents learn to live both a public life and a private life [96]. Their public life is often consciously devoid of references to their deceased child because of social admonition and rejection. Their private life, by contrast, often includes remembering, sharing, and cherishing memories of their dead child, and sensing an ongoing connection to their deceased son or daughter. She states, "Death ended your child's life but not his or her relationship to the family" [96, p. 6] and, in another source [97, p. 5], "You give up the old person who was physically connected to a now deceased child, and you must make different connections with your child who has died."

Reflecting on data gathered over several years of observing bereaved parents, Klass [43-44] identified some deeply rooted spiritual dimensions—what Fowler [90-92] would call a transformed faith consciousness. Klass argued that, for parents, bereavement resolution requires transcending the transitoriness of human existence [44]. Parents' recovery involves gaining a sense of solace—that is, a comfort within an enduring pain—and remaining connected to the inner representation of their dead child [43]. This inner representation provides an encounter with a reality transcending the momentary, fleeting nature of human experience. When Klass presented his views at the Eleventh International King's College Conference in London, Ontario, Canada, bereaved parents in his audience affirmed his portrayal of their experiences.

Do bereaved adolescents relate this same sort of new consciousness as reported by bereaved parents? Some adolescents do, and the name we have given to this phenomenon is "ongoing attachment."

First, we present some data regarding adolescents of high school age, and then adolescents of college age.

Bereaved High School Students

In a recent nation-wide study, 157 bereaved adolescents who had experienced a sibling death were asked the question, "If you could ask or tell your dead sibling something, what would it be?" [15]. Content analysis of responses revealed six mutually exclusive categories: regretting, endeavoring to understand, catching up, reaffirming, influencing, and reuniting in heaven. Pervasive throughout the qualitative data was the theme of "ongoing attachment" illustrated by a sense of the timelessness of adolescent bereavement and the infiniteness of the sibling bond. Grieving was characterized as a process whereby "the bereaved siblings learn to live with the physical absence and the simultaneous emotional presence of their deceased brother or sister" [15, p. 174].

Respondents in the Hogan and DeSantis study also completed the Hogan Sibling Inventory of Bereavement (HSIB), a measure using a 6-point Likert scale ranging from 1 (almost always true) to 6 (does not apply to me) [15]. Forty-nine percent said they still feel close to their dead sibling, 47.6 percent said they mostly remembered good things about their dead sibling, and 41.7 percent said they think about their dead sibling daily.

In two separate studies, the highest mean score on the HSIB scale was associated with the item "I believe I will see him or her in heaven." Data from a sample of 144 bereaved adolescents showed 73.2 percent of these adolescents said it is almost always true that they believe they will see their sibling in heaven, and the mean score for all the respondents was 1.7 [13]. In a study with forty bereaved adolescents this same item had the highest mean score (1.4) [11]. The triangulation of qualitative and quantitative data from these various studies [11-13, 15] plus the replication of the finding from the HSIB challenge the prevailing conceptualization that healthy grief necessitates a finite end-point.

Bereaved College Students

Kirsten Tyson-Rawson recently completed a dissertation on female college students bereaved over the death of their father [99]. She conducted extensive, in-depth interviews with twenty students, all in their late adolescence, and used the constant-comparative approach [100-102] to analyze her data.

One of Tyson-Rawson's findings is that all of her interviewees expressed marked changes in how they think about the world, "including the presence or absence of a sustaining spiritual belief" [99, pp. 221-222]. These observations included altered perceptions of the extent to which they can control their lives and an awareness of how unpredictable life can be. These young women see themselves as more vulnerable than they were prior to their father's death, and they refuse to take things for granted.

Tyson-Rawson reported that fourteen of her twenty research participants "indicated an ongoing attachment to the deceased, indicating a continuing bond with the significant other who died" [99, p. 166]. Half of the students (10) experienced this ongoing attachment as a welcome presence. Tyson-Rawson noted that each respondent was hesitant to report her experiences of her father's presence lest people consider her crazy. These women "were also more likely to report that they viewed themselves as having reached some resolution of their grief" [99, p. 171].

Four students were troubled by the sense of their father's ongoing presence in their lives. Tyson-Rawson said their grief expressions seemed no more powerful than the expressions of the other women in her study, but these four reported "nightmares, intrusive thoughts, and high levels of anxiety that debilitated the subject in one or more areas of functioning" [99, pp. 172-173]. In these four women's lives, there was a sense of unfinished business about their fathers' deaths specifically linked to ambivalent relations with their fathers during life. None of these four women reported any sense of having resolved their grief.

In Balk's work with bereaved college students, feelings of identification with the person who had died marked the responses of a significant portion of these students [78]. For instance, since the death:

- 16 percent thought of themselves as being very much like the person who had died,
- 20 percent wanted very much to become more like that person,
- 23 percent acted more often like that person,
- 24 percent had become more interested in that person's occupation or field of study.

In addition, Oltjenbruns identified positive outcomes for eighty-nine of ninety-four bereaved college students whom she studied [103]. These positive outcomes all denote a changed perspective on human existence. The most commonly reported positive outcomes were a deeper appreciation of life (74%), greater caring for loved ones (67%), increased emotional attachment to others (56%), and emotional strength (53%).

A hallmark of the Oltjenbruns' study is her investigation of ethnicity and grief. Two-thirds of her research participants were Anglo and one-third were Mexican-American. She found no differences in ethnic group bereavement responses. The fact that her study included such a significant portion of Mexican-Americans and Anglos supports her assertion that most persons, regardless of ethnic group membership, "may experience something positive as a result of death . . . and that there is much similarity as to what those outcomes are" [103, p. 51].

CONCLUDING DISCUSSION

In this concluding section we discuss six topics: appraisal of a crisis and coping; detachment versus ongoing attachment; bereavement research on adolescents; fruitful areas for investigation; the concept of bereavement recovery; and religion and spirituality. We begin with a central component in life crisis models, namely, appraisal of a crisis and coping.

Appraisal of a Crisis and Coping

We have argued that coping with a death requires correctly appraising the demands of the crisis. One aspect of correct appraisal is to understand that grief feelings last longer and recovery from grief proves harder than people typically expect. The adolescents, with whom we worked, no longer had a sanguine appraisal of what grief work demands. Bereaved college students now understood that grief work is harder, lasts longer, and produces sadder feelings than unaffected persons understand.

As indicated in the responses of college students to the Grant Foundation Bereavement Inventory, perceptions of the help that religion provided did interact for adolescents on at least six dimensions of bereavement: reminiscing about the deceased; thoughts of reunion with the deceased; less difficulty believing the death happened; identifying with the deceased; phenomena indicating recovery from bereavement; and using different coping strategies to deal with grief. It was not the case, however, that adolescents who perceived religion as helpful had bereavement responses unlike either 1) the college students who found religion distressing or 2) the college students who reported religion neither helpful nor distressing. Students for whom religion offered neither help nor distress reminisced less about their deceased loved one and did not think as often about times of reunion. Are we to take such actions as signs of detachment and indications of a healthier state of mind? Would such conclusions not be logical given the bereavement recovery model which says the task is to disengage one's investment in the person who died?

Note that the students for whom religion was neither helpful nor distressing indicated that coping practices were more upsetting to them. Did coping practices involve more disquiet for them because they had no religious foundation on which to base their appraisal of the situation? Appraisal of the situation covers more than the individual griever's current state of mind. As in the life-arc model offered by Leighton [65], appraisal covers transcendence of the moment and assessment of the ultimate meaning of human existence and death.

What led students for whom religion was distressing to spend significantly more time, than the other students, wondering about the reality of the death and spending more time measuring themselves against their image of the person who had died? These students felt different from their friends, felt awkward around their friends, and were unsure about the future. One could say that the temporal thickness of their grief was infected with a loss of social and emotional support, thereby indicating obstacles to fulfilling the human sentiments of securing love, obtaining recognition, and giving love. Their vigilance to detect signs of something bad that could happen indicates a bleak anticipation about the future. Their imaginations were clouded with a sense of dread rather than of hope.

College students found grief work was harder, lasted longer, and involved more sadness than they would have predicted prior to becoming grief-stricken. They were caught unaware of what grief entailed. Underestimating the characteristics, the intensity, and the duration of bereavement continues to be common in American society. The media perpetuates the idea that grief is a brief event to be completed privately and quickly.

Detachment versus Ongoing Attachment

Implicit in underestimating the characteristics, the duration, and the intensity of grief feelings is the expectation that people should become detached—preferably within six months to a year—from the person who died. This expectation may be a factor in producing the very uncomfortable feelings that many non-bereaved persons experience around someone who manifests grief or who even mentions the death of someone they loved. In addition, the expectation that recovery means detachment leads professionals to express concern for persons who remain attached to a loved one who died.

Expectations about detachment, as the sign of recovery from bereavement, have seeds in Freud's seminal paper "Mourning and Melancholia" in which he maintained grief work requires detaching libidinal energy from the inner representation of the person who had died [93]. We hear colloquial expressions of this concept in the phrase "letting go." Bowlby [94] and Parkes [37, 104] agree that the purpose of grief work is to sever ties to the deceased and—as Bowlby argued—to reinvest in new social attachments.

Before the onset of a significant crisis such as death, we live on contrived time or positivistic time which is linear and includes a discrete, simplistic sense of past, present, and future. Following a death, time is simultaneous, and past, present and future is more of a summative knowing, more in keeping with timelessness and "time without end, Amen." Bereaved adolescents manifest emotional bonds with their deceased siblings, emotional bonds which blend the past, present, and future of their life-arcs into an "everywhen" [105].

We have argued that ongoing attachment occurs in the lives of bereaved adolescents. There is overwhelming cultural evidence to suggest on-going attachment is not peculiar to adolescents. A remarkable bit of evidence for ongoing attachment is the millions of people who visit The Vietnam War Memorial each year to remember and leave literally tons of connections for their deceased loved ones. Another example is afforded by the pilgrimages to the Wailing Wall in Jerusalem.

Bereavement Research on Adolescents

The findings we discuss in this chapter represent responses of adolescents who have experienced the deaths of persons with whom they have bonded—parent, sibling, other relative, or friend. Other than a few cases of late adolescents who are widowed, our findings do not include death of a spouse. Most bereavement research has been done with middle-aged or elderly widows, and we cannot uncritically accept application of those findings to an interpretation of the experiences of bereaved adolescents. An especially troubling phenomenon is the scholarly work which makes no distinction between children and adolescents. It is mistaken to base conclusions about the phenomena of adolescent bereavement on research peculiar to another group or on research which makes no effort to test whether differences mark adolescent bereavement from the grief of other age groups.

A great gap in adolescent bereavement research involves the lack of culturally diverse sampling. Most of the studies include middle-class, White American adolescents. A fine exception to this rule is the study by Oltjenbruns [103]. Cook and Dworkin provide excellent discussion of cultural considerations for grief therapy [106]. Further research needs to address the bereavement experiences of adolescents from other racial/ethnic groups.

One question that troubles us is whether the researchers will be sensitive to the concerns and values of adolescents from different cultures. Insensitivity to the religious sentiments and values of people from another culture is not easily overcome. For instance, it is not uncommon for Anglos to be ignorant of, and even dismissive of, the spiritual values of Mexican and Native American peoples. How can researchers, who are not members of the culture being investigated, obtain information which enlightens them about bereavement in that other culture? We suspect that investigators skilled in ethnography, not in the administration and analysis of standardized instruments, will make the initial research inroads with bereaved populations of other cultures.

Fruitful Areas for Investigation

We invite efforts to test our findings and assertions. We hope that investigators use multiple methods to conduct their studies. We firmly believe that triangulation of methods offers the best promise of generating a verifiable substantive theory of the role of religion in adolescent bereavement. We suggest some areas that could be investigated:

- Grounded theory studies using the constant-comparative method can enrich our understanding of the theme of ongoing attachment [100-102].
- Longitudinal (or sequential) approaches can explore the effects of time since the death and the relationship of the griever to the deceased (e.g., immediate family, friend, or other relative).
- Longitudinal (or sequential) approaches can explore the trajectory of grief for the bereaved adolescent *vis-à-vis* such factors as ethnicity, culture, gender, religion, and other personal and background factors.
- Experimental designs can test the efficacy of interventions to assist bereaved adolescents to cope with grief and prevent the development of debilitating consequences due to unresolved grief.
- One critical analysis that is overdue is a review of the assumptions that the central bereavement theorists [25, 37, 39, 94, 104, for instance] have with regard to both religion and spirituality.

The Concept of Bereavement Recovery

We want to touch on the issue of the ferment over re-thinking what it means to recover from bereavement. If an ongoing attachment to the deceased is common, we need to reconsider what we understand about complicated mourning. Another issue, of course, is whether encouraging acceptance of an ongoing attachment endorses pathology. The criterion of pathology in the received traditions of bereavement recovery—that is, in the work of Freud and Bowlby—is refusal to rend one's bond with the person who died.

Certainly some continuing attachments with the person who died are signs of pathology. One of the more complicated signs is endowing a replacement child with the identity of the child who died.

However, clinical experience with bereaved adolescents and with bereaved spouses has taught us that some bereaved persons with ongoing attachment manifest no signs of pathology. Stroebe et al., in fact, assert that the insistence on severing ongoing attachments is a recent phenomenon and is not evident in other historical eras [98].

Religion and Spirituality

In this increasingly secularized and post-modern world, what role does religion play in coping and recovery? Some may think we are encouraging adherence to an illusion [46]. We appreciate that many of our colleagues feel skeptical about what appear to them to be appeals to superstition and magic.

There are bound to be questions directed at our ideas about religion and spirituality. While we think religion has been shunned for the most part in research circles, we have problems with certain operational understandings assigned to religion by researchers. For instance, we do not think of religion as simply an adherence to a religious dogma, membership in a religious denomination, or church attendance. We also do not endorse religious expectations of *deus ex machina* intrusions into the natural world.

Given all these disclaimers, you might therefore ask, "What are your ideas about religious faith?" The answer for us lies in understanding more deeply what Fowler means by a growth in faith consciousness [91, 92]. We contend that part of this growth involves deepening one's personal understanding of the meaning of human existence. Clinical experience and research has convinced us that a deepening understanding of human existence does occur in the lives of some bereaved adolescents. We believe this deepening understanding is a possibility open to all human beings.

REFERENCES

1. D. E. Balk, *Sibling Death during Adolescence: Self-Concept and Bereavement Reactions*, unpublished doctoral dissertation, University of Illinois, Urbana-Champaign, 1981.
2. D. E. Balk, Adolescents' Grief Reactions and Self-Concept Perceptions following Sibling Death: A Case Study of 33 Teenagers, *Journal of Youth and Adolescence, 12*, pp. 137-161, 1983.
3. D. E. Balk, The Self-Concepts of Bereaved Adolescents: Sibling Death and Its Aftermath, *Journal of Adolescent Research, 5*, pp. 112-132, 1990.
4. D. E. Balk, Death and Adolescent Bereavement: Current Research and Future Directions, *Journal of Adolescent Research, 6*, pp. 7-27, 1991. (Special issue on Death and Adolescent Bereavement.)
5. B. Davies, Long-Term Outcomes of Adolescent Sibling Bereavement, *Journal of Adolescent Research, 6*:1, pp. 83-96, 1991. (Special issue on Death and Adolescent Bereavement.)
6. E. J. Deveau, The Impact on Adolescents When a Sibling Is Dying, in *The Dying and the Bereaved Teenager*, J. D. Morgan (ed.), The Charles Press, Philadelphia, pp. 63-77, 1990.

7. J. H. Fanos and B. G. Nickerson, Long-Term Effects of Sibling Death during Adolescence, *Journal of Adolescent Research, 6*:1, pp. 70-82, 1991. (Special issue on Death and Adolescent Bereavement.)

8. M. Guerriero, *Adolescent Bereavement: Impact on Physical Health, Self-Concept, Depression, and Death Anxiety*, unpublished master's thesis, York University, Toronto, Ontario, 1983.

9. M. Guerriero and S. J. Fleming, *Adolescent Bereavement: A Longitudinal Study*, paper presented at the Annual Meeting of the Canadian Psychological Association, Halifax, Nova Scotia, June 1985.

10. M. Guerriero-Austrum and S. J. Fleming, *Effects of Sibling Death on Adolescents' Physical and Emotional Well-Being: A Longitudinal Study*, paper presented at the Annual Convention of the American Psychological Association, Boston, Massachusetts, August 1990.

11. N. S. Hogan, *An Investigation of the Adolescent Sibling Bereavement Process and Adaptation*, unpublished doctoral dissertation, Loyola University, Chicago, Illinois, 1987.

12. N. S. Hogan, The Effects of Time on the Adolescent Sibling Bereavement Process, *Pediatric Nursing, 14*, pp. 333-335, 1988.

13. N. S. Hogan, Unpublished data from the National Sibling Bereavement Study, 1988.

14. N. S. Hogan and D. E. Balk, Adolescents' Reactions to Sibling Death: Perceptions of Mothers, Fathers, and Teenagers, *Nursing Research, 39*:2, pp. 103-106, 1990.

15. N. S. Hogan and L. DeSantis, Adolescent Sibling Bereavement: An Ongoing Attachment, *Qualitative Health Research, 2*:2, pp. 159-177, 1992.

16. N. S. Hogan and L. DeSantis, Things That Help and Hinder Adolescent Sibling Bereavement, *Western Journal of Nursing Research, 16*:2, pp. 132-153, 1994.

17. N. S. Hogan and D. B. Greenfield, Adolescent Sibling Bereavement Symptomatology in a Large Community Sample, *Journal of Adolescent Research, 6*:1, pp. 97-112, 1991. (Special issue on Death and Adolescent Bereavement.)

18. I. M. Martinson and R. G. Campos, Adolescent Bereavement: Long-Term Responses to a Sibling's Death from Cancer, *Journal of Adolescent Research, 6*:1, pp. 54-69, 1991. (Special issue on Death and Adolescent Bereavement.)

19. I. M. Martinson, E. B. Davies, and S. G. McClowry, The Long-Term Effects of Sibling Death on Self-Concept, *Journal of Pediatric Nursing, 2*, pp. 227-235, 1987.

20. A. Morawetz, The Impact on Adolescents of the Death in War of an Older Sibling: A Group Experience, *Series in Clinical and Community Psychiatry: Stress and Anxiety, 8*, pp. 267-274, 1982.

21. R. A. Goodman, *Adolescent Grief Characteristics When a Parent Dies,* unpublished doctoral dissertation, University of Colorado, Boulder, Colorado, 1986.

22. R. E. Gray, *Adolescents Faced with the Death of a Parent: The Role of Social Support and Other Factors*, unpublished doctoral dissertation, University of Toronto, Toronto, Ontario, 1987.

23. R. E. Gray, Adolescent Response to the Death of a Parent, *Journal of Youth and Adolescence, 16*, pp. 511-525, 1987.
24. R. E. Gray, The Role of School Counselors with Bereaved Teenagers: With and Without Peer Support Groups, *The School Counselor, 35*, pp. 188-193, 1988.
25. B. Raphael, *The Anatomy of Bereavement*, Basic Books, New York, 1983.
26. E. Wakerman, *Father Loss: Daughters Discuss the Man that Got Away*, Doubleday, Garden City, New York, 1984.
27. J. N. McNeil, B. Silliman, and J. J. Swihart, Helping Adolescents Cope with the Death of a Peer: A High School Case Study, *Journal of Adolescent Research, 6*:1, pp. 132-145, 1991. (Special issue on Death and Adolescent Bereavement.)
28. C. Podell, Adolescent Mourning: The Sudden Death of a Peer, *Clinical Social Work Journal, 17*, pp. 64-78, 1989.
29. S. J. Fleming and R. Adolph, Helping Bereaved Adolescents: Needs and Responses, in *Adolescence and Death*, C. A. Corr and J. N. McNeil (eds.), Springer, New York, pp. 151-166, 1986.
30. D. W. Adams and E. J. Deveau, Helping Dying Adolescents: Needs and Responses, in *Adolescence and Death*, C. A. Corr and J. N. McNeil, (eds.), Springer Publishing Company, New York, 1986.
31. E. Pendleton, *Too Old to Cry, Too Young to Die*, Thomas Nelson, Nashville, Tennessee, 1980.
32. M. W. Trautmann, *The Absence of the Dead... Is Their Way of Appearing*, Cleis Press, Pittsburgh, Pennsylvania, 1984.
33. H. Wass, and J. M. Stillion, Death in the Lives of Children and Adolescents, in *Dying: Facing the Facts*, H. Wass, F. N. Berarado, and R. A. Neimeyer (eds.), Hemisphere, Washington, D.C., pp. 201-228, 1988.
34. I. O. Glick, R. S. Weiss, and C. M. Parkes, *The First Year of Bereavement*, Wiley, New York, 1974.
35. H. G. Koenig, L. K. George, and I. C. Siegler, The Use of Religion and Other Emotion-Regulating Coping Strategies among Older Adults, *The Gerontologist, 28*, pp. 303-310, 1988.
36. D. N. McIntosh, R. C. Silver, and C. B. Wortman, *Religion's Role in Adjustment to a Negative Life Event: Coping with the Loss of a Child*, paper presented at the Annual Convention of the American Psychological Association, Boston, Massachusetts, August 1990.
37. C. M. Parkes and R. S. Weiss, *Recovery from Bereavement*, Basic Books, New York, 1983.
38. P. G. Reed, Religiousness among Terminally Ill and Healthy Adults, *Research in Nursing & Health, 9*, pp. 35-41, 1986.
39. E. Lindemann, Symptomatology and Management of Acute Grief, *American Journal of Psychiatry, 101*, pp. 141-148, 1944.
40. G. R. Cox and R. J. Fundis (eds.), *Spiritual, Ethical, and Pastoral Aspects of Death and Bereavement*, Baywood, Amityville, New York, 1992.
41. K. J. Doka (ed.), *Death and Spirituality*, Baywood, Amityville, New York, 1993.

42. D. Klass, *Parental Grief: Solace and Resolution*, Springer Publishing Company, New York, 1988.
43. D. Klass, Solace and Immortality: Bereaved Parents' Continuing Bond with their Children, *Death Studies, 17*:4, pp. 343-368, 1993.
44. D. Klass, *Spiritual Dynamics in the Resolution of Parental Grief*, paper presented at the Eleventh International King's College Conference on Death, Dying, and Bereavement, London, Ontario, May 1993.
45. J. D. Morgan (ed.), *Personal Care in an Impersonal World: A Multidimensional Look at Bereavement*, Baywood, Amityville, New York, 1993.
46. S. Freud, *The Future of an Illusion*, W. D. Robson-Scott (trans.), Doubleday, Garden City, New York, 1957. (Original work published in 1927.)
47. K. Barth, *The Word of God and the Word of Man*, D. Horton (trans.), Harper & Brothers, New York, 1957. (Original work published in 1928.)
48. D. Bonhoeffer, *Prisoner for God: Letters and Papers from Prison*, R. H. Fuller, (trans.), Macmillan, New York, 1960. (Original work published in 1953.)
49. R. Bultmann, *Jesus and the Word*, L. P. Smith and E. H. Lantero (trans.), Scribners, New York, New York, 1958. (Original work published 1934.)
50. P. Tillich, *The Courage to Be*, Yale University Press, New Haven, Connecticut, 1952.
51. R. H. Moos (ed.), *Coping with Life Crises: An Integrated Framework*, Plenum, New York, 1986.
52. R. H. Moos, and J. A. Schaefer, Life Transitions and Crises: A Conceptual Overview, *Coping with Life Crises: An Integrated Approach*, R. H. Moos (ed.), Plenum, New York, pp. 3-28, 1986.
53. K. B. Bryer, The Amish Way of Death: A Study of Family Support Systems, *American Psychologist, 34*, pp. 255-261, 1979.
54. C. S. Lewis, *A Grief Observed*, The Seabury Press, New York, 1961.
55. X. Leon-Dufour, *Life and Death in the New Testament: The Teachings of Jesus and Paul*, T. Prendergast (trans.), Harper & Row, San Francisco, California, 1986.
56. B. Baldwin, A Paradigm for the Classification of Emotional Crises: Implications for Crisis Intervention, *American Journal of Orthopsychiatry, 48*, pp. 538-551, 1978.
57. G. Caplan, *Principles of Preventive Psychiatry*, Basic Books, New York, 1964.
58. G. Caplan, Recent Developments in Crisis Intervention and in the Promotion of Support Services, in *A Decade of Progress in Primary Prevention*, M. Kessler and S. E. Goldston (eds.), University Press of New England, Hanover, New Hampshire, 1986.
59. S. J. Danish and A. R. D'Augelli, Promoting Competence and Enhancing Development through Life Development Intervention, in *Primary Prevention of Psychopathology*, Vol. 5, University Press of New England Hanover, New Hampshire, pp. 105-129, 1980.
60. S. J. Danish, M. A. Smyer, and C. A. Nowak, Developmental Interventions: Enhancing Life-Event Processes, in *Life-Span Development and*

Behavior, Vol. 3, P. B. Baltes and O. G. Brim (eds.), Academic Press, New York, pp. 340-346, 1980.

61. K. I. Pargament, God Help Me: Towards a Theoretical Framework of Coping for the Psychology of Religion, *Psychologists Interested in Religious Issues Newsletter, 13*:2, pp. 1-6, Summer 1988.

62. K. I. Pargament, God Help Me: Towards a Theoretical Framework of Coping for the Psychology of Religion, in *Research in the Social Scientific Study of Religion*, Vol. 2, D. O. Moberg and M. L. Lynn (eds.), JAI Press, Greenwich, Connecticut, pp. 195-224, 1990.

63. K. I. Pargament, R. E. Hess, and K. Maton (eds.), *Religion and Prevention in Mental Health: Conceptual and Empirical Foundations*, Haworth Press, New York, 1991.

64. C. C. Hughes, M-A. Tremblay, R. N. Rapoport, and A. H. Leighton, *People of Cove and Woodlot: Communities from the Viewpoint of Social Psychiatry*, Basic Books, New York, 1960.

65. A. H. Leighton, *My Name Is Legion: Foundations for a Theory of Man in Relation to Culture*, Basic Books, New York, 1959.

66. D. C. Leighton, J. S. Harding, D. B. Macklin, A. M. Macmillan, A. M., and A. H. Leighton, *The Character of Danger: Psychiatric Symptoms in Selected Communities*, Basic Books, New York, 1963.

67. W. F. Lynch, *Images of Hope: Imagination as Healer of the Hopeless*, Helicon, Baltimore, Maryland, 1965.

68. V. F. Frankl, *Man's Search for Meaning: An Introduction to Logotherapy* (3rd Edition), Simon and Schuster, New York, 1984.

69. M. Fox, *Original Blessing: A Primer in Creation Spirituality*, Bear and Company, Santa Fe, New Mexico, 1983.

70. S. Moore, *The Inner Loneliness*, Crossroads, New York, 1982.

71. D. E. Balk, Sibling Death, Adolescent Bereavement, and Religion, *Death Studies, 15*, pp. 1-20, 1991.

72. L. E. LaGrand, Loss Reactions of College Students: A Descriptive Analysis, *Death Studies, 5*:3, pp. 235-248, 1981. (Journal entitled *Death Education* from 1977-1984.)

73. L. E. LaGrand, *Coping with Separation and Loss as a Young Adult: Theoretical and Practical Realities*, Charles C. Thomas, Springfield, Illinois, 1986.

74. D. Floerchinger, Bereavement in Late Adolescence: Interventions on College Campuses, *Journal of Adolescent Research, 6*:1, pp. 146-156, 1991. (Special issue on Death and Adolescent Bereavement.)

75. D. E. Balk, *The Many Faces of Bereavement on the College Campus*, paper presented at the Annual Convention of the American Psychological Association, Boston, Massachusetts, August 1990. (ERIC Document Reproduction Service No. ED 326794.)

76. D. E. Balk, *Death, Bereavement, and College Students: A Description of Research at Kansas State University*, paper presented at the Annual Meeting of the American Educational Research Association, Chicago, Illinois, 1991.

77. D. E. Balk, *The Meaning of Death and the Prevalence of Bereavement in College Students' Lives*, unpublished manuscript.
78. D. E. Balk, *Trajectory of Grief among Bereaved College Students: Longitudinal Results of a Preventive Intervention*, paper presented at the Eleventh International King's College Conference on Death, Dying, and Bereavement, London, Ontario, 1993.
79. D. E. Balk, K. Tyson-Rawson, and J. Colletti-Wetzel, Social Support as an Intervention with Bereaved College Students, *Death Studies*, 17, pp. 427-450, 1993.
80. D. Offer, *The Psychological World of the Teenager: A Study of Normal Adolescent Boys*, Basic Books, New York, 1969.
81. J. Marcia, Identity in Adolescence, in *Hand-book of Adolescent Psychology*, J. Adelson (ed.), Wiley, New York, pp. 159-187, 1980.
82. E. Erikson, Identity and the Life Cycle, *Psychological Issues*, 1 (Whole No. 1), 1959.
83. E. Erikson, *Childhood and Society*, Norton, New York, 1963.
84. E. Erikson, *Identity: Youth and Crisis*, Norton, New York, 1968.
85. L. Kohlberg, The Cognitive-Developmental Approach to Moral Education, *Phi Delta Kappan, 46*, pp. 670-677, 1975.
86. J. Piaget, *Psychology of Intelligence*, Routledge and Kegan Paul, London, 1950.
87. J. Piaget, and B. Inhelder, *The Growth of Logical Thinking from Childhood through Adolescence*, Basic Books, New York, 1958.
88. L. Kohlberg and C. Gilligan, The Adolescent as a Philosopher: The Discovery of the Self in a Postconventional World, *Daedalus, 100*, pp. 1051-1086, 1971.
89. D. A. Austin and J. E. Mack, The Adolescent Philosopher in a Nuclear World, in *Adolescence and Death*, C. A. Corr and J. N. McNeil (eds.), Springer Publishing Company, New York, 1986.
90. J. W. Fowler, Stages in Faith: The Structural-Developmental Approach, in *Values and Moral Development*, T. Hennessy (ed.), Paulist Press, New York, 1976.
91. J. W. Fowler, *Stages of Faith: The Psychology of Human Development and the Quest for Meaning*, Harper and Row, San Francisco, California, 1981.
92. J. W. Fowler, *Stages of Faith and Religious Development: Implications for Church, Education, and Society*, Crossroad, New York, 1991.
93. S. Freud, Mourning and Melancholia, in *The Standard Edition of the Complete Psychological Works of Sigmund Freud*, Vol. 14, J. Strachey (ed. and trans.), Hogarth Press, London, pp. 243-258, 1957. (Original work published 1917.)
94. J. Bowlby, *Attachment and Loss: Loss, Sadness, and Depression*, Vol. 3, Basic Books, New York, 1980.
95. M. Osterweis, F. Solomon, and M. Green, (eds.), *Bereavement: Reactions, Consequences, and Care*, National Academy Press, Washington, D.C., 1984.

96. N. S. Hogan, Commitment to Survival, Part One, *Compassionate Friends Newsletter, 6*, pp. 1, 5-6, Summer 1983.
97. N. S. Hogan, Commitment to Survival, Part two, *Compassionate Friends Newsletter, 6*, pp. 5-6, Fall 1983.
98. M. Stroebe, M. M. Gergen, K. J. Gergen, and W. Stroebe, Broken Hearts or Broken Bonds: Love and Death in Historical Perspective, *American Psychologist, 47*:10, pp. 1205-1212, 1992.
99. K. Tyson-Rawson, *College Women and Bereavement: Late Adolescence and Father Death*, unpublished doctoral dissertation, Kansas State University, Manhattan, Kansas, 1993.
100. B. G. Glaser and A. L. Strauss, *The Discovery of Grounded Theory: Strategies for Qualitative Research*, Aldine degruyter, New York, 1967.
101. A. L. Strauss, *Qualitative Analysis for Social Scientists*, Cambridge University Press, Cambridge, United Kingdom, 1987.
102. A. L. Strauss and J. Corbin, *Basics of Qualitative Research: Grounded Theory Procedures and Techniques*, Sage, Newbury Park, California, 1990.
103. K. A. Oltjenbruns, Positive Outcomes of Adolescents' Experience with Grief, *Journal of Adolescent Research, 6*:1, pp. 43-53, 1991. (Special issue on Death and Adolescent Bereavement.)
104. C. M. Parkes, *Bereavement: Studies of Grief in Adult Life*, International Universities Press, New York, 1972.
105. W. E. H. Stanner, The Dreaming, in *Reader in Comparative Religion: An Anthropological Approach*, W. A. Lessa and E. Z. Vogt (eds.), Harper and Row, New York, pp. 269-277, 1965.
106. A. S. Cook and D. S. Dworkin, *Helping the Bereaved: Therapeutic Interventions for Children, Adolescents, and Adults*, Basic Books, New York, 1992.

CHAPTER 4

Long-Term Effects of Sibling Death in Childhood

Betty Davies

PAULA'S STORY

Paula, age forty-eight, sat having tea at her kitchen table and recalled the events of her sister's death. Paula was four when her baby sister, Sophie, died at sixteen months of age:

> Sophie was ill from the day she was born. She would get screaming fits and cry a terrible high pitched cry. I can remember thinking, most of the time, I felt invisible because she was such a worry for my parents and took most of their time.
>
> One winter's night, the baby convulsed and my mother walked half a mile through a blizzard to get to the nearest phone to call the doctor. My grandmother stayed with the baby and me. When the baby died, I sat on the bed, lifting her arms and letting them fall—they were so limp—for once she was quiet. My grandmother let me do that, let me look at her and everything. When my mother came in, she screamed at me, "Get away from her!" She was just hysterical.
>
> They did an autopsy on my sister to find out what exactly had been the problem (she had a tumor of some sort), and then returned her to the house and her casket was kept at the house until her funeral. They had the little casket right beside Mom's side of the bed, and Mom would hold Sophie and fondle her, and people were coming in and out, just visiting. My crib was in the same room as my parents' bed. I can remember one man coming over to the crib and saying, "You shouldn't be in here, you know." I thought that I was totally invisible until he talked to me. But I still stayed there.

The next thing was the funeral, and I think Mom took it really hard, because after the funeral, all I remember is that I was sent to live with my aunt. Nothing was explained to me—but my Mom had a "nervous breakdown." My aunt wasn't very healthy either . . . she was sick all the time and was really skinny. Today, she would be called "anorexic." They lived in the same little town. I think my cousin really resented my being there. She was mean to me . . . she made me drink a full glass of castor oil one day when she was babysitting me, and then she made me clean up the bathroom. I used to hide in the basement and play with my imaginary friend.

I did go back home, but I don't remember when. Mom was still totally preoccupied with Sophie's death. She was trying to communicate with her spirit, and she was visiting the grave every day. Dad was doing his thing, off to work. And this went on . . . they were told that the best thing to do was to have another baby. That was their big goal. So, I have another sister, eight years younger than me . . . it took four years for her to come. Looking at an old family photograph which included Paula at about seven years, when her mother was pregnant with the new baby, Paula said, " I was quite tall and lanky . . . and sad." Mom and Dad really wanted that child. I guess because of that, they spoiled her rotten. She couldn't cry without being picked up. They just doted on her, afraid something might be wrong with her too.

When I went to school I was painfully shy. My imaginary friend was fine, but when I got with real kids, I just didn't know how to play. The next thing was that I had trouble reading, I had trouble in school. I've always had the feeling of not belonging. It definitely affected me with interacting, with playing games at school. I would hang back. I was always the one to isolate myself. It was weird. I still tend to do that. I can be outgoing on a superficial basis, but not in any depth. It definitely has something to do with feeling different. Even with my husband who had a happy childhood, and who has been supportive of me, there are times that I feel really different . . . because not even he, nobody, really understands what happened to me.

As long as I'm in a learning situation and I'm helping others, I feel good. I feel very awkward when the focus is on me. I relate well to children too . . . I guess because I have an empathy for children and how much they can remember. I have always been sympathetic to other people, and I could relate to the dying parts of things . . . but I don't think I was as helpful as I could have been, because I hadn't thought this all through until recently.

No one ever talked about Sophie's death. My mom was out of it for a long time—I knew there must be a reason why I couldn't live at home for a time—but nobody explained anything to me. She had lots of little keepsakes of Sophie, but I really didn't understand it. If she was alive now, I would have a lot of questions for her. My father, he is seventy-five now, still won't talk about Sophie or anything like that—because it's "negative" and you never talk about the dead—that's his line of thinking.

I had dreams for a long time . . . but they were more like nightmares. There was always a young small child in my dream, and it's following me and I can't get rid of it. I used to have this repeating dream for years, right through my twenties and thirties. The only way you could tell whether this child was alive or dead was to put a mirror under its nose to see if was breathing. And there was no breath, and I was terrified. I was just trying to get away.

I never talked to anyone about the dream, or anything else about Sophie because I never thought that her death was significant in my life. I even went to a psychiatrist at one point in my life when I was feeling that I should have been happier, but Sophie's death never came out at all. I never told him about my dreams or my sister's death, but they were pertinent things that I overlooked.

My sister's death was the trouble, but I never thought of it. I have always had mood swings. One day when I was sitting here, feeling really down, I said to my husband, "I don't belong. I've got shallow roots. Here I am in a nice house . . . why aren't I really happy?" I decided that my roots were too shallow . . . I don't feel close to my own family, to my sister and my dad. I started to think back and I thought, "I wonder if it has something to do with Sophie."

So, it's only been recently that I have thought about this experience, and it seems to explain so much. I didn't have anyone to help me . . . it's so important to have an adult who could talk to you or help you, and parents need help in remembering that they have other children. Letting children get their feelings out . . . that's so important. If you could just have a way of finding out that you are not alone in these feelings, in the dreams. Being alone is the difficult part . . . when a child is alone, who does she talk to? You make up a friend . . . it isn't much help, mind you! I was lonely, not so much because I missed my sister, but more because nobody understood. So, you feel different, like you don't belong. Those are basically the feelings, and that's sort of a burden you carry through your life and you don't know why, until you sort of figure it out— wow! that's a breakthrough!

If my sister had not died? Well, maybe I would have been more important to my parents . . . I think I might have felt more loved and like I belonged . . . which would have made me feel more . . . given me more self-esteem. It just snowballs . . . I would have been better adjusted at school, and on down the line. I try to pass on what I have learned to my own children, so that if they have any loss like this in their families, they will remember . . . they will remember that they have other children.

Paula's story is only one of many accounts of adults, who in their childhood, experienced the death of a brother or sister. Her story highlights many of the findings from research projects which have focused on exploring the long-term effects of sibling bereavement.

BACKGROUND

Two research projects provide the basis for these findings. The first was a follow-up study of fifty-eight families who participated in Martinson et al. Home Health Care program in Minnesota for children who were dying of cancer [1]. These families have been assessed at periodic intervals since the death of the children; the most recent assessment occurred at seven to nine years following the death. In this assessment, semi-structured interviews were held with forty-six mothers, thirty-three fathers, and seventy-one siblings. At the time of the deaths, siblings ranged in age from three to sixteen years, and were now between the ages of eleven and twenty-four. Only the sibling interviews contribute to the data for this chapter [2].

The second study focuses on interviews with twenty-five adults who, during childhood, lost a sibling from any cause. These individuals ranged in age from twenty-one to seventy-five.

All interviews were tape recorded, transcribed, and subjected to content analysis. Selected aspects of the siblings' experience are emphasized here.

SELECTED FINDINGS

Thinking about the Deceased Sibling

All respondents indicated that they continued to think about their brother or sister, some as often as every day. These thoughts were reflected by responses such as "He is always in the back of my mind, and often right in the middle of my thoughts." Such thoughts were frequently triggered by a variety of events or activities which included tangible reminders, such as old photographs or the child's belongings [3]. Attending other funerals also brought back memories and a resurgence of grief: "When I go to a funeral or see someone else's death, I can remember . . . I can remember the scene of the whole thing. I relive it all over again." Paula remembered thoughts of Sophie permeating her whole life. More recently, her thoughts stemmed from recognizing her personal reaction to Sophie's death.

Other triggers were less tangible, such as just growing older. For example, eighteen-year-old Laura stated:

> As I watch myself get older . . . I remember as I started wearing makeup and started dating, I looked back and said, 'Gosh, Mary never got to experience anything like this', and that kind of got to me . . . she never got to be a regular teenager.

Older siblings also expressed such thoughts:

> I still think about my brother, wondering what it would be like if he were here to be the uncle of my children . . . what would he be like? What would his family be like?

In some cases, thoughts of the deceased sibling were aroused by a sense of still missing the companionship of the brother or sister who died. Barry, now twenty-four, missed his brother very much:

> Put it this way, I think of Dick almost every day. I really do miss him. I don't know what it is really. We used to do a lot of things together . . . we played together when we were real young because we were only two years apart, you see . . . we did a lot of stuff together.

Talking about the Deceased Sibling

Participants indicated that they thought about their siblings much more than they talked with anyone about their memories [3]. At the time of the death, Paula did not talk about her thoughts and feelings, and this behavior remained consistent for most of her adult life. Even as a young woman, Paula did not discuss her sister, her thoughts, or her dreams with the psychiatrist whom she consulted for help with her persistent sadness. At the time, she did not recognize the impact of Sophie's death on her own development.

Much of Paula's experience at the time of her sister's death set the tone for later reactions. No one talked with her to explain events and activities, no one encouraged her to share her thoughts and concerns. She knew that her mother treasured some of Sophie's belongings, but mother and daughter never shared their perceptions. Discrepant views about the belongings of the deceased child is indicative of problematic grief in siblings [4]. Her father, now an elderly man, still refused to discuss the death. It was only through her own reflecting that she realized the significance of the event, and shared her story for the first time during the interview.

For most siblings, if talking about the death at the time had not been part of their experience, it was less likely that they shared their thoughts now with anyone: "For the most part, I just keep it to myself, just a little memory of Sam."

Dreaming about the Deceased Sibling

Paula was not alone in dreaming about her sister. Many participants indicated that such dreams about their brother or sister continued for many years following the death. For Paula, her recurring dream was frightening, and she discussed it with no one, not as a child or as an adult. For some other siblings, the dreams were comforting, providing a "link" to the deceased sibling. Still, these siblings did not share their dreams either, usually out of fear of being ridiculed. Some siblings did not discuss their dreams because they regarded them as "private treasures" and preferred to keep them to themselves.

Feeling Different

Many siblings talked about how their experience made them "feel different." As children, they felt different from their peers, and for many, as it did for Paula, this feeling continued into adulthood. In the words of one woman, now age thirty-five, recalling her experience as a thirteen-year-old:

> I always felt that nobody really understood how I felt . . . I did feel very different. I was, as I say, more serious than other people. I always took offense to the jokes that were in—"dead baby" jokes and "frogs in the blender" jokes, things like that. Things that the other kids were finding sort of funny, I thought were sort of stupid and pathetic and disgusting.

Withdrawing

In response to feeling different, and not being understood, some siblings withdrew [5]. They preferred solitary activities, such as reading, or walking alone, or, as Paula had done, playing with imaginary playmates. Paula was among nine participants in the longer term study who reported long-term effects of sadness and depression. Some had sought professional help, and others, like Paula, realized on their own, that much of their sadness was related to the deaths of their siblings.

Following the deaths and to the present time, all siblings in this study felt different from others, particularly others of their age group. However, all except the group that included Paula, had at least one person they could talk to and share their day to day experiences at the time of the death. Those in Paula's grouping did not have anyone to talk to. They withdrew from others, particularly their peers. Their feelings of being different were reinforced, and they tended to miss out on developmental tasks of learning how to form and sustain relationships with friends. This was especially notable for participants who were young adolescents when their sibling died [6].

Feeling Lonely

Nearly all siblings indicated that at the time of the death, loneliness was a major problem which persisted. Recurring loneliness was especially painful for those who continually thought about their deceased brother or sister, like Barry whose words were quoted earlier, or Mark who, at fourteen said:

> She was my only sister and after she died (when Mark was 6), I was lonely . . . the loneliness is building up again now. That loneliness is the hardest.

For Paula, and for all siblings, the loneliness was compounded by the reactions of others. As children, they perceived that no one understood what the experience was like for them. Consequently, their sense of being alone was magnified, and continued to the present time.

Experiencing Growth

Many siblings perceived that they had gained maturity and had grown psychologically as a result of their experience. Their comments frequently expressed sentiments such as, "I have a better outlook on life now; I mean, I realize how important life is as a result of my sister's death." Such feelings also stemmed from many siblings' subsequent "comfort" with death events. Their exposure to death enabled many siblings to comfort others during similar traumatic times, and they felt good about such interactions. Such feelings, reflective of psychological growth, may account for the higher self-concept scores calculated for the bereaved siblings in the first study [7]. Even Paula, who endured long standing feelings of isolation and sadness, was positive about what she had learned. She believed that by sharing her experience with her own children and others, she could contribute to the overall well-being of children.

Feeling "I'm Not Enough"

Not all surviving siblings had higher self-concepts. These were the siblings who thought that they compared unfavorably with the sibling who died. Such thoughts and feelings of inadequacy were usually long-standing and present even before the child died. For others, their inadequacy was reinforced by thoughts that they should have been the child to die. In some cases, one or both parents explicitly expressed this belief and their children thought that could "never be enough" to make their parents happy again.

From the time of Sophie's death, Paula felt "invisible." Her mother's overwhelming grief precluded any awareness of her surviving child's emotional needs. Paula felt alone and excluded. Then, her parents looked forward to another child . . . as if Paula was not enough to keep them happy. Paula's new sister was the center of attention, and again, Paula felt forgotten. She withdrew into a world with an imaginary playmate, and over time, gained some sense of personal satisfaction from meeting the needs of others. It was as if she was not worthy of having her own needs met. When asked what would be different if her sister had not died, Paula indicated that she would have felt loved, and as if she "belonged" in the family. Her sadness still persists, but was partially alleviated when she experienced her "breakthrough" and recognized the personal impact of her sister's death.

Perceiving How Life would be Different

All of the siblings wondered how life would be different if their brother or sister were still alive. Most perceived that their lives would be different if the death had not occurred. Some siblings thought that the family composition would have been different: parents would not have divorced, or subsequent siblings would not have been born. Had the child not died, participants also believed that a personal aspect of themselves would be different. They said that:

> I would not be as close to my other sister as I am;
> I would be more outgoing than I am because the sadness got in the way;
> I would have done better in math because my brother would have helped me along the way.

Siblings commonly attributed current attitudes and behaviors to the experience of having lost their brother or sister. Forty-year-old Martha indicated that she, and her remaining siblings, learned to "be sick at the drop of a hat if they wanted a little more attention from their mother." She went on to say that she is aware that she still uses illness as an "escape" when life gets a little exasperating. Several indicated that the experience made them more appreciative of life itself: "I learned early that you can die, and that life is precious." The death had been a marker event in the lives of the siblings. Even with advancing age, siblings still identified the death as a critical event in their lives, even when it had not been acknowledged as such at the time of the death, or since.

IMPLICATIONS

The responses of siblings to the death of a brother or sister have only recently received attention as a subject worthy of serious investigation. Very seldom have such investigations explored the long-term effects of sibling bereavement. For some time, it has been assumed that grief is a series of steps leading to resolution if the death was accepted, or to pathological grief if intense grief reactions continued longer than expected. Findings indicate however that resolution does not occur by one year for many bereaved siblings. Rather, the effects of losing a sibling to death are long-lasting and pervasive. Sibling grief is an individual journey that should not be expected to follow time limits and a specific path.

The findings also support what seems like common sense: parents are instrumental in creating optimal environments for their grieving children. There is much to be done in offering assistance to families grieving the death of a child. There is much support that can be given to the surviving children. As a minimum, there is the acknowledgment that a child's death impacts on the lives of siblings. Siblings who continue to feel sadness for many years can be assured that they are not alone, that someone understands, and that they are in fact, "enough."

REFERENCES

1. I. M. Martinson, D. G. Moldow, G. D. Armstrong, W. F. Henry, N. D. Nesbit, and J. H. Dersey, Home Care for Children Dying of Cancer, *Research in Nursing and Health, 9*, pp. 11-16, 1986.
2. B. Davies, *Long-Term Bereavement in Siblings Following a Child's Death from Cancer*, Final report submitted to American Cancer Society, California Division, Psychosocial Oncology, San Francisco, California, 1986.
3. B. Davies, After a Sibling Dies, in *Bereavement: Helping the Survivors*, M. A. Morgan (ed.), King's College, London, Ontario, 1987.
4. B. Davies, Family Responses to the Death of a Child: The Meaning of Memories, *Journal of Palliative Care, 3*:1, pp. 9-15, 1987.
5. B. Davies, Long-Term Outcomes of Adolescent Sibling Bereavement, *Journal of Adolescent Research, 6*:1, pp. 83-96, 1991.

6. B. Davies, Long-Term Follow-Up of Bereaved Siblings, in *The Dying and Bereaved Teenager*, J. Morgan (ed.), The Charles Press Publishers, Philadelphia, Pennsylvania, pp. 78-89, 1990.
7. I. M. Martinson, E. Davies and S. G. McClowry, The Long-Term Effects of Sibling Death on Self-Concept, *Journal of Pediatric Nursing, 2*:4, pp. 227-135, 1987.

CHAPTER 5

Re-Grief as Narrative:
The Impact of Parental Death on
Child and Adolescent Development

Mary Anderson Miller

Give sorrow words, the grief that does not speak
Whisper's the o'er-fraught heart and bids it break.
— W. Shakespeare, *Macbeth*

Two desserts stood side-by-side both saturated with symbolic
meaning representing past, present, and future. The cake, her
father's favorite dessert, was always ordered from their hometown
bakery for special occasions. The cookies, part of a project for which
Anne had just received a very prestigious award, forecasted a
bright and promising future.

It had been more than seven years since they had that cake. He
died that long ago. Yet, here it was again, marking another family
ceremony—albeit one of a very different nature. This one re-opened
a tragic family episode, long closed and tightly shut. But "tragedy is
partly a matter of where a story ends" [1, p. 35], and this story was
far from over.

In this chapter, the author examines the narrative strands of
a young adolescent's life that freshen an understanding of latent
bereavement and describes a process which helps the adolescent
accommodate and integrate the loss several years after her father's
death. The task of the psychotherapy, in a narrative framework, was
to examine Anne's life story, reopen it, and move it forward. The
adolescent provided the raw material; the therapist provided "support,
inspiration and editorial acumen" [1, p. 40].

99

CHILDHOOD BEREAVEMENT AND ITS IMPACT
ON ADOLESCENT DEVELOPMENT

Although the debate regarding age and developmental capacity of children to mourn may continue, the impact of childhood bereavement is profound and long-term, but is not necessarily indicative of subsequent psychopathology [2-7]. The death of a parent also means death of a way of life [7]. The event of the death itself is stressful, and the aftermath pervades most aspects of life reaching to the "inner workings of the child's meaning-making system and to the way his or her world was structured" [8, p. 102]. According to Rando, significant adults in the lives of bereaved children must understand, legitimize, and help them accommodate the loss and concomitant changes in their lives [5].

Most information on childhood bereavement has come from clinical data and retrospective studies. A recent prospective longitudinal study by Silverman, Nickman and Worden [7] and Silverman and Worden [8, 9] provides data from a non-clinical sample population of children ages seven to seventeen about their experience when a parent dies. This study contributes significantly to a growing knowledge-base on childhood bereavement and explores the process of grief from a different perspective. According to this study, the death of a family member is not an isolated event but one that occurs in a social context of which the deceased is a part [7].

For children, as well as adults, bereavement is a cognitive and emotional process that weaves the experience of the death, the meaning of the loss, and a changing relationship with the deceased into the fabric of their lives over time. This process is not static, coming to an end marking "recovery," but rather one of ongoing, episodic accommodation in relation to the child's developmental level. In this framework, accommodation for children refers to "a continuing set of activities—related both to others and to shifting self-perceptions as the child's mind and body change—that affect the way the child constructs meaning" [7, p. 502]. This requires not only "an understanding of the meaning of the death, but a sense of the meaning of this now-dead parent in his or her life" [7, p. 502].

In a second case example, Jenny illustrates how children find ways to maintain a connection with the deceased parent which is consistent with their developmental level and family dynamics:

> After Jenny's father died, the first grade teacher, who had the best of intentions, quietly suggested that Jenny might want to make a father's day card for her uncle or grandfather. Jenny emphatically replied that, of course, the card would be for her father—she could take it to the cemetery and put it on his grave, maybe with a flower.

Children establish a set of memories, feelings, and actions referred to as "constructing the deceased" [7]. These may help them to maintain a positive connection to the deceased parent. The following categories formulated from a study by Silverman, Nickman, and Worden reflect children's efforts to maintain this connection [7, p. 497]:

- making an effort to locate the deceased (74% believed in "heaven");
- actually experiencing the deceased in some way (81% believed their parents to be watching them);
- reaching out to initiate a connection;
- remembering;
- keeping something that belonged to the deceased (linking objects).

Developmental transitions, such as adolescence, may precipitate a resurgence of grief which provide opportunities for further accommodation of the loss in relation to the current life stage [4, 10]. In adolescence, grief-related responses may take on familiar forms of mourning or find release in other ways, such as exaggerated pseudo-adult behaviors, identification with the dead person, care-eliciting behaviors, sexual acting-out, withdrawal, and depression [4]. Adolescence may offer a "second chance" to rework conflicts from childhood [11]. According to Raphael: "Some children may not have the opportunity, ego resources, or support to grieve and mourn for losses they experienced during childhood and this may only come with adolescence or, for some, with adulthood" [4, p. 169].

Issues of bereavement are superimposed on those of adolescent development [4, 12-18]. Many biological changes occur as adolescents mature physically and sexually. Factors of cognitive development which are important in bereavement include those leading to the ability to know one's self and others and to gain mastery over one's situation [7, 18, 19]. Simultaneously, a variety of psychosocial tasks leading to adulthood must be accomplished.

The impact of parental death shapes both reconciliation of conflicts from the past and direction in the future. When a parent dies, adolescents may be expected to assume adult roles, possibly forcing a premature foreclosing of their identity [4]. Issues of identity and gender identification may be complicated by the sex of the deceased parent [4]. For example, adolescent development may differ for males and females and the absence of a father may be significant in the development of heterosexual relationships and social roles for girls [14, 20-22]. For both genders in early adolescence, peers are sought from one's own sex. While in middle adolescence, most often, there is a shift toward the opposite sex [11]. This natural shift away from parents toward peers often represents a sense of loss for the adolescent; in reality, the death of a parent compounds this process [4, 14]. At a time when peer group acceptance is so important, bereaved adolescents often report "feeling different" and may feel set apart [4, 14, 23]. They may receive little comfort, have few opportunities to express grief, or share memories of the deceased [4]. Their distress may be acted out or internalized, perhaps appearing later in life. Their coping abilities may be strengthened or compromised.

If we consider the consequences of latent bereavement on adolescent development, how will the absence of a parent due to death affect an adolescent's capacity to manage such a pivotal transition period? Research suggests that much will depend upon the "interaction among the social context, the family system, and the personal characteristics of those involved" [8, p. 94].

In the following case study, there are three predominant narrative strands. The strands are concurrent and intertwined, each contributing to the process of healing:

1. A medical emergency reveals the undercurrent of latent bereavement in the larger narrative of a young adolescent's life;
2. The reconstruction of her father's life and death re-opens the family history; and
3. A ritual service, symbolizing resolution and transition, integrates the past and present with lifelong implications for her growth and development.

ANNE'S NARRATIVE

Anne's story began in the emergency room of a local hospital where she had been admitted for acute gastrointestinal distress. During treatment, she cried out for her father who had died some six and a half years earlier. Clearly her pain was more than physical; her symptoms indicated emotional pain as well. Following this emergency, she was referred for psychological counseling.

Over the course of her psychotherapy, the narrative of Anne's life began to unfold:

Anne's father died of cancer just a few months before her seventh birthday, at a time when her two younger brothers were three years and one-year-old. Her mother volunteered little information about his illness or death, responding to Anne's questions in a distant and restrictive manner. Anne did not attend the funeral service nor were there opportunities to inquire about it later.

Family life after her father's death was described as "chaotic." With few exceptions, relationships with extended family and friends were severed. Over the next few years, Anne encountered several changes including a new stepfather, a move out of state, a new sibling, and two new schools.

Any of the changes in Anne's life could have precipitated her physical distress and her cry for her father, but none did. Why then, in the middle of the year during her seventh grade, did her symptoms become acute? According to Raphael, a resurgence of grief may appear in adolescence [4]. When direct expression of grief is precluded, related responses may find other forms of release, as in Anne's situation.

It is important to examine what could have been done to help Anne accommodate the loss of her father relative to her developmental tasks of adolescence. Research suggests that "the bereaved child must deal with how and why the parent died and what the parent's presence may have been like had it continued over time" [7, pp. 495-496]. Finding ways to maintain a connection to the "now-dead" parent which are consistent with the developmental level and family dynamics "are aspects of an accommodation process that allows the child to go on living in the face of loss" [7, p. 496].

Significant others in the child's life play an important role in this process [24]. Small children may need assistance until puberty to remember an absent loved one [25]. Pictures, especially those of the deceased with the child, stories and symbols that characterize their relationship, possessions which serve as keepsakes and mementos, and recollection of important dates and special occasions all serve this purpose. By keeping memories of the deceased alive for children, the feelings associated with the dead parent remain available for resolution [5].

For Anne, memorabilia, tangible and symbolic, would be needed to provide a picture of her father and a review of their relationship. However, reconstructing the life and death of Anne's father, with sufficient clarity to help Anne examine her repressed feelings and beliefs about him, would require reopening the door to an era of family history that had been tightly closed. At her mother's request, Anne's family was included in the psychotherapy.

REOPENING ANNE'S NARRATIVE

Photograph albums, providing a pictorial history of family life at that time, reopened that door with relative ease and stimulated interaction among family members. An oral history about her father and family life was first evoked from the pictures and continued throughout the psychotherapy. The stories and the pictures brought into clear focus a vibrant portrait of a father involved in the routines of family life and highlighted a warm and close relationship with his children. Detailing stories in everyday life help to clarify elusive experiences [1]. On her own initiative, Anne created a photo collage from these family albums that had remained intact for seven years, and brought it to the therapy session.

> This beautifully framed photo collage pictorially opened and closed the children's history with their father. Pictures of each child with the father had been carefully chosen, beginning with his presence at their birth and ending with a family picture taken outside the hospital during his fatal illness. In the only family picture, the camera angle captured the father's eyepatch (a result of the later stages of his illness) and the name of the hospital where he died. There were no "special occasion" pictures, only ones reflecting their daily life and portraying the relationship of Anne's father with each of his children.

According to Polster, it is "those simple events which give context and continuity to life" [1, p. 7]. Anne's decision to create the collage, as well as its content and arrangement, reflect tasks associated with both bereavement and adolescence [26]. The collage symbolically integrated Anne's story of the life and death of her father into a coherent whole. Its creation, as well as its permanence, signified her need to keep memories of him alive so that feelings associated with him would remain available for reconciliation [5]. He was no longer such a "nebulous" inner representation, because Anne had clearly placed her father in the family and faced his fatal illness and death. Pictorially, she had captured the cause and circumstances surrounding his death as well as the patterns of relationships within the family, particularly those between her father and his children. All were important to her; all reflected key variables influencing the outcome of childhood bereavement [2]. This symbolic representation of her father was "an active effort to make sense of the experience of loss and to make it part of . . ." her reality [7, p. 496]. Her need to know him and understand his relationship with her and her siblings, at this time in her life, may reflect a developing ability to know herself and others [18-19, 21-22]. Anne's connection to her father will continue to evolve and will be important throughout her life.

The energy and power of the feelings generated by this compilation of family history needed to be put into constructive action and incorporated appropriately into present day life. Since there had been little commemoration for Anne's father, a ritual activity might be beneficial.

THE THERAPEUTIC FUNCTION AND
VALUE OF RITUAL

Rituals symbolize transition, healing, and continuity [27]. Perhaps, a ritual would help to integrate and direct Anne's unfolding narrative, but would it be "bearable"? Would it avoid the "level of pain or discomfort beyond which people are no longer able to function well?" [1, p. 33]. Rituals provide many therapeutic properties for this purpose. According to Rando, preparation for, and acting out of, rituals cuts through intellectualization, directly reaching the emotions and providing acceptable outlets and symbols through which to express inner feelings [5]. Furthermore, these feelings can be made more manageable because the ritual activity has a clear purpose and a distinct beginning and end. As a familiar and accepted part of every society, rituals provide a measure of safety for all participants during an emotionally-charged event.

Anne reviewed several options and decided that she and her siblings would create a memorial service to commemorate the seventh anniversary of their father's death. In essence, their father could be "with them again and they with him" in their present family life.

CONNECTING THE NARRATIVE STRANDS:
INTEGRATING PAST AND PRESENT

The activities of ritual preparation and enactment would provide constructive outlets for feelings connected to Anne's experience of her father's death. Significant symbolic strands of her past with their attached affect could be acted out and incorporated into her present life. There was as much therapeutic value in the process of the preparations as in the enactment of the ritual. Narration of the family history continued throughout the planning and preparatory activities. During this time, Anne's knowledge of her father was augmented by important information which was revealed about her mother including the nature of the relationships with the nuclear family, extended family, and friends, before and after her father's death.

Ritual Preparations

To whom, where, and how would the children tell this very personal and significant segment of the family's life story? Such decisions would greatly affect the tenor of the memorial service but, more important, the therapeutic value of the experience for Anne and her family. The family's preferences were not always possible, and the seemingly serendipitous nature of events, in retrospect, became significant.

The questions—where and to whom—provided form and direction to the preparations and enactment of the service. What could have been a real stumbling block for the family turned into an opportunity that, probably in the end, contributed to a much more meaningful activity.

> Originally, the family had chosen their local church and a prescribed liturgy appropriate for the occasion. Since the church was unavailable on that date, the priest decided that a traditional liturgy would be conducted in a non-traditional location—their home. The setting would make the service less formal, more personal, and self-contained. Flowers and photographs could be placed with more flexibility and the service would be videotaped by Anne's stepfather. The invitation list could be more relaxed or perhaps restricted.

Who do the children invite to commemorate the seventh anniversary of their father's death? Since stories are used to "join our lives with those of other people" [1, p. 30], it seemed likely that relational ties with ritual participants could be strengthened and deepened. Remembering the deceased with others provided an opportunity to integrate memories into the present time and into current relationships [28-31]. In opening the service to those outside the immediate family, discussions about who to invite and who not to invite entailed one of the most tense and risky moments in Anne's narrative.

> Do they invite only those who knew their father? And, of those, who should they include? Do they include new people with whom they feel especially close and, therefore, want to witness this important event which links their past with their present? Do they include people who knew their father and by all standards had a "right" to be there, but with whom relationships were strained?

After much discussion and debate, the family chose to include old and new friends, maternal relatives, certain teachers, and of special importance, their father's best friend. Ultimately, they excluded their paternal relatives, choosing instead to protect themselves from re-opening old wounds. The risk of compromising the therapeutic value of the service outweighed the potential healing of the rift between the families.

People spanning three generations, relatives and friends—old and new—and those from relevant community institutions, came together to support and participate in the narration of this important segment of Anne's family history. For those who knew Anne's father, it was a time of recollection and reunion. For those who did not, it was an opportunity to learn about him and his significance to Anne at this time in her life. Anne's new knowledge about her father, the nature of their relationship, and the meaning of his death to her were validated by "those who count." These factors will be important in Anne's ongoing accommodation of her loss as she develops and matures.

All participants were invited to a luncheon following the memorial service. Planning the menu enhanced the storytelling.

> The menu for the luncheon developed from discussions about her father's favorite foods. However, items reflecting current family life had a way of just "slipping in". The food symbolically represented past, present, and future. For example, in addition to the cake, her father's other favorite dessert was Anne's cookies. These had been part of a recent award-winning project and predicted the possibility of a promising future for Anne.

Ritual Service

The most significant aspect of the memorial service was the story telling, a process that began in the family room—the center of their family life.

> The photo collage, a pictorial narration of her father's life and death, stood alone on an easel surrounded by flowers that would be planted to bloom anew each spring. The easel was the focal point around which all gathered with the priest to participate in the traditional liturgy—a simple, yet touching commemoration to honor Anne's father.
>
> The storytelling continued with vigor during lunch. Her father's best friend had an eclectic collection of stories about their father that described a side of him that the children did not know, enhancing and amplifying their knowledge of him as a person and a friend. There was laughter as well as tears, as the diverse array of stories were filled with humor, irony, adventure, mystery, and love. These aspects are often omitted when people are suffering the unbearable pain of mourning [1].

Through a total sensory experience, the memorial service integrated the fragmented past into Anne's present life with long-range implications for her growth and development. By anchoring such an experience in the present, the family will have years to recall it among themselves and with friends. The stories, the memorial service captured on film, the poignant family history portrayed in the framed collage, and the rebirth of the memorial flowers each spring will serve as ongoing symbolic connections to her father and help to sustain Anne through many transitions in her life. Her new relationship with him is not static, but will be redefined over time. She may draw on this new-found knowledge of him to influence her judgments about herself and her relationship to the world.

The memorial service symbolized transition, healing, and continuity. The juxtaposition of past, present, and future threaded throughout Anne's narrative also frames the experience of adolescence because "at no other period of life are past and future so insistently present" [14, p. 30]. This may reflect an unconscious striving for continuity and integration, the core of Erikson's definition of a developing identity: "A striving within to bring together the self that one is with the self that one was, with the self that one wants to be . . ." [32, p. 120]. During this period, conflicts from childhood that resurface may be reworked more successfully [4, 11]. These conflicts, as well as their accommodation and integration, do not exist in a vacuum but within the context of an adolescent's significant social group. Linking innovation with tradition through the use of familiar symbols and rituals may be helpful in bringing order and control over psychic conflicts [33]. We may need to "look anew at rituals that facilitate dialogue and other kinds of relationships to the past" [7, p. 502].

NARRATIVE AND PSYCHOTHERAPY

> People think and make judgments from the confidence of narrative; anyone at any age is able to tell the story of his or her life with authority. . . Everyone all the time is in the act of composition, our experience is an ongoing narrative within each of us [34, p. 22].

Narrative in its many and varied forms is important in facilitating the process of bereavement for the accommodation of the loss and "requires the development of a common language for talking about the death and the person who died" [7, p. 502]. Life stories, play activity, psychodrama, and ritual are some ways children and adolescents may develop this language and act out the experience of the death, the meaning of the loss, and a changing relationship with the deceased parent.

Adolescents, like everyone else, engage in an ongoing process of self-construction, composing stories about their life experiences. Animate and inanimate objects that they choose and the relationships they form are expressions of their feelings, beliefs, and values. "The language they use and connections they make reveal the world that they see and in which they act" [21, p. 2]. These real-life stories and their narration not only provide important information about how adolescents compose their lives but how others may assist them in that composition. For example, sometimes stories put 'bearable' distance between the narrator and the experience, referred to by Wolfenstein as "mourning from a distance" [12, p. 118].

Psychotherapy provides a supportive framework for eliciting and amplifying life stories and for guiding their integration, direction, and emotional bearability [1]. Fragmented and disparate strands of the narrative are integrated, with "each part eventually belonging to the whole" [1, p. 31]. Direction not only guides the forward movement of the narrative but mobilizes the energy required to fuel that movement. Emotional pain, which inhibits integration and direction, gradually becomes bearable. Only after the pain has lessened may "the drama inherent in the tragedy . . . be honored" [1, p. 17].

Therapists, like editors, must exercise keen judgement in guiding narrative development. By recognizing key elements in life stories, they are in a unique position to guide clients through their bereavement. From their narrative, therapists highlight those elements that are important and significant. Some elements may be apparent while others may be undercurrents, providing only subtle clues of their existence. Drawing from this pool of possibilities, clients are assisted in choosing roles, writing scripts, and designing sets replete with relevant and meaningful symbols. These catalyze the integration, direction, and emotional bearability of their unfolding narrative. With each choice comes a set of consequences. For example, some have positive cathartic potential and stimulate psychological growth while others may inhibit such growth. Support, as well as inspiration, must be provided as clients confront possibilities, make choices, and then live with the consequences.

Real life stories need to be narrated; they need to be "said, painted, danced, dramatised, put into circulation" [35, p. 37]. The narration of real-life stories and their validation by significant others affirm one's experience, one's self, and provide the basis for a "genuine relationship" with others [22]. Such connections form strong, healthy relationships, past and present, and may ease the pain of "emotional isolation". This feeling of "being lonely in the midst of others" may be a root of human loneliness so often expressed by those who are bereaved [36, 37].

Rituals, memorials, and other cultural forms of expression provide rich mediums for the narration of these "real-life" stories as the experience of the narrator is legitimized by significant others and integrated into current life [29-31]. Special occasions and family events also provide opportunities to acknowledge and connect with the deceased [31, 38]. For example, at the remarriage of two widowed persons, the priest acknowledged the deceased spouses by name. In lieu of attendants, their children and grandchildren were summoned to the alter to witness the marriage vows, connecting family members past and present in the familiar ritual. The benefits of ritual are ongoing. For example, in one study two years after the death, children and adolescents report that attending the funeral of their parent helped them acknowledge the reality of the death, honor their parent, and accept support and comfort from others [9].

CONCLUSION

Death of a family member and bereavement of the mourners occur in a social context. Adults who interact with bereaved children and adolescents need to understand their grief process, legitimize their experience, and help them to cope and master the tasks of mourning as they grow and develop [5]. Developmental transitions and life events may precipitate a resurgence of grief which provide opportunities for further accommodation of the loss in relation to their current life stage [4, 15]. Grief-related responses may be readily identifiable or disguised as in Anne's case.

However, like Anne, many children live in a world where adults often misunderstand childhood bereavement and want to shield them from the realities of death. In trying to protect children (and perhaps themselves as well) from suffering unbearable pain associated with the loss, the reverse often happens as repressed pain intensifies. Anne's case study illustrates that attempts to circumvent the death and allay feelings connected to the loss do not alleviate grief and may set up risk factors for various disorders later in life.

Silverman, Nickman and Worden make three recommendations to help children and adolescents accommodate the death of a parent:

1. Develop a common language for talking about the death and the person who died.
2. Dialogue to help children and adolescents learn to remember the deceased and maintain an ongoing connection.

3. Initiate rituals that facilitate dialogue and other kinds of relationships to the past [7, pp. 501-502].

Can we be open, listen carefully, and ask the right questions? Children and adolescents can help us to develop the language, rituals, and social support that are needed to help the bereaved accommodate and integrate the experience of the death, the meaning of the loss, and a changing relationship with the deceased into the fabric of their lives over time.

REFERENCES

1. E. Polster, *Every Person's Life is Worth a Novel*, W. W. Norton & Co., New York, 1987.
2. J. Bowlby, *Attachment and Loss, Volume III: Loss*, Basic Books, Inc., New York, 1980.
3. P. R. Silverman, The Impact of the Death of a Parent on College Age Women, *Psychiatric Clinics of North America, 10*:3, pp. 387-404, 1989.
4. B. Raphael, *The Anatomy of Bereavement*, Basic Books, New York, 1983.
5. T. A. Rando, *Grief, Dying, and Death: Clinical Interventions for Caregivers*, Research Press Co., Champaign, Illinois, 1984.
6. J. L. Krupnick, Bereavement During Childhood and Adolescence, in *Bereavement, Reactions, Consequences, and Care*, M. Osterweiss, F. Solomon, and M. Greene (eds.), National Academy Press, Washington, D.C., 1984.
7. P. R. Silverman, S. Nickman, and J. W. Worden, Detachment Revisited: The Child's Reconstruction of a Dead Parent, *American Journal of Orthopsychiatry, 62*:4, pp. 494-503, 1992.
8. P. R. Silverman and J. W. Worden, Children's Reactions in the Early Months After the Death of a Parent, *American Journal of Orthopsychiatry, 62*:1, pp. 93-104, 1992.
9. P. R. Silverman and J. W. Worden, Children's Understanding of Funeral Ritual, *Omega Journal of Death and Dying, 25*:4, pp. 319-331, 1992.
10. J. E. Baker, Psychological Tasks for Bereaved Children, *American Journal of Orthopsychiatry, 62*:1, pp. 105-116, 1992.
11. P. Blos, *On Adolescence*, Free Press, New York, 1962.
12. M. Wolfenstein, How is Mourning Possible? *Psychoanalytic Study of the Child, 21*, pp. 93-123, 1966.
13. M. Rutter, *Children of Sick Parents*, Oxford University Press, London, 1966.
14. K. Dalsimer, *Female Adolescence*, Yale University Press, New Haven, 1986.
15. S. Altschul (ed.), *Childhood Bereavement and its Aftermath*, International Universities Press, Madison, Connecticut, 1988.

16. E. Harris, Adolescent Bereavement Following the Death of a Parent: An Exploratory Study, *Child Psychiatry and Human Development, 21*:4, pp. 267-291, 1991.
17. E. Berlinsky and H. Biller, *Parental Death and Psychological Development*, Lexington Books, Lexington, Massachusetts, 1982.
18. J. Piaget, *The Construction of Reality in the Child*, Basic Books, New York, 1954.
19. R. Kegan, *The Evolving Self: Problem and Process in Human Development*, Harvard University Press, Cambridge, Massachusetts, 1982.
20. N. Chodorow, *Feminism and Psychoanalytic Theory*, Yale University Press, New Haven, Connecticut, 1989.
21. C. Gilligan, *In a Different Voice: Psychological Theories and Women's Development*, Harvard University Press, Cambridge, Massachusetts, 1982.
22. L. M. Brown and C. Gilligan, *Meeting at the Crossroads*, Ballentine Books, New York, 1992.
23. S. J. Fleming and R. Adolph, Helping Bereaved Adolescents: Needs and Responses, in *Adolescence and Death*, C. A. Corr and J. N. McNeil (eds.), Springer Publishing Co., New York, 1986.
24. A. M. Rizzuto, *The Birth of the Living God: A Psychoanalytic Study*, University of Chicago Press, Chicago, Illinois, 1979.
25. E. Furman, *A Child's Parent Dies: Studies in Childhood Bereavement*, Yale University Press, New Haven, Connecticut, 1974.
26. J. W. Worden, *Grief Counseling and Grief Therapy: A Handbook for the Mental Health Practitioner*, Springer, New York, 1982.
27. O. van der Hart, *Rituals in Psychotherapy: Transition and Continuity*, Irvington, New York, 1983.
28. M. White, Saying Hullo Again: The Incorporation of the Lost Relationship in the Resolution of Grief, *Dulwich Centre Newsletter*, Spring 1988.
29. P. C. Rosenblatt, R. P. Walsh, and D. A. Jackson, *Grief and Mourning in Cross Cultural Perspective*, Human Relations Area Files, (microfilm), 1976.
30. S. M. Silverman and P. R. Silverman, Parent-Child Communication in Widowed Families, *American Journal of Psychotherapy, 33*:3, pp. 428-441, 1979.
31. P. Rosenblatt and C. Elde, Shared Reminiscence About a Deceased Parent: Implications for Grief Education and Grief Counseling, *Family Relations, 39*, pp. 206-210, 1990.
32. E. H. Erikson, Identity and the Life Cycle, *Psychological Issues, 1*:1, 1959.
33. G. Obeyesekere, *The Work of Culture*, University of Chicago Press, Chicago, Illinois, 1990.
34. E. L. Doctorow, The Passion of Our Calling, *New York Times*, Book Review, p. 22, August 25, 1985.
35. V. Turner, Dewey, Dilthey, and Drama: An Essay in the Anthropology of Experience, in *The Anthropology of Experience*, V. W. Turner and E. M. Bruner (eds.), University of Illinois Press, Chicago, Illinois, 1986.

36. R. S. Weiss, *Loneliness: The Experience of Emotional and Social Isolation*, M.I.T. Press, Cambridge, Massachusetts, 1973.
37. C. M. Parkes and R. S. Weiss, *Recovery From Bereavement*, Basic Books, New York, 1983.
38. D. Becker and F. Margolin, *Implications: Therapies for Children*, C. E. Schaefer and H. L. Millman (eds.), Jossey-Bass, Inc., San Francisco, 1977.

CHAPTER 6

The Legacy of AIDS:
The Untold Stories of Children

Ruth Rothbart Mayer

INTRODUCTION

A child's earliest human interaction is most frequently with his parents. They represent his entire world, his first and most significant relationship. A parent's death creates a violent disruption of that relationship which, in addition to the chaos such a tragedy introduces into the child's life, occurs without the child having the ability to share his feelings, fears, and beliefs with others. "He does not have the 'vocabulary' for discussion, thereby causing him to believe, temporarily or permanently, that the world is a dangerous and painful place" [1, p. 10].

When AIDS is the cause of death, children are further silenced. Discussing death with children is difficult, but discussing an AIDS death is even harder. More often than not, families protect themselves by retreating into isolation and keeping AIDS a secret. Such protective blinders may inhibit the parent's ability to understand their children's needs. Children under the age of two will sense change but are not able to ask questions. Toddlers and school-age children learn to do what adults impose; they do not ask questions or pretend not to hear. They may assume more responsibility in the home, by being brave, by becoming caretakers, or by providing emotional support for the ill parent or other family members. Teenagers may stay out of the house more frequently or act out and be labeled "unruly." They often cope on their own.

In lower socio-economic areas where there is an increase in AIDS, children's lives may already be complicated by poverty, abuse, homelessness, and violence. Their lives are fragmented and their emotional needs may remain unmet in an environment in which the external demands of living take precedence. Many families struggle with such practical concerns as food, clothing, and shelter. They may experience multiple deaths and fear for their own lives in neighborhoods where gun shots punctuate the night air. "Inner-city individuals and families, constantly struggling to cope with the general life conditions under which they reside, rarely have the luxury to anticipate the demands of death and grief" [2, p. 137].

A great tragedy of AIDS is the number of children who will be orphaned by the disease. Recent statistics indicate that there will be a higher number than anticipated. In poverty areas where women are more often the sole caregiving parent, Michaels and Levine estimate that by the year 2000, as a result of AIDS-related deaths, there will be up to 125,000 motherless children orphaned in the United States. Most of these children will not be HIV infected. There are no estimates of how many HIV negative children of two parent homes will lose a father to AIDS, and continue to live under the care of their HIV negative mothers [3, p. 3476].

We are only beginning to learn how children's lives are affected when a parent dies of HIV/AIDS, especially how secrecy, stigma, and isolation affect families. There is still a great deal more to learn about how these factors work themselves out in children's lives. The following is an account of my son Zachary Mayer. Unlike many children affected by AIDS today, his life began without complications. At age two and a half years, when his father was diagnosed with HIV, Zachary became one of a growing number of children who lived through the illness, then lost a parent to this disease.

Being a social worker for over twenty years did not prepare me to live through this experience without excessive stress. Looking back, my husband and I did lay the groundwork for Zachary to understand his father's illness, but I was too deeply affected by the dramatic changes in our lives to give conscious thought to our son's needs. We represent one scenario, that of an intact traditional family in which one parent has AIDS and the other HIV negative family members learn to cope, both during the illness and after the death. Hopefully, one family's experience will help others in a similar situation.

Several major themes have continued to develop from the time of my husband's diagnosis late in 1986, through his death in 1988, to the present, just before Zachary's ninth birthday. The issues discussed in this chapter address the developmental phases of the young child, between the ages of four to eleven years. While the concerns relate directly to general phases of bereavement, the reality of AIDS as the cause of his father's death has created for Zachary an unusual, if not completely new, set of circumstances. It is important to understand how children are traumatized as a result of losing a parent to AIDS. To survive, children must be given the tools to enter adolescence and then adulthood. In order to express their vulnerability and fear, children need to feel safe and be encouraged to grieve their losses.

SECRETS

A family may keep the presence of AIDS a secret because the stigma, which causes them to feel shame, creates too much stress. They may also maintain secrecy for religious or cultural reasons, to avoid problems with employment or housing, or to shield children from rejection by their peers. While a family's reasons for holding the secret deserve respect, it is important to understand how such secrets affect children.

Unlike adults or older children, young children have limited experiences to help them interpret events. They may sense that their parents' reactions are different, but most likely they do not understand why. Often adults may deny how much children see—"He didn't see me crying, he just saw me wiping my eyes. He probably thinks I have a cold." The truth is that children can sense distress, anger and fear and will eventually react in one way or another.

> During the early course of Michael's illness, we thought that Zach, at age two and a half, was too young to understand our discussions about treatments, hospitals and doctors. We "protected" him from hearing about his father's illness by huddling in a corner to talk on the phone and we hoped he wouldn't notice us spelling words. One afternoon, following a conversation in which Michael and I talked about his worsening condition, we noticed that Zach was missing. I called for him and finally found him in the corner of his bed, hugging his animals and singing in the darkened room. Suddenly I understood that we had been treating him like a shadow in our midst.
>
> At dinner Zach said, "I'm sad." I asked him why and he replied, "Because Mommy's sad." I told him his father had a bad cough which bothered him a lot. Zach nodded vigorously but when I added that he and I were healthy, he giggled and ran away from the table.

When children are in nursery or grade school their world expands and they may feel less in control as they see and hear things from which they were protected at home. Seeing other children come to school hand-in-hand with both parents may arouse resentment, anger, and feelings of loneliness. A child's upset, which he may experience as a sudden volcanic reaction, is certain to confuse him. The transition from home to an unprotected world in which he tries to cope silently enlists him in his parents' conspiracy. He may suppress what he senses or knows as he begins to understand his home life is a secret.

> Zachary kicked and scratched children at nursery school, didn't want to be touched, and sometimes urinated in his pants because he said that other people, not his mommy, picked him up from school. His teacher was mystified by this strange behavior from a child who had been so cheerful and cooperative. The teacher and principal called us in, not knowing if Zachary needed to be disciplined or sent to a school for children with special needs.
>
> Since Zach seemed to come to and go from school happily, it never occurred to us to explain our situation to the school authorities. We were surprised when we were told of his poor behavior. Even then we were reluctant to say anything, fearing his teacher would ask questions about the nature of the illness. After much debate I told her and the principal that Zachary's father had been ill, but was on the mend. They thanked me because it explained Zachary's behavior but they never asked about the nature of the illness. However, by giving only partial information, each time Michael became ill, and Zachary's upset erupted, we were forced to revise our statement.

Because AIDS has become a more chronic illness, the family must cope with a child's growing awareness of his parent's condition, as he matures. His questions will change, he will ask for more details, and, seeing his parent become ill more often, he will persist until the answers are more satisfactory.

> In the winter of 1987 both Zachary and Michael were ill. Zachary was frightened by his cough which sounded much like his father's, and insisted on taking the same cough drops. Once, tired and frustrated at being up most of the night, I yelled at him to "just stop coughing." Realizing he was confused and frightened by the thought that his cough could make him as sick as his father, I explained that his daddy had a virus in his blood which makes him cough but it was different than the cough children get.
>
> From the beginning Michael and I had decided not to tell the pediatrician about Michael's illness, believing that "the illness didn't affect Zachary." But I did not want to tell him simply because I felt too ashamed. I thought he might judge us for bringing AIDS into our home and worried that he would talk about us. A year later, I informed him of my husband's illness because I needed reassurance that my son's health was sound. He was sympathetic

and responsive to my request for support. From that time on he reminded me that Zach's periodic illnesses, mostly ear infections, were typical of children his age.

Once, after an examination, I was mortified when the doctor told my son he had a virus. Zachary's eyes widened in fear. He remembered being told his father had a virus. It was an honest mistake—doctors tell children they have a virus all the time—but one that cost us dearly because Zachary had bad dreams for more than a week. Despite the doctor's explanation of the difference between a little virus and a big virus and even after he was well, Zachary asked when his virus would go away.

When children sense stress but do not understand the cause, they begin to wonder if *they* are the cause. A very young child is vulnerable and can become angry at both the circumstances and himself, even if the reasons are ambiguous. There is no such thing as a child being too young to internalize guilt. Early on, they think they can be "bad" or can be made to feel "at fault" and this causes them to feel shame. Lenore Terr explains how children swap guilt for shame:

> Everybody has trouble with the idea of bad luck. Inadvertently wandering under a cloud somehow feels disgraceful. Shameful. Often children would rather put together some made-up reasons for tragedies and feel guilty about these made-up causalities than experience the humiliation of being victims to the world's randomness . . . As a protection against feeling ashamed, in other words, young people make delayed, unconscious trade-offs—"guilt" for "shame" [4, p. 113].

> It should have come as no surprise to me when one day, Zach swore like an adult at his gymnastics teacher and then called him "poopy and doody." His shocked teacher told him he was bad. When I picked him up, Zachary announced, "I am bad." This set a tone for Zachary's behavior, especially during the last year of his father's life when Michael withdrew from family life. They took one long trip together during which Zach learned when to ask his father to do things with him and when Michael needed to rest. At home again, Michael retreated to his work and private thoughts and Zachary let out his anger on me.

Around age three, children become interested in the life and death process, fascinated by dead bugs and animals and wanting to know why things and people die. They often develop, what adults consider, a morbid interest and sometimes kill bugs to observe the crushed carcass. They ask what happens to people when they die and where the body goes. "Though children may seem to accept the idea of death they do not understand, and are frightened by, its finality" [5, p. 325].

> A friend gave us the book *Lifetimes* [6] which explains the life cycle to children. Zachary was fascinated that something living could disappear after it died. It was during this process of exploration that Michael died, five days after Zachary's fourth birthday. He said, "Now I don't have a daddy any more. It's like a butterfly, when it dies you never see it again." At first, Zachary embraced all of Michael's belongings. "Now that Daddy is dead, this is ours." But as the months wore on and Michael didn't return, Zachary's behavior changed to anger.

It is common for children to fantasize about a parent after he or she has died. They want to recapture life as it was, have their parent back, and be a family again. To accomplish this, children may make up stories to explain where a parent has gone, when he will return, or other "facts" that address the child's own needs and fears. When it is too hard for a parent to explain AIDS as the cause of death, children may rely on fantasy because reality can be like living under the water, where facts float by, unclear and distorted by confusion.

> By the time Zachary turned five, and for the next year, his stories became more and more incredible. There were many disruptions in our lives at that time—we moved, I changed jobs, he changed schools, therapist, and babysitter. For the first time, he traveled by bus to a new day camp. In kindergarten, with an unsympathetic, highly structured teacher, Zachary's behavior became disruptive. He loved going to school but couldn't stay still, made silly faces, and refused to sit in any kind of group.
>
> At the same time, he was asking more questions about how his daddy got the virus, but I was unable to answer him clearly. Zachary told plausible stories about two non-existent older brothers, one who was in college and didn't need a bed in our house, and another who shared Zach's bunk bed. He gave money away and crammed his pockets full of little toys from his kindergarten class. Worse, Zachary began to harbor his own secrets. He never told me anything that happened during the day. He often lost memos from school or I found them stuffed in the bottom of his backpack. When asked why, his big brown eyes would meet mine as he said, "I don't know." At first, it was understandable for him to create a fantasy life which he controlled, but I was becoming aware of how the secrets I held were affecting him.

"AIDS is a family problem that transcends illness and death. It is uniquely one that causes families to feel they have failed and have a 'skeleton in the closet' " [2, p. 108]. Telling this secret to children is to reveal things which evoke in you shame, uncertainty, and fear of your children's wrath. The burden is passed on, not just to one child but, to the next generation of children.

> For almost two years after my husband's death, I believed it was best to keep the word AIDS a secret from my son, even though my professional life included working with women who, like me, were HIV negative and had spouses who were living with, or had died from AIDS. I pretended Zachary didn't hear my conversations, justifying my behavior by worrying that he would tell his friends or their parents and certain he would feel stigmatized. The real reason I didn't tell him was out of my own fear of his anger. Once I acknowledged that Zachary had been angry with me for a long time I was able to put such fears aside and think about how to impart information to him about AIDS. I started to think about the difference between secrets and privacy, having forgotten that our "secret" did not preclude our right to privacy.

Secrets are hidden concerns that reflect shame, while privacy describes matters that families choose not to share because they are important only to them. Personal habits, salaries, family disputes, or family members with chronic illnesses are not talked about outside the family unless there are specific reasons. Stating the value of the private realm, Schneider writes, "Some phenomena are intrinsically private affairs. That is, they ought to be kept private—protected by limited access . . . the private sphere is essential both for the maintenance and the improvement of the self and society" [7, p. 41].

> I could state the facts without fear once there was a clear difference established between revealing "the secret" from the privacy to which we were entitled. Now, within the privacy of our home, we could talk about the events in our lives. I began by telling Zach how, when I was a little girl, the adults in my house talked amongst themselves, but didn't include me. "You were too young before, but you're six now and I don't want you to feel a secret has been kept from you. The name of Daddy's illness scares people because they don't know much about it, so I waited until you were old enough and could understand." Zach asked, "What's the name of the illness so I'll know if it will scare me." When I said, "AIDS," he shrugged and said, "That doesn't scare me."

HOW PARENTAL COPING AFFECTS CHILDREN

"It is perhaps no accident that in the traditional marriage vows, the pledge to remain constant places 'in sickness' before 'in health'; sickness tests family strength and resiliency as few other crises do. In this context AIDS is the supreme test of family strength" [8, p. 33].

Parents cannot explain HIV to a child until their own feelings about the illness have at least been talked about, if not resolved. Children are more likely not to be told when the diagnosis is first made, especially when the affected partner is asymptomatic. Though a partner may remain reasonably healthy for several years, an overwhelming tension can infuse the air with stress. Some people report that, at the point of diagnosis, they begin grieving the loss of the relationship. Often the infected partner chooses denial as a coping mechanism, insisting that his/her spouse not tell anyone thus leaving her/him further isolated.

While other illnesses and tragedies may foster embarrassment, AIDS is unparalleled in the way that stigma, guilt, and shame influence every day and every interaction. Couples may be mired in discussing how a partner contracted the disease, sometimes revealing behavior of which the spouse was not aware. Tragically, AIDS may have resulted from behavior that occurred years earlier, leaving the couple feeling cheated by bad luck and misfortune. Hemophiliacs and people who contracted AIDS through tainted blood feel victimized by the medical community and by a disease they did not deserve. However the disease was contracted, the healthy spouse feels stigmatized by association and has few places to go to receive support and sympathy.

In addition, the healthy partner must deal with the daily responsibilities of child care, employment conditions, diminished finances, medical and social support systems, as well as household chores. As a result, they experience low self-esteem, depression, and anger which they often do not feel entitled to express. Also, unlike other illnesses in which a couple may strive to maintain sexual intimacy, this aspect of their relationship often becomes strained. Some couples stop having sex because one or both are afraid of transmission. Couples who continue their sexual relationship may feel resentment at having to limit their sexual activity and become dependent on condoms, which are now symbolic of AIDS. Though couples know better, some engage in unsafe sex practices to feel "normal" again or because they think it is worth the risk to try to get pregnant. This strained intimacy may make a woman feel frustrated as her role of wife shifts to that of caregiver. Engaging in unsafe behavior becomes another secret, another shame, and this often speaks to the degree to which self-destructive feelings can develop. These unremitting stresses may make it difficult for parents to adequately nurture and communicate with their children.

Unexplained changes may lead some children to become resigned and compliant, while others express distress by acting out and appearing to be problem children. Adults are less likely to acknowledge their own uncertainties and their children's fear and anger. Instead, they tend to focus on, and react to their children's aggressive behavior.

Every time Zachary acted out in public I was mortified that we would be judged—he as a "spoiled brat" and I as an inadequate mother. In the back of my mind I was sure people knew my husband had AIDS.

The first time Michael was hospitalized Zachary was not quite three. He had been learning how to express himself, to say that he missed his father and even to say that he was angry because his daddy got sick. But when, on the way to the hospital, Zachary threw himself to the ground screaming because he was fearful of seeing his father for the first time in weeks, I felt enraged at his behavior.

"Walk slower, Mommy. Don't walk so fast." He wasn't listening to me. Telling him there was nothing to worry about, that Daddy was fine, was not consoling. We made our way, stopping and starting. In calm, more rational moments I understood his pain and fear, but on our way to the hospital where it was my job to reunite father and son, my resentment welled up inside.

Zachary expressed his unhappiness and anger daily but I chose to ignore it. He threw all his stuffed animals around the room, acted out in nursery school, and refused to listen to me. However, I needed to believe that his adjustment was remarkably good. I resorted to lecturing, cajoling, or sometimes slapping his hand to teach him more reasonable behavior. Finally, I realized that my behavior was not rational, which made me feel guilty. I found a therapist who assessed Zachary to be a fearful and constricted child. Her goal was to help make him feel safe and to give him a place to communicate anything he felt, mostly through play.

Each week when Zachary was with his therapist, I fell into a deep sleep in the waiting room. There, in a moment of quiet, knowing that someone was taking care of my son, the stress lifted long enough for me to rest peacefully. Once Zachary had a tantrum in the waiting room. With the therapist present he vented his anger while I, under her tutelage, talked quietly to him. I understood for the first time how little attention Michael and I had been paying to his fears.

In their discussion of a parent's ability to cope with a child's bereavement, Hummer and Samuels point out that, "a factor which should not be underemphasized is the degree of ego strength at that period of life in which the death occurs, and the resources and limitations brought to bear upon the adaptation by the overall personality of the bereaved . . . The parent may also limit the child's comprehension by distorting information, using ambiguous euphemisms, and/or excluding the child from sufficient concrete experiences with the death" [9, p. 41; 10] or, in the case of HIV, during life.

> Michael withdrew during the last months of his illness. He continued to work but refused to participate in household responsibilities—bills, taxes and Zachary's care. The things I would be left with, he had already left behind. Michael suffered great disappointment and anger at knowing he would not see our son grow up. When it happened, his death was unexpected, but quiet. For a brief moment, relief flooded our home.
>
> After Michael died Zachary demanded my attention by alternately acting out or lovingly inviting me to sit and play with him. Often I was distracted and had a hard time just sitting still. When I got angry with him, Zachary would say, "you're a wolf, Mommy." He was learning to defend himself but still he was a vulnerable little boy with few answers to many complex questions, many of which were hard to articulate, no less to try to understand.
>
> He wanted to know how his daddy looked when he died and once, asked if I had taken a picture. I could answer those questions but when he asked how his daddy got "that virus," I avoided answering, saying I was too tired or I would offer to read to him. He complied, but looking back I realize how my lack of clarity served to fuel his confusion and anger.

With death comes the dilemma for the living: how to survive? Most spouses experience survivor's guilt not only because they do not have the disease but also because the stigma of AIDS is too great to bear alone. AIDS widows usually do not feel comfortable in bereavement and widows' groups where, most if not all, the people who attend have lost a spouse to other more respectable diseases, like cancer.

> I read books about widowhood and learned that widows felt ashamed at their loss of status. I clung to Zachary. He became my source of strength and my *raison d'être*. I censored what I told people about the cause of death, feeling denied a proper widowhood because I could not freely tell the truth and when I did, eyebrows would raise. I was asked, "How do you know you are safe?" or "How did he get it?", more often than, "Oh, I'm so sorry to hear that."
>
> In order to get sympathy from friends or people whom I had carefully screened, I first had to persevere through their questions. I clarified information about AIDS, the routes of transmission, and

the safety measures I took in my home to ensure that Zachary and I would not be exposed. People were often confused about the HIV test, not understanding the difference between the length of time it takes for the virus' antibodies to appear in the blood versus *if* the test is positive, how long the virus can lay dormant in a person's body. Not only was I asked to clear their confusion on these matters but I was asked my opinion about whether or not they should be tested.

I felt like a pariah. I wanted to hide, but instead I resolved to get through this time by mastering information.

AIDS AND DEVELOPMENTAL LEARNING

Palombo describes eight variables that distinguish the death of a parent for a child:

1. The cause and type of death—violent, peaceful, accidental, from natural causes, sudden and delayed deaths
2. The factors associated with which of the parent dies, father or mother, adoptive parent, surrogate parent
3. The factors related to the child's age, sex, and developmental level
4. The manner in which the child is informed of the event and whether the event was witnessed or not
5. The nature of the relationship of the child to the parent
6. Whether the child suffered prior psychopathology
7. The child's cognitive grasp of what occurred
8. The nature of the support system around the child [11, p. 18].

An AIDS death involves two additional stresses which may increase a child's confusion:

1. A child may be unclear or not know about the behavior that caused a parent to become ill with AIDS. When discovered, it may be frightening, especially as he matures and is tempted to try drugs or experience sex. For most children this behavior would be considered experimentation but for him, it elicits a fear of repeating the past.
2. Unlike other extreme causes of death, this child must live with the realization that the illness could have been transmitted to him. This fear which he may live with forever, can be even more injurious as the child continues to hear people say HIV testing is still unreliable and must be done regularly. Children may also be victims of the cruelty—intentional or not—of neighbors, friends, or even relatives who shun them.

Children whose parent is suffering with, or has died of AIDS, carry a double burden. They mourn the imminent loss, or death, of the parent and struggle to understand an illness that often is poorly explained. Some children may know about AIDS and ask questions, most cannot. They either have not been told or sense it is a secret they too must protect. Initially, a young child wants reassurances and is less interested in the details of the disease: "Can I get the illness?" "What will happen to me if he dies?" "Will I die?" "Will Mommy die?"

Zachary seemed satisfied with the explanation that his father had a virus in his blood for almost a year. Having grown up with an ill parent he had time to observe and to ask more direct questions. In kindergarten, after learning about Martin Luther King, Zachary came home excited to have discovered such an interesting man, but sad because he had been shot. A few days later, our friend Raymond died of AIDS. Zachary never asked questions about his illness so it came as a surprise when he said, "He was young, wasn't he, Mommy? Like Daddy? Daddy was young. Martin Luther King was young but he got shot. Daddy and Raymond were sick. Did Raymond die of the same thing my Daddy died of?"

A year later, when Zachary was six and I first introduced the word AIDS, his first reaction was relief because he had not heard of it before. But over time his questions were more urgent and more frequent. First he asked if AIDS traveled through the air, then if fevers traveled through the air. The analogy of chicken pox, which he had, helped him understand the difference between airborne diseases and those transmitted through the blood.

One morning while taking a shower he beckoned me, "Can children get AIDS?" I dreaded telling him about perinatal transmission and my assurances that we did not have the virus sounded less convincing to him. He had a hard time grasping that AIDS could be confined to contact by blood or bodily fluids, especially since, to a child, a bodily fluid means spit or urine. Sex was a "special cuddle" which was the description given in one of his books about how babies were born. He didn't quite believe that AIDS was not airborne and didn't believe it was safe to be in a room with a person with AIDS. I reminded him we lived with his daddy and we didn't get AIDS, but still, the mystery lingered. For months, when he heard of someone dying, he was sure it was due to AIDS.

Although Zachary was now initiating the questions, it was evident he was scared. His quest for information was complicated by grief. He felt vulnerable and angry that his father had died. He refused to believe that he was dead, and refused to cooperate at home until I brought his father back. Zachary's anger was formidable, as powerful as his need for reassurance, love, and consistency.

When he asked what a virus was and how it gets into the blood, I explained the routes of transmission in simple terms, not being specific about how his father acquired it. He tried to understand why people feared AIDS and why doctors could not cure it. In these discussions Zachary was learning about physiology, biology, sexual functioning, substance abuse, and medicine.

In mourning, a child must learn to separate from the dead parent, to form new relationships, and to believe that he can go on with his own life. Children want to feel a part of the family, to be valued, and made to feel important. An anxious parent may want to rush the process to enlist the child's support or, in the name of honesty, be aboveboard. If this occurs after a parent dies, the remaining parent, or caregiver, is left to transmit information while they are grieving. It is not just the information a child hears that can overwhelm him but also the adult's grief and fear.

Over a two year period Zachary asked many questions. Each time I gradually added a little more information, knowing he understood more and was listening attentively to news about AIDS on TV and radio. We talked about who got AIDS and why people react so negatively. While it was good that he grasped the information, I made a point to remind him of other things about his father that would help balance the picture.

There was one incident that made me realize how intertwined AIDS had become with death for Zachary. I had bought a book called *Rachel and the Upside Down Heart* [12] about a little girl whose father died. It told of her sadness and how her Mommy said she would remember her father in her heart and in her mind. As she got older, Rachel was conscious of being the only girl in her class without a father. Just then, Zachary jumped up in excitement, "That's like ME, Mommy. That's like me. I didn't know anyone else who had that happen and they feel like I do!" Zachary had met other children whose fathers had died, including one whose father died of AIDS. But this book only addressed the sad feelings a little child has when a parent dies. It helped me understand how the simultaneous process of mourning and learning about AIDS was such a difficult one.

Despite a parent's best efforts to warn a child not to tell people about AIDS, it is understandable why a child would do so. Some may want to hear what other people know, to get a reaction, or to enlist a friend who will offer support. Like the parent, the child is isolated with the knowledge and may feel cheated at not being able to talk openly.

Eventually, Zachary told the parent of one of his friends that his father died of AIDS. I asked him why, he just said he thought she would want to know. I asked if he was looking for a reaction, he nodded. The parent did not mention their discussion until months later. Zachary was testing the waters and had chosen someone he thought was trustworthy. Periodically, and unpredictably, he made such announcements.

At the end of the last school year, he said he didn't want to talk about AIDS any more and asked, "If someone wants to know what my daddy died of, what should I say?" I told him he only had to say he didn't feel like talking about it. In the same conversation he asked if he ever cried about his daddy dying. I reminded him of the time, three years earlier, when he was feeling sick and he burst into tears. For the first time, understanding the finality of death, he sobbed, "My daddy's dead, my daddy's dead." He was relieved to know he had cried because now, almost five years after his father's death, Zachary doesn't remember his father as clearly. But he reminds us both that his daddy loved him and if he were here today, he would be very proud of his son.

Now, at the beginning of third grade Zachary came home and with a big smile said, "We're going to learn about AIDS in school, Mommy. I already know a lot because you taught me so much."

Some families prefer not to shelter their children from an AIDS diagnosis and include them when attending doctor's appointments, social service agencies, and even adult support groups. They do not feel shame and believe the family unit is maintained when there are no secrets. Some families make their situation public, take a stand by organizing their lives around the fight against AIDS, and become politically involved to fend off the shame imposed by an unjust, judgmental world. As adults, it is their right, but children are not always given a choice. Children will comply with their parent's actions because they want to be included, to feel they are valued members of the family. They may simply accept the sentiment that AIDS is an enemy against which the family must fight. But prematurely bringing a young child into adult activities may be overwhelming, especially where the focus is primarily on the parent's needs.

Likewise, telling a child how a parent actually got HIV/AIDS may be incomprehensible to a child who is not developmentally prepared to understand the specifics of sexual choice and substance abuse. Children may not be ready to hear such information because they have their own primary needs which focus on feeling safe, being a part of the family, and understanding all of the changes that have occurred. While parents may not be able to guarantee absolute safety with regards to the future, they can create an atmosphere in which children can ask questions, repeatedly if necessary, and be reassured about their own health and well-being.

THE LATE EFFECTS OF TRAUMA

The combination of grief and trauma affect a child in very specific ways. Children express grief intermittently and often act as if nothing significant has taken place. Some continue to play with friends and participate in activities, while others may vent sadness or anger through negative behavior. In either case, grief is present and does not stand still.

A prolonged and painful illness, or the sudden death of a parent will traumatize a child, "flooding" or overwhelming the psyche with conflicting emotions. For children, a traumatic event often "freezes" their ability to understand or cope with events as they unfold. They may remain confused and uncomprehending for a long time. According to Samuels:

> The death of a parent is a traumatogenic agent and affects the child in that the impact of the death shatters the child's comprehension, his reasonable sense of security, and the belief in his parent's omnipotence. It is on the one hand an overwhelming stimulus sorely taxing the child's ego capacities, and on the other, may interfere with his sense of self, self-esteem, and the differentiation of certain aspects of fantasy from reality [10, p. 32].

Given permission, time, and a wide latitude, children will absorb change and learn to express their grief more freely. Without encouragement, a child may suppress his grief which may surface later on the occasion of other deaths and crises. Or, more likely, his grief may remain buried but be signaled by poor school performance, erratic behavior or depression.

The study of historic events and their devastating aftermaths have helped us to understand how silence and repression can influence people's lives and the group psyche. Research, such as Bergmann's, "The Generation of the Holocaust," on the long term effects of trauma in Holocaust survivors offers powerful images: the "curtain of silence . . . a silence maintained because the world needed to forget . . . the degradation of their seed as not worthy of propagation . . . and the expectations and the need for children to make up for parental trauma . . ." [13, p. 8]. Such impressions help elucidate the feelings evoked in families who survive an AIDS death. It is especially true for families in which there are multiple deaths due to AIDS, or where AIDS is one of many frightening life conditions.

Parents or guardians, in an attempt to put the past behind them, may treat children as problems to be solved, rather than children who have sustained a terrible loss. An uneasy parent may project the deceased parent's behavior onto the child each time he or she errs or ventures out in the world. The adolescent who is defiant or caught experimenting with drugs may be accused of being "just like your father."

These children, not only have to make up for the sins of their parent but, often they need to be perfect in the eyes of the surviving parent, achieving what the spouse could not. As the surviving parent works out unresolved anger through the child, the child is denied his own mourning and the positive development of his personality.

As children get older they will have a better understanding of the discriminatory statements that they hear about drug users, homosexuals, and people's feelings about AIDS. In school, where AIDS is being taught more regularly, many of these children cannot talk about or show emotion in front of their peers for fear of recrimination. What is it like for a child to be silenced? What price does such silence play on a child's need to be like other children, knowing he is not? How does a healthy, active teenager approach dating without wondering if he is really safe and being concerned about the reactions he might get if he disclosed his family's situation?

Long after a person with AIDS dies, the families struggle with the legacy of the disease. Too often, they must remain silent as the public continues to stigmatize, rather than appreciate, what these families endure. Their pride in being good caregivers, keeping the family together, and learning to reconstruct their lives is constrained. Children, who lose both parents or who are shunted through foster care systems, have little opportunity to reflect on their lives in a healthy supportive atmosphere. It is likely that unresolved trauma and mourning are themes which may follow them into adulthood.

At this point it is critical that children come to understand that a disease does not define the parent, a family, or themselves. While children who have gone through this experience do not come out unscathed, it is important to help them reconcile their anger at their parent for dying. Such reconciliation is complicated when the cause of death is AIDS. In this case, children need to learn how to forgive their parent for not only dying and leaving, but for a condition which makes their families feel stigmatized and ashamed.

SURVIVING AN AIDS DEATH

We are at the beginning of a new era in which AIDS will affect more and more children. While statistics indicate that it will be most prevalent in poverty areas, AIDS has already permeated all aspects of society. Ironically, it will take the growing prevalence of the disease to lessen its stigma. As more people are personally affected, AIDS will come to be viewed as one of many terrible illnesses. Until that time, and because the number of children orphaned to AIDS is growing, we must make every effort to reach families as early as possible and begin working with children while their parent is ill with AIDS, and not just after death occurs.

AIDS is an unpredictable illness in its duration and degree of severity, therefore, it does not effect everyone in the same way. While each family has their own unique way of coping with and responding to the illness, the consequences of AIDS can strain a family's ability to cope. Below are guidelines for professionals to use in helping to prepare families.

1. Communicate

Telling children something about their parent's health does not mean that they have to be "told all." Often, parents first think about what they *do not* want their children to know and need encouragement to think about what they *can* say. Some parents feel that giving partial information is not being honest, but the fact is, children do not always want the name of, or the details about, an illness. They may be more interested in knowing how it can affect a person, whether or not it can be transmitted, and if they have to worry about their healthy parent's, or their own, health. Like the rest of us, children need accurate and clear information which can be kept simple, "I have to see the doctor because my throat has been bothering me and the doctor isn't sure why." Or, "I'm on special medication to help me breathe better and I think it has helped a lot." When there is no more new information, children may benefit from hearing less about their parent's illness and having that parent re-focus attention back to them: "I am telling you as much as I can now. I want you to be happy, to work hard in school, and to play with your friends. Just be a kid! If anything changes with me, I promise to tell you."

2. Develop an Extended Family Network

It may be difficult for parents to know who to trust but involving other people will become more important to children as the illness progresses. People in the extended network, such as family, friends, "buddies," or professionals, should be chosen because they can help with practical matters and have a comfortable relationship, or are interested in developing such a relationship, with the children. By offering children praise and support, the people in this support network can help nurture their inner resources and strengths. Also, while children may refuse to talk about the illness or even themselves, they may take comfort in the presence of other adults who make them feel safe.

3. Provide a Safe Place

Children may want to know about any possible changes in their living circumstances—will they continue to live with their healthy parent or will the family have to move? Including them in the planning may be as simple as letting them choose what to take, going to the new community, or introducing them to people or children in the new neighborhood. For some children, home will be where their hearts are because change in their lives may include not only a different home but new caregivers. In this instance, the family network may provide the "home" to which children can go for visits or talk to on the telephone. Another way to establish a "home" is to talk about or take children to places that are special to them or to the parents and children. Photographs and treasured objects can become the basis of an ongoing project of "memory storing."

4. Work Together

It is important to secure a place or a role for the children in the family. Little children can run simple errands such as getting something from the refrigerator, changing the television station, or answering the telephone. When older children help with caregiving or chores, their efforts can be acknowledged verbally. They can also be rewarded with a free day or two that will provide them with relief from their duties and may help them feel appreciated.

Parents can keep children engaged by talking about things that have always been of mutual interest—friends, sports, the news, a television program, school, or happenings in the neighborhood. When a parent's health is good, families can plan special outings, visit friends and relatives, or plan a holiday party at home.

5. Respect a Child's Timing

Parents can heed children's messages much like following the rules of a traffic signal. The "red light" is on when children walk away, act as though they do not hear, or change the subject. They should not be pushed into hearing information that they may not be ready to receive. The "yellow light" appears when children express uncertainty. They may say, "Yes, I want to know" but fidget or are uncomfortable. Or, they may listen because they think that it will please their parents. By the same token, children may not be sure if they are ready but in the course of a conversation find that they are interested, rather than afraid, therefore, the "yellow light" turns "green."

6. Understand How Children Mourn

When children are mourning, they may draw on fantasy to help cope with their loss. They may make up new family members or tell stories about their lives that have no bearing on reality. By listening, parents can learn more about their children's fears and concerns. Many children benefit from participating in bereavement groups for children. A play therapist may help children "use" fantasies to cope with loss and fear. While parents may not understand all that children are experiencing, they can help by introducing children's books which explain death and by learning to listen to, but not stop, their children's fantasies.

7. Develop Rituals

AIDS forces us to categorize people by their behavior. In order for children to overcome the stigma of the disease in their own families, they must learn that a person's behavior does not define the whole person. Developing rituals to mourn and honor the deceased parent helps children handle the death and places more focus on the parent as he or she was, rather than on the illness that took him or her away. Including children in the funeral or memorial service is the first step in helping them honor their parent, especially in the company of others who also cared about the parent. Observing holidays and anniversaries which were special to the deceased parent helps children, whose memories fade so quickly, resolve their grief. Pictures of the family and objects that children have collected from their deceased parent's belongings are invaluable ways of developing and preserving a memory bank which can be housed in a photo album, a box, or another place chosen by the children.

CONCLUSION

In the best possible world and with the best help available children may continue to be confused and saddened for a long time. Since the loss of a parent is a new experience and most likely without precedent, children may not understand many of the precepts that adults learn to accept—"each day heals and offers new hope" or "death is a part of life." But children do like the idea of growing up and becoming "big kids" with more privileges. Helping children look to the future may offer them a new perspective.

> I told Zachary there were many things he might not understand at this point because he was learning a lot and children need time to think about what they learn. "But," I said, "some day, everything that we have talked about will suddenly be clear to you. As you get older you will understand much more than you do now." His eyes lit with understanding and he smiled broadly. I finally believed that I had given him something to look forward to.

REFERENCES

1. R. Burrell, Entering the World of the Grieving Child, in *Worlds of the Grieving Child*, S. Sunderland and R. Burrell (eds.), Fernside: A Center for Grieving Children, Cincinatti, Ohio, 1989.
2. B. O. Dane and S. O. Miller, *AIDS: Intervening with Hidden Grievers*, Auburn House, Westport, Connecticut, 1991.
3. D. Michaels and C. Levine, Estimates of the Number of Motherless Youth Orphaned by AIDS in the United States, *Journal of the American Medical Association, 286*, pp. 3456-3461, 1992.
4. L. Terr, *Too Scared to Cry: Psychic Trauma in Childhood*, Harper and Row Publishers, New York, 1990.
5. R. A. Furman, Death and the Young Child: Some Preliminary Considerations, *Psychoanalytic Study of the Child, 19*, pp. 321-333, 1991.
6. B. Mellonie and R. Ingpen, *Lifetimes*, Bantam Books, New York, 1983.
7. C. D. Schneider, *Shame, Exposure and Privacy*, W.W. Norton, New York, 1977.
8. C. Levine, AIDS and Changing Concepts of Family, *The Milbank Quarterly, 68*:1, pp. 33-58, 1990.
9. K. M. Hummer and A. Samuels, The Influence of the Recent Death of a Spouse on the Parenting Function of the Surviving Parent, in *Childhood Bereavement and Its Aftermath*, S. Altschul (ed.), International Universities Press, Connecticut, pp. 37-43, 1989.
10. A. Samuels, Parental Death in Childhood, in *Childhood Bereavement and its Aftermath*, S. Altschul (ed.), International Universities Press, Connecticut, pp. 19-36, 1989.
11. J. Palombo, Parent Loss and Childhood Bereavement: Some Theoretical Considerations, *Clinical Social Work, 9*:1, pp. 3-33, 1991.

12. E. Douglas, *Rachel and the Upside Down Heart*, Price Stern Sloan, Los Angeles, California, 1990.
13. M. S. Bergmann, Prelude, in *Generations of the Holocaust*, M. S. Bergmann and M. E. Jucovy (eds.), Columbia University Press, New York, pp. 3-29, 1992.

CHAPTER 7

Helping Bereaved Children and Adolescents Cope with the Aftermath of Suicide

Sandra L. Elder

Suicide is a tragedy. When someone close commits suicide, children and adolescents are plunged into confusion, emotional upheaval, and pain that affects everyone involved. The intensity of their loss and the complicated path of mourning may leave them with emotional scars that last a lifetime.

Stevenson points out that suicide is sudden, usually unanticipated, frequently violent, and may take place in the "presence of other stresses" [1, p. 134]. He also notes that for the survivors, a suicide evokes guilt, "loss of control," a "flood of emotions," and the potential for being distanced from and discriminated against by others [1, pp. 134-135]. Even when distancing and discrimination do not occur, the survivors may feel apart from others [1].

This chapter will:

- discuss factors influencing children's perceptions of suicide
- determine how to facilitate the healing process
- examine personal stories of survivors
- list the danger signs associated with adolescent suicide
- review the differences in the grief process between suicide and other deaths.

FACTORS INFLUENCING CHILDREN'S
PERCEPTIONS OF SUICIDE

Cognitive Development

Cognitive development is a key component in children's ability to conceptualize the meaning of death and understand why the person took his or her life. Young children's egocentricity and their ability to think in a cause-and-effect manner may make them believe that something they did or did not do caused the death [2]. They believe that if they are good, the world will be good, and if they are bad, the world will be bad. So when things go wrong, they think it is their fault.

If these thoughts and feelings are left unchecked, young children may weave in more information based on their imagination and fantasy in order to round out the story of what happened to their loved one. They may be angry with themselves for their wrongdoing and may withdraw or act out if they believe that they are responsible for the suicide. The fact that young children think in concrete terms and have a difficult time understanding abstractions means that they must rely on their parents, siblings, and other adults to interpret what has happened [2]. When they are confused and upset, they are more apt to respond to the emotional tone of the person who is conveying the information and to their perceptions associated with the manner in which information is provided. They also tend to mourn in bits and pieces because they have difficulty dealing with the intensity of their grief on a continuing basis.

By the time they have reached the age of seven or eight years, many children have developed the capacity to understand that death is irreversible, body functions cease, everyone including themselves will die, and there are a variety of causes of death [3]. However, the trauma of the suicide may make them so unsettled that they may feel responsible, puzzled by the death, anxious about their own bodies, and concerned about what happens after death [4].

During pre-adolescence and early teen years, they begin to think in an abstract manner, more like adults. They are often more capable of managing the emotions of grief than younger children, but their ability is still limited by developmental constraints. The developmental process known as separation-individuation during adolescence involves a shift from a partially dependent to an increasingly autonomous relationship with their parents [5]. When a parent or close family member dies, adolescents developmental processes may be interrupted. Raphael considers parental death as being "the greatest loss for the adolescent, especially in the earlier years when he or she has not completed the separation process" [6, p. 145].

The sudden separation by death, especially death by suicide, at a time when independence is slowly being achieved, awakens tremendous conflicts and may interfere with the natural progression of intellectual-emotional-psychological "growing up." Changes that might normally be expected may be averted, avoided, or may not transpire. Such an arrest of developmental unfolding may put adolescents "on hold" in one phase, and thus interfere with the development of the skills and energy necessary to meet subsequent phase-appropriate demands [5].

The Meaning of the Relationship to the Person Who Died

The nature of the relationship with the suicide victim has a direct influence on the adaptation of children and teens to the suicide. For children at any age, the death of a parent may signify the permanent loss of emotional support, comfort, security, and guidance. They may feel abandoned, isolated, and for older children in particular, betrayed by the person whom they had relied upon and always expected to be there for them. On the other hand, in less favorable situations such as the suicide of a violent and abusive parent, children may feel ambivalent and torn by a confusing mixture of love and hate. Teens are especially prone to symptoms associated with post-traumatic stress reactions including acting out, truancy, delinquency, violent behavior, and substance abuse [4, 7]. This is particularly true if the person they wished dead has actually fulfilled their wish.

When a brother or sister commits suicide, the gap left in the family may irreparably damage or destroy the sibling sub-system and its role as a training ground for life. Sibling relationships are replete with interactions that promote personal growth including companionship, co-operation, love, compassion, conflict, rivalry, role modeling, and identification [8]. Surviving siblings may be left to deal with their younger brothers and sisters, especially when their parents feel overwhelmed. They struggle to understand why their sibling died, may be constricted by adult rules concerning how and where they can discuss what happened, and grapple with whether or not they played a part in the death. A major concern arises from the fact that siblings identify with each other, link their fate to one another, and may be prone to taking the same course of action [8].

When a close friend commits suicide, teens, in particular, lose a peer who usually had similar attitudes, beliefs, and perceptions to their own. The fact that many adolescents live more intensely in their peer group than they do in their families means that a cluster of friends are likely to be affected. They will require special attention because of the increased possibility of romanticization and contagion.

The Personality of the Surviving Child or Adolescent

The composition of the personality of each child and teen has a direct bearing on their response to a suicide. This includes their ability to feel loved, valued, confident, and positive about themselves. After a suicide, any or all of these personality components may be affected. A suicide may take away a major source of warmth, comfort, and caring from their lives and they may feel unwanted, insecure, embarrassed, and less confident [9]. They change how they think and feel about themselves and the world around them, and experience an intense array of emotions that include:

- **guilt** based on a belief that they had the power to create such a tragedy because they were angry at the suicide victim and had wished the person would die. For adolescents, in particular, guilt may be associated with their inability to prevent the death. At any age guilt may be a defense against the terrible feelings of helplessness that surround a suicide.

- **anger** or rage associated with being abandoned by a family member or friend. They may be angry that their lives have changed, they have been forced into silence due to family dictums, or they have been embarrassed by the suicide. In some situations, anger may be related to the fact that nobody prevented the death, hopes and dreams involving the dead person were decimated, and they had no opportunity to correct misunderstandings or say goodbye.

- **denial** that can be used to protect them from facing the reality of the death, the possibility that they had contributed to the circumstances leading up to it, or recognizing that they had prior knowledge that the suicide would occur. Denial may also provide respite from replaying the real or imagined picture of the suicide, being preoccupied with thoughts of their own death or dealing with their emotions.

- **depression** characterized by flattened affect, morbid thinking, lack of energy, sleep disturbances, anorexia, and psychosomatic symptoms. Although depression is a normal part of mourning, following a suicide it may be more intense and lasting and characterized by prolonged bouts of tearfulness, helplessness, and hopelessness.

Availability of Emotional Support

After a suicide in the family, children and adolescents are affected by the reaction of their parent(s). They take their cues from them and for young children especially, parents control the amount of information children receive about the death and influence how they behave within and outside of the family. When a parent dies, Edelman says:

> Researchers have found that children who lose a parent need two conditions to continue to thrive: a stable surviving parent or other caregiver to meet their emotional needs and the opportunity to release their feelings [10, p. 8]:.

When a parent commits suicide, the surviving parent may be so distraught that the needs of the surviving children are overlooked. As a result, they may delay their grief or release their feelings elsewhere such as in their peer group, the classroom, or the playground. Older children and teens may be forced to take on increased responsibility in the family and assume some of the tasks of the deceased parent. Some of these responsibilities may be inappropriate and too difficult or overwhelming. Some may also increase the intensity of their feelings as they remember the behavior of the deceased parent.

In a single parent family or an abusive family, suicide of an estranged or a violent parent may have more impact on the surviving children than the surviving parent. Children and teens may be left without permission to mourn their loss or participate in rituals and ceremonies.

In dysfunctional families, the lack of an operational framework for family functioning and absence of a clear definition of roles and responsibilities, consistent emotional support, cohesion, boundaries, and decision-making mechanisms may add to children's confusion, and may inhibit, prolong, or intensify their grief [4, 7, 11].

When a close friend dies, children and adolescents may turn to their parents for varying degrees of emotional support and guidance. However, teens especially are apt to turn to their peers, sharing their thoughts and feelings with them because they are mourning the same loss. The benefits provided by mutual peer support may involve a greater opportunity to express their feelings, sort out what has transpired, and determine how they will commemorate the death. Stillion and her associates point out that teens are apt to be less judgemental than their parents, less apt to base their thinking on moral or religious beliefs, more willing to attribute the suicide to the failure of society than to personal failure, and more willing to evaluate suicide as a choice available to anyone who is competent. They also note that older teens and more intelligent children are less likely to approve of suicide or romanticize it [7].

HOW TO FACILITATE THE HEALING PROCESS

Children and adolescents can recover from the aftermath of a suicide if they receive adequate psychological support from family members, friends, other survivors, and skilled professionals. If the conspiracy of silence surrounding the suicide is allowed to perpetuate, they will have difficulty rebuilding their lives. However, if an open, honest, and supportive environment is provided that enables them to express their thoughts and feelings without judgment or criticism, they can learn to come to terms with their loss and move on to lead healthy lives. As part of the process, the "emotional wound" must be lanced in order for healing to begin. Their loss will never be forgotten, but they do not have to remain "frozen" or at a standstill for the rest of their lives.

Lukas and Seiden discuss the long-term effects of silence surrounding suicides through the work of Fraiberg:

> In our efforts to protect children from painful emotions we may deprive them of their own best means of mastering painful experiences. Mourning . . . is a necessary measure for overcoming the effects of loss. A child who is not allowed feelings of grief . . . is obliged to fall back on more primitive measures of defense, to deny the pain of loss, and to feel nothing [12, p. 171].

If we withhold information from children and adolescents in order to protect them from the pain of a suicide, we are leaving them open to the possibility of "complicated grief" reactions. These may include: reality distortion; difficulty with object relations; distorted self-concept; self-destructive behavior; and over-identification with the deceased [13, 14]. The first task of grieving is to accept the reality of their loss [15]. It is crucial, however, not to give them more information than they are asking for or are capable of understanding and handling.

Over time, children and adolescents also need to incorporate or accommodate their loss as they mature and their perceptions of death change. Edelman refers to the words of Therese Rando:

> I use the term accommodate, because at different points in time you can have accommodated the loss, made room for it in your life, . . . but then something else can bring it up again later on. Grief is something that continues to get reworked [10, pp. 23-24].

The anniversary of the death, special occasions, or certain objects may bring forth unexpected difficult feelings. The fact that death by suicide is sudden and self-inflicted makes children and adolescents subject to profound and lasting emotions that are extremely difficult to resolve and may impact on their lives for years to come.

PERSONAL STORIES OF SUICIDE LOSS

Interviews with individuals who have experienced a death by suicide during childhood or adolescence help to illustrate the impact of such a death on the survivors. Participants were invited to tell their stories as they remembered them. Those who had experienced a suicide over ten years ago were surprised at the intensity of their emotional reaction to certain parts of their stories. Some remembered things that they had never before recalled or discussed. They frequently commented, "I thought I was over this!" Rando explains:

> The hurt can be a connection to the loved one for a long time. It may be the only thing you have that keeps you connected to the person who died. Sometimes pushing the pain away is a way of holding on, and sometimes holding it close is . . . We need to find other ways to stay connected [13, p. 13].

Three female survivors willingly recounted the following stories.

Sarah

Sarah, now thirty-eight, was twelve years old when her mother died of a drug overdose. For a number of years she was never certain if her mother committed suicide. She remembered the ambulance attendant asking, "Where are the pills?" No one talked to her or her siblings about what had transpired. Immediately after her mother died, Sarah realized that her life had changed completely. In the kitchen, her father told the children as they held hands in a circle praying, "Everything is going to be all right. Mom has gone to heaven."

She vividly recalled that "no one was talking to us, no one was talking about it, or saying that this was awful . . . instead everyone was talking about normal things." She remembered hiding under the bed for a long time after the ambulance attendants took her mother away on a stretcher. No one came to find her. Her radio was still playing music, and she wondered how it could do that when her mother had just died.

Sarah's father thought that it would be a "nice idea" for the children to help buy their mother's casket. She recalled going to the bank to take money out of each of their bank accounts and holding the crisp new one hundred dollar bill.

Sarah remembered the funeral and having to look at her mother lying in the casket. Her mother looked like "someone that wasn't my mom." Her face was made up in a way that was very different from her mother's true appearance. On the way to the burial, her father suggested that they all sing hymns together. She lamented that it looked like they were "such a happy family . . . but we weren't!" She recalled the continuous fighting between her parents and the fact that they had even fought on the day of her mother's death. On that day, her father had left the house and her mother had gone to her room and locked the door.

After the funeral, Sarah felt like she "never had a mom because you couldn't talk about her." When asked about the impact of her mother's death on her life, she said, "I was never a kid any more. I couldn't be mad. I couldn't feel. I had to just understand." She said, "We were referred to as those four kids. We weren't wanted! At least that is how it felt. If we were good, we were not needed, and if we were bad, we were too much trouble." Her family was the "bad family on the block."

When asked how her life might have been different if her mother had not died by suicide, she said, "My wedding would have been different because my mother would have been there to help me buy my dress, and at the birth of my children my mother would have been there to know them." She expressed sadness concerning the past and anxiety about the future. She said, "Anything that I have loved, I have lost!"

In concluding, Sarah was asked what she would say to her mother if she was with her right now. She said, "I would tell her I love you! I miss you! I would ask her, why did you go? Then I would look at her for awhile."

Lois

Lois, a twenty-four-year-old, was fourteen when her father died by suicide. Her parents had separated when she was seven and divorced when she was twelve. One day, the police called to tell her that her father was missing. Two days later, they called again to tell Lois that he had taken his life. When her mother heard the news, she was very distraught. Lois said, "I felt responsible for her and felt that it was my job to see that everything was okay."

Her father's funeral was the first one that she had ever attended. It was a difficult experience for her, "watching everyone fall apart." After the funeral, she did not want to go back to school. She felt sick, tired, afraid, and trapped. She did not feel safe, and had great difficulty facing people.

Lois became very angry toward her father. She resented "all the things he took away from me—like walking me down the aisle when I got married, teaching me to drive a car, taking me on horseback riding trips, doing neat things with me, and protecting me." He had always made her feel secure.

For Lois, her father's death was "like being in a plane crash." After he died, it seemed as if "all the rules had changed." She could no longer trust men, and she saw them as being "unreliable." Lois felt deceived by her father because he called her the night before he disappeared and nothing seemed unusual. She said she realizes now that he was trying to say goodbye, but then she lamented, "I never thought that he would do this!"

After her father's death, Lois also thought that "nobody was the same, especially her mother." She began taking antidepressants, felt constantly sad and weepy, and had little self-esteem. She felt extremely vulnerable and was no longer a "go-getter." She continued to look to Lois "for strength." Lois felt as if she had grown up very quickly and that she did not really have a childhood.

Her father's suicide had also changed Lois. She said that she had developed a greater need for control and saw herself as being very needy. Her cat, Prince, became her guardian angel . . . "he totally saved me." Prince also filled the void left by her father. Later, when the first male that she had allowed to become close to her, sexually abused her, the cat once again became her significant other, helping her through another traumatic time in her life. Lois believes that her father's spirit is in the cat. At times, when she has experienced suicidal thoughts, Prince and her other cats have made her feel so needed she has not hurt herself.

When Lois was asked what would have happened if her father had not died, she stated that she would have finished high school, won a scholarship to the University of British Columbia, and graduated with a degree. His death made her more determined and unwilling to allow men to control her life or be subjected to their authority. She added that she probably would not have met the husband she loves.

At this time, Lois believes that a suicide is the worst possible death because the survivors feel so cheated. She feels especially frustrated because she believes that her father knew what an impact this kind of death would have on her since his own brother died by suicide. She remains angry with her father because "he purposely and knowingly did something that would hurt me."

When asked what she would like to say to him now, Lois said, "You cheated yourself, not me. You missed a lot of things, and it is such a waste!"

Julie

Julie is now nineteen years old. She was eighteen when a male friend died by suicide. She described his death as being the most difficult death to handle because it leaves too many questions unanswered. Initially, Julie was unable to talk about his death. Today, she is still puzzled, and says, "It is hard to understand that he couldn't see that it would get better and that so many people cared about him."

For Julie, her friend's funeral was not a celebration of his life, it was a tragedy. His suicide was such a waste of a life. In her mind he was too young to die, and the fact that he died by suicide made her very uncomfortable.

After the funeral, Julie tended to isolate herself and was unable to return to school for the rest of the year. She admitted that she had her own suicidal thoughts both before and after his death. In fact, she and Barry had talked about death and shared a mutual fascination with it. At that time, they both believed that being dead would mean "no stress, no problems, no worries!" In the interview, Julie stated sadly, "There is nothing to offer in this world and there is only one disappointment after another."

When asked how she would like her world to be changed, Julie said, "The way families communicate. They are too busy to take time and show that they care. Everyone goes their separate ways." In continuing, she said that no one cared about her and that she felt worthless and distrusting of men.

Julie stated that the impact of Barry's death on other teens has caused some of them to use drugs and alcohol excessively. For some, his death has been so upsetting that they do not want his name mentioned around them.

It was a long and difficult year before Julie could feel angry at Barry for taking his life. The people who helped her then and have helped her most since have been friends from work. They just listened to her, did not judge her, and told her that they cared.

In closing, when asked what she would say to Barry now, she said that she would like to tell him, "I miss him and I love him!"

RESEARCH STUDY OF BEREAVED
ADOLESCENTS

In addition to the case examples cited previously, it is helpful to include some brief thoughts, feelings, and perceptions provided by five adolescents, ages twelve to sixteen years, whose fathers died from suicide. These bereaved teens were part of the cohort used in a study by the author that was completed in 1993.

When Paul was thirteen, his father died by suicide. Paul said, "I still love my father, but I don't like the choice he made to take his life." Carol, age twelve, who was seven years old when her father died, said, "I thought it was my fault that my father took his life because I burnt his toast that morning and he was upset." Susan, age twelve, was ten years old when her father died as a result of an alcohol-related accident. She had difficulty understanding the fact that this kind of death was labeled as a passive suicide. Two other participants, aged thirteen and fourteen years, experienced the same confusion when their fathers died in alcohol-related accidents, and these deaths were also labeled as passive suicides. Such suicides are viewed as being self-willed and are the combination of alcohol consumption and personal destruction.

Three males in this study who were seven, nine, and thirteen years old when their fathers died, were unable and unwilling to discuss their thoughts and feelings about the death of their fathers. However, they were very willing to participate by answering the study questionnaires. Their non-verbal communication indicated that they thought this study was important, even though they could only be partially involved.

ADOLESCENT SUICIDES: DANGER SIGNS

Teen Generation (T/G), a magazine found in the school libraries of most Canadian junior and senior high schools, included a useful article for adolescents about suicide [16]. It outlined the primary issues pertaining to suicide including: how a person may feel just before they take their life; how teens can help themselves when they feel this way; the danger signs of suicide; how to comfort the survivors; and where to find more information or assistance. The danger signs include:

1. extreme personality changes
2. lack of emotion
3. changes in eating habits
4. changes in sleeping patterns
5. irrational behavior—believing that there is nothing worth living for

6. risk-taking behavior such as use of drugs and alcohol, and reckless driving
7. sexual promiscuity
8. an obsession with death through their writings, conversations, and thoughts
9. giving away their prized possessions.

DIFFERENCES IN THE GRIEF PROCESS

Is there a difference in the grief process of death by suicide as opposed to other types of death? I believe there is a difference in the intensity of the experience and the depth of feelings involved. Survivors of suicide may encounter greater degrees of trauma, bewilderment, denial, anger, blame, and guilt than survivors of other types of death. It may be especially difficult for them to live with the social stigma that is associated with suicide. There tends to be a conspiracy of silence surrounding a suicide that often prevents the survivors from moving through the grief process. This may cause them to be caught in their grief. When they are trapped, they may exhibit the following reactions:

1. a loss of trust which could result in an inability to establish any kind of relationship
2. reality distortion caused by using denial and repression to avoid the truth
3. inner dialogue which is often very negative and critical
4. a disturbed self-concept due to feelings of shame, rejection, and feeling unloved and unlovable
5. continued guilt associated with feeling responsible for the death or believing that they could have prevented it
6. strong feelings of rage with nowhere to direct it
7. prolonged depression
8. a continual search to make sense out of what happened, and looking for answers to the "maybe" and "why" questions
9. an over-identification with thoughts of suicide which sometimes can lead them to committing suicide themselves.

Lukas and Seiden refer to the following comments by Shneidman:

Working with survivors/victims of a committed suicide to help them with their anguish, guilt, anger, shame and perplexity involves providing postventive mental health care for them. Postvention is prevention for the next decade and next generation [12, p. 209].

According to Lukas and Seiden, survivors of suicide need:

* encouragement to talk
* therapy designed for the survivor
* dissemination of information about self-help groups
* an end to the stigma of suicide particularly for the survivor
* an understanding that there is a class of people called survivors [12, p. 209-210].

Children and teens need our help to successfully walk the complicated path of mourning. As Lukas and Seiden tell us, "It's time to end the silence" [12, p. 210].

ACKNOWLEDGMENTS

Appreciation is extended to the survivors of a death by suicide who provided their personal accounts for this chapter.

REFERENCES

1. R. Stevenson, Teen Suicide: Sources, Signals and Prevention, in *The Dying and the Bereaved Teenager*, J. D. Morgan (ed.), The Charles Press, Philadelphia, 1990.
2. R. Lonetto, *Children's Conceptions of Death*, Springer Publishing Company, New York, 1980.
3. A. Lazar and J. Torney-Purta, The Development of the Sub-concepts of Death in Young Children: A Short Term Longitudinal Study, *Child Development, 62*, pp. 1321-1333, 1991.
4. A. Leenars and S. Wenckstern, Suicide Postvention in School Systems: A Model, in *The Dying and the Bereaved Teenager*, J. D. Morgan (ed.), The Charles Press, Philadelphia, 1990.
5. S. Elder, *The Impact of Parental Death During Adolescence on Separation-Individuation Process*, Dissertation, University of Victoria, Victoria, Canada, June 1993.
6. B. Raphael, *The Anatomy of Bereavement*, Basic Books, New York, 1983.
7. J. Stillion, E. E. McDowell, and J. H. May, *Suicide Across the Life Span: Premature Exits*, Hemisphere Publishing Corporation, New York, 1989.
8. S. P. Banks and M. D. Kahn, *The Sibling Bond*, Basic Books, New York, 1982.
9. B. Day, *Suicide: The Ultimate Abandonment*, Lecture, Association for Death Education and Counselling Conference, Boston, March 6-9, 1992.
10. H. Edelman, *Motherless Daughters, The Legacy of Loss*, Addison-Wesley Publishing Company, Reading, Pennsylvania, 1994.
11. J. O. Brende and R. Goldsmith, Post-Traumatic Stress in Families, *Journal of Contemporary Psychology, 21*:2, pp. 115-124, 1991.

12. C. Lukas and H. Seiden, *Silent Grief: Living in the Wake of Suicide*, Charles Scribner's Sons, New York, 1987.
13. T. Rando, *Treatment of Complicated Mourning*, Research Press, Champaign, Illinois, 1993.
14. S. M. Valente and J. Rifkin Sellers, Helping Adolescent Survivors of Suicide, in *Adolescence and Death*, C. A. Corr and J. N. McNeil (eds.), Springer Publishing Company, New York, 1986.
15. W. Worden, *Grief Counselling and Grief Therapy: A Handbook for the Mental Health Practitioner*, Springer Publishing Company, New York, 1991.
16. D. Douglas, Suicide, Helping Yourself, *Teen Generation: Voices of Today's Generation 51*:1, March 1991.

BIBLIOGRAPHY

Berman, A. and D. Jobes, *Adolescent Suicide: Assessment and Intervention*, American Psychological Association, Washington, 1991.

Carlson, G., Depression and Suicidal Behavior in Children and Adolescents, *Affective Disorders in Childhood and Adolescence: An Update*, D. P. Cantwell and G.A. Carlson (eds.), Spectrum Publications, Jamaica, 1983.

Dietrich, D., The Bereaved Child's Psychological Health Several Years Later, *Children and Death*, G. Paterson (ed.), King's College, London, Canada, 1985.

Fraiberg, S., *The Magic Years*, Charles Scribner's Sons, New York, 1959.

Furman, E., *A Child's Parent Dies: Studies in Childhood Bereavement*, Yale University Press, New Haven, Connecticut, 1974.

Gaines, D., *Teenage Wasteland: Suburbia's Dead End Kids*, Harper Perennial, New York, 1990.

Garbarino, J. and F. Stot, *What Children Can Tell Us*, Jossey-Bass Publishers, San Francisco, 1989.

Gordon, S., *When Living Hurts*, Union of American Hebrew Congregations, New York, 1985.

Gravelle, K. and C. Haskins, *Teenagers Face To Face With Bereavement*, Julian Messner, Englewood Cliffs, New Jersey, 1989.

Jaco, R. M., Suicide-proofing Youth: A Survival Technique for the Eighties, *Suicide: Helping Those At Risk*, J. D. Morgan (ed.), King's College, London, Canada, 1986.

Jewett, C., *Helping Children Cope With Separation and Loss*, Harvard Common Press, Harvard, Connecticut, 1982.

Johnson, K., *Trauma In The Lives Of Children*, Hunter House, Inc., Claremont, California, 1989.

Kaysen, S., *Girl, Interrupted*, Vintage Books, New York, 1993.

Kolehaimen, J. and S. Handwerk, *Teen Suicide*, Learner Publications Company, Minneapolis, Minnesota, 1986.

Leenaars, A. and S. Wenckstern, *Suicide Prevention In Schools*, Hemisphere Publishing Company, New York, 1991.

Orbach, I., *Children Who Don't Want To Live*, Jossey-Bass Publishers, San Francisco, 1988.

Shamoo, T. and P. Patros, *I Want To Kill Myself: Helping Your Child Cope with Depression and Suicidal thoughts*, D. C. Heath and Company, Lexington, Massachusetts, 1990.

Shengold, L., *Soul Murder: The Effects of Childhood Abuse and Deprivation*, Ballantine Books, New York, 1989.

Sternberg, F. and B. Sternberg, *If I Die and When I Do: Exploring Death with Young People*, Prentice-Hall, Englewood Cliffs, New Jersey, 1980.

Teicher, J. D. and J. Jacobs, Adolescents Who Attempt Suicide, *American Journal of Psychiatry, 122*, pp. 1248-1257, 1966.

Wertheimer, A., *A Special Scar: The Experiences of People Bereaved by Suicide*, Routledge, New York, 1991.

CHAPTER 8

Domestic Violence, Children and Their Losses

Barbara C. Zick

The literature on domestic violence primarily focuses on the impact on women and less is written about the losses that children experience. Major aspects of their childhood are drastically changed as family life is disrupted. Support groups for children, who experience domestic violence, provide opportunities for them to express their feelings, talk about the abuse, and learn new coping skills.

"In the next minute four more women or children will be beaten, raped or killed. Once every fifteen seconds a woman or child is victimized by domestic violence" [1, Fact Sheet]. "Severe spouse abuse is the single major cause of injury for which women seek medical attention; it is more common than auto accidents, mugging, and rape combined" [2, p. 5].

Domestic violence is a continuum of behavior which progressively becomes more intense, frequent, and lethal. It is the seeking of control by one individual over another. The individual who is seeking the control is the batterer and the sense of powerlessness the victim feels results in the control being maintained. Richard Gelles and Murray Straus, pioneers in the study of domestic violence, suggest that individuals are more likely to be injured by another family member in their own home than by anyone else in our society [3].

153

CYCLE OF VIOLENCE

If you imagine a circle and divide it into thirds, each third comprises one phase of the cycle of violence. Lenore Walker describes the following phases in *The Battered Woman* [4].

1. "Tension Building" Phase

The batterer criticizes, makes demands of, yells at, threatens destruction of important belongings, isolates the family from extended family and friends, is very hard to please, or uses any means to keep the family environment feeling "crazy-like." His behaviors may not be a tangible ingredient, that is, one that is visible to the "outside world." In fact, the batterer may be portrayed to the "outside world" as a nearly perfect citizen and family member. Many times he is a person very involved in the community, either in his professional career or his recreational endeavors. Yet, a level of stress and strain permeates all activities in the family. The victim will attempt to keep the household calm, withdraw from friends, keep the children quiet when the batterer is present, and keep the children away from extended family members in order to prevent the sharing of nuclear family information. Every effort is made to create a home that seems as perfect and harmonious as possible. It is difficult to maintain such an environment where everyone feels like they are "walking around on eggshells," just waiting for them to crack wide open.

2. The "Acute Battering Incident"

An incident may occur for no apparent reason. The batterer may or may not be using drugs and alcohol. The family may not know exactly what has triggered his outburst. The batterer will, for example, humiliate, hit, kick, choke, beat, sexually abuse, and/or imprison the victims. The victims—the wife and children—may try to protect themselves, call the police, attempt to calm the batterer, try to reason with the batterer, or fight back. Often they are injured in the process. This is a scary time for all involved. The "explosion" can also come in the form of verbal and psychological abuse. It does not take bruises and broken bones to qualify as bona fide abuse.

3. The "Kindness and Contrite Loving Behavior"

The time that follows the "acute battering" is often called the "honeymoon" because it is a time of wonderfulness and hopefulness. It is a time when the victim feels "swept off her feet" with gifts, candy, flowers, or positive activities. Often the batterer comes forth with apologies and promises to go to counseling or to church. He brings gifts for the children and gives them outward affection. Some victims relate that their batterer's crying and assurances that the abuse has stopped, persuade them to deny the severity of the situation in their lives. The victim may see this time as a hopeful opportunity to increase the family unity and end the chaos that they have been experiencing. It is a time to put their "family dream" back on track. Any legal proceedings may be stopped, charges are usually dropped, and counseling appointments may be made.

Painfully, for most of the families involved in domestic violence, the predictable cycle repeats itself over and over again, with increasing speed and lethality. The good intentions do not materialize, promises are not kept, and counseling appointments are canceled.

WHAT KEEPS THE CYCLE GOING?

The questions that are often asked of these women include, "Why do you stay?" or "How can you allow this to happen around your children?" Women frequently struggle with these questions. The violence is the source of their own grief over the loss of their unfulfilled dream of an intact and well-functioning family. Denial, power, and control also keep the cycle going. In each phase of the cycle there is denial by everyone that the abusive behavior is present. Initially, the abuse can be subtle in nature and destruction to the family fabric is not seen. Denial also provides the "defense" that the family is not being abused. Abusers tell their partners, "You are just imagining things," "I treat my kids the way my Dad treated me." Women report that it is easier to deny the severity of the events inside the home to family and friends, rather than to explain and receive more criticism from them about the marriage.

Power and control by the abuser keeps the cycle intact. "Often abusers use the children to maintain power and control over their partners. They may belittle or degrade the children as a means of harassing the victim. Men who abuse may control their partner's activities, companions, whereabouts, etc." [2, p. 4].

The hope that things will change and they can be a "normal" family keeps many families together. Hope is present in the "kindness and loving" phase of the cycle and it helps the family to remember the "good" times of the past. Women who stay in their relationships say that they do not want to take their children away because there is always the possibility, and the hope, that these happy events will occur again.

BATTERED CHILDREN

"Although the extent of wife abuse has been well documented over the last ten years, relatively little attention has been given to the effect of this violence on the children who grow up in these families" [5, p. 278]. The man is able to keep physical, emotional, and environmental control over the woman and her children, therefore maintaining a constant level of tension and fear in their lives. The "propensity of batterers" to abuse their children has been widely mentioned in the literature on family violence. It has also been reported that the father, or the father substitute, is three times as likely to be the abusive parent in a family where the mother is also battered [6]. Women have witnessed the physical and emotional abuse of their children when the family was living together. In the support groups these mothers report that the safety of their children is their main worry, especially when the children are with their father during visitation times.

Children grow up in all kinds of households where the list of adults present may include parents, grandparents, aunts, and/or uncles. They can also be in a household where a non-relative is the intimate partner of the care-giving parent. This chapter focuses on those relationships in which one individual is abusing the other members in the household, and when one individual does not seem to grasp the impact of his violent behavior on the lives of the children.

Children observe and experience the feelings that are expressed by the adults in their lives. When they observe destructive and abusive patterns, they learn that the world in which they live is not safe, predictable, or trustworthy, and is often out of their control. "Thus the phrase, children of battered women, refers to children who have repeatedly witnessed severe acts of emotional and physical abuse directed at their mother by her intimate partner. In too many cases, these children have observed acts of violence perpetrated by multiple partners throughout their childhood" [7, p. 16].

Studies on childhood development report that children learn from a significant role model, the parent, that violence toward a loved one is acceptable. Children, after the age five or six years, show strong tendencies to identify with the aggressor and lose respect for the victim [2]. It is within this turbulent framework that the children are developing, growing, and living. The way in which this violence impacts on children is profound. The developmental, psychological, and sociological stages of growth for children are influenced by the effect of the violence on them. Their developmental need at the time of the incident may increase the depth of their loss. Children have feelings about the violence and are not always equipped to express those feelings in

appropriate ways. Their developmental and psychological growth may no
their homes.

Batterers have abused and killed family pets in the children's presence or with their knowledge. Pets can mysteriously disappear with no explanation provided. Bobby found his dog shot and hanging from a tree in the woods. His father denied knowing anything about the killing, but Bobby knew how his father hated the dog. He was convinced that his father was the one who killed and hung his friend. Pet bunnies have been found with their necks mysteriously broken. Children who are old enough to understand that such behavior can easily be transferred to them may act out aggressively and exhibit severe disobedience, destructiveness, or cruelty to animals.

PREGNANCY AND INFANTS

What happens when a child has been exposed to physical abuse while still within the mother's uterus? Abuse to pregnant women is common, by their self-reports. A baby in utero can not be protected by a woman who is subjected to physical assaults. Many women who have been interviewed state that physical violence became more acute during pregnancy and during their child's infancy. The number of infants who have been born deformed because of in utero abuse is unknown [4].

If a mother must function in a state of fear for herself and her child, it is difficult for her to nurture and love her child in a relaxed and caring way. A dramatic loss of the mother's love and attention, without proper substitution, can lead to acute infantile depression. Women who are being abused must be concerned about their own basic safety needs and this decreases their available energy to care for their children. It is stressful to avoid abuse, experience it when it happens, and recover from the effects of that occurrence. The continuum of physical and psychological trauma affects the ability of a mother to be a nurturing parent to her children [8]. As a result, many of these women seek resources from domestic violence services to assist them in being available to their children.

INFANTS AND SMALL CHILDREN

Women in domestic violence support groups relate how they look back on their early days of motherhood. They recall many times when they were emotionally unavailable to their children because they were trying to keep the environment calm to please their partners. Mothers relate how they kept the children playing in another part of the house when the father came home, so that no noise or toys would "set off" an incident. If a child cries or needs the mother, the abusive partner may abuse the mother or child until the child is calmed. Children lose the security of being able to count on their parents to be available to them as they need them—to cuddle or to play with them.

Infants and small children have nearly been dropped from their mother's arms when these women were trying to protect themselves and their children from being battered. Many women report that it is very difficult and dangerous to leave the house during a battering incident. They talk about trying to gather up their child, a purse, or the car keys while struggling with their partner who is trying to pull the child from their arms. Mothers have reported letting go of their child temporarily because they were afraid that the child would be injured in the tug-of-war. Sue said, "I was afraid he was going to pull the baby's legs off, he was pulling on him so hard. I did not want Tommy hurt, so I let Paul take him. It was terrible, I still can hear Tommy crying." The grief and guilt is intense for these women, as they hear their child crying for them, and yet physically they cannot do anything. Mothers report the feeling of helplessness in caring for their children when they are not able to keep them safe. The confusion for a small child must be great, as parents pull and tug, yell and scream, with the child caught in the middle. The research of Jaffee et al. verified what mothers have been reporting about their babies, "Infants who witness violence are often characterized by poor health, poor sleeping habits, and excessive screaming" [7, p. 40].

SCHOOL AGE CHILDREN

The kind of violence that occurs and the duration of the violence is directly related to children's losses and the resulting physical effects on them. Observations of children at battered women's shelters have provided anecdotal information on the large number of problem areas for these children. The problems relate to health, socio-emotional development, and behavior [9]. These children may experience intestinal difficulties, enuresis, sleeping problems, ulcers, phobias, distractibility, confusion, tantrums, aggressiveness, extreme passivity, and self-mutilation. The range of responses vary as much as the children do, but each response is one child's way of reacting to the chaos.

If a parent takes the child to a physician with some of these physical complaints, a treatment could be started, relief could be accomplished, and the real underlying reason for the symptoms missed. If the symptoms return, the child may interpret them as "their fault." They may wonder, "What did I do to create so many problems?" or "If I was a better kid, Mommy and Daddy wouldn't fight."

Findings by Moore et al. indicate that children of battered women perceive themselves to have significantly less control over events in their lives than children from non-violent homes [10].

SCHOOL

Family chaos is easier to escape from during the school day, but battered children carry many of their difficulties into the school environment. Gelles and Straus report that children who experience severe violence are two or three times more likely to have failing grades in school, experience difficulty forming friendships, become discipline problems at school, and physically assault others outside of school [3]. Boys are especially at risk for becoming involved in juvenile crime.

Children who move from school to school experience additional difficulties. They must start with a different teaching curriculum which includes other textbooks, and they must contend with new teachers, school rules, and children. Children from violent homes have learned to be cautious around adults and trusting new adults may become a serious issue. The lack of trust centers around the unpredictable nature of adults in the home environment of these children. A child may be vigilant at school so as not to do anything to make an adult angry. Low self-esteem, depression, and confusion about why they are changing schools, combined with a lack of trust that adults will treat them appropriately, frequently makes them feel scared and powerless. These feelings, combined with the stigma of family violence and the possibility of having to move again, may contribute to their difficulties in making new friends.

KIDNAPPING AND MOVING

Fear of losing a parent is very real for these children. They may be afraid that their father will be so abusive to their mother that she will die, he will end up in jail, and they will be left without either parent.

It is not uncommon for the fear to include being kidnapped by one parent and taken to another state or country. In one situation, Helen's husband took the children to his homeland in the Middle East to hide them from her. When Helen went to get the children, his family tried to kill her and the children to prevent them from returning to their home in the United States. This is not an isolated incident. In another situation, Cynthia's husband has kept her two children in another state, hundreds of miles away from her. For more than a year, she has not been able to talk to them on the phone. Cynthia's children were told that she did not want them and Helen's children were told that their mother was never coming for them. These families demonstrate that children can be used as pawns when control over the relationship by an adult is an issue.

A woman may need to take the children out of their home because she does not feel it is safe for them to live there. As a result, these children must make a number of changes and experience several losses in the process. They leave familiar surroundings including their own rooms, friends, toys, clothes, activities, and even pets. Children may not be permitted to play outside their new home because of concern for their safety or the possibility that their location may be identified if they are seen. Molly took her son from their Midwestern home so they would not be killed by his father. They had to change their name and how they received any mail. Decisions had to be made concerning who could know where they were. All the necessary personal documentation that allows us to operate in our society, such as a driver's license, library card, and bank statements also had to be changed. Applications for housing services, such as utilities or rental agreements, give individuals the means to find a safe refuge. But such applications require identification and, therefore, are also a means by which victims can be tracked by the abuser. It is a complex process to erase the identity of two people to reappear as two other people. Schools have a difficult time when parents cannot present past school records and it is hard for children to remember, "What is my name today?"

Health care also becomes difficult, either because they lack financial resources or because the mother knows that this is a public record which could lead the batterer to them. Routine, which provides security and structure in children's lives, changes dramatically. They no longer have a reliable way to measure what is normal and okay in order to feel safe and secure.

The children often feel a sense of guilt that they have somehow caused the abuse. If their names were mentioned during fights between their parents, children may assume that they were the cause of the fight or that they should have stopped the violence. Some children believe that if they are "super good," Mom and Dad will get along and they can return to the family home.

Societal status symbols are often lost to these children and their parent. Women have told us that the losses they have felt included knowing that they will not be "moving up" to a larger home, driving the latest automobile, or having the comforts available to them that were once a part of their lives. Many of these newly defined families move from comfortable dwellings to very compact apartments or mobile homes.

When a battered woman decides to leave a relationship she is confronted with many decisions regarding her children's well-being, custody and visitation rights, and economic settlements [11]. The cycle of violence is based on power and control; who is going to have the power and how is it going to be used? Batterers tend to try to control the negotiations concerning children's custody and financial arrangements. Battered women more frequently need to settle for less than their fair share, at the expense of their children [12].

GRANDPARENTS AND EXTENDED FAMILY

Many individuals have images of the major holidays that include a multi-generational family sitting around the dining room table pleasantly eating a meal. It is not that way for many of these children. The acknowledgment of abuse in the household may divide grandparent relationships. Grandparents tend to take sides to support the parent that they see as right or most deserving of their attention and help. Their input may increase the stress to such an extent that the children's custodial parent must limit or discontinue contact with the grandparents for a period of time, or forever. Gatherings, as they once were, may not be safe or possible any more. New "traditions" need to be defined and established during the holidays. This can be a lonely time for the women and children, but most of them state, "it is so much better than before because there is no violence."

VISITATION

Visitations are very stressful for all parties involved. Visiting and playing with their father may be very different now because children may receive gifts, attention, or go to new recreational places. Women relate their own sadness over the gifts and attention that the children now receive from their father, that were absent when the family was together. The children get confused by what their father is doing for them and wonder why mother does not do the same. Sarah said it best, "Don never did anything for the kids when we were a family, now he is trying to give the kids anything they want. I can only afford food and housing for them and sometimes they ask me why is Dad being so nice now, Mom? It is very hard to answer them and not show my anger at him."

Visits can be at his new residence, in a "neutral location" like a restaurant, park, or a state agency with an intermediary person present as a required safety feature for the children. This is a loss of freedom for the children who must meet their father at an appointed time, in an appointed place, and possibly with supervision. Many of the children do not like this visitation arrangement and ask their mothers if they have to go. The father may say that this is his time with the children and insist that no other events interfere. Nancy's children became very upset with their father when he would not take them to their dance or gymnastic classes on "his" time. When Nancy tried to intercede for them the outcome only became more conflicted. She was accused of trying to make decisions about her ex-husband's time with the children and he became more belligerent. Consequently, she let the children voice their feelings to her about their father's behavior, knowing she could not change the situation. They went on the scheduled visits and missed their own activities when he chose not to honor them.

If other events come up that conflict with the scheduled visitation times, many of these families cannot negotiate a compromise. The need of an abusive individual to have "the control" in a relationship remains the focus even after the family separates.

THE LEGAL SYSTEM

Frequently, the legal system becomes a major component in the follow-up of the violence. New events further disrupt the family including an arrest, jailing of one or both parents, and the setting of court dates. When the police officers are not sure what has happened in the dispute, both adults can be arrested. As a result, the children can be placed with extended family, neighbors, or county foster care. They are not sure who will care for them, when their parents will be back, or if their parents will be back. Legal papers and court orders become part of the family's tension and focus, including custody of the children and financial arrangements. Even though the children are not making these decisions, they are very aware of the energy and the new vocabulary around them. They can easily misunderstand what they hear and interpret custody as never seeing one or the other parent again. If the mother does not have the financial means to seek legal aid, her fear and tension can compound the children's anxiety about their future.

Sometimes older children, who do not want visitation with their fathers, encounter the legal system. They experience a loss of power and voice when the court system demands that they must obey. Karen, at age thirteen, refused to see her father. Her refusal pulled her and her mother back into the court system because her father filed a contempt of court against her mother for not "making" Karen participate in the visitation order. Karen's mother responded to her attorney,

"How am I going to make her go, I can not physically carry her there. What does he expect of me?"

THE MEDIA

The media may become a part of this picture, especially if either parent has a public occupation, any notoriety, or the violence was covered by the press. As family details become public domain, the mother and her children must contend with a violation of their privacy. Women verbalize their feelings of hopelessness and helplessness when they are unable to protect their children from the intrusion of the exposure by the media. The media will come to families and ask for the details that are beneficial for their service, but potentially dangerous for the woman and her children. Safety can be compromised if a victim of domestic violence talks with the media and their whereabouts, name, or future plans are disclosed.

SUPPORT

The amount of support, that a mother is able or not able to receive throughout the process, is also a factor in how the children experience the violence. They need her attention when her energy is low. If she receives emotional support for herself, she can then focus more readily on her children's needs. They all benefit most when she seeks educational information on domestic violence and how to stop the cycle. They can receive this support and information through domestic violence support groups for children and women, individual therapy by a therapist who is well-versed in domestic violence issues, or the victim can call one of the domestic violence crisis lines available in many communities.

Provide a safe place for the victim and encourage her to talk about the possibility that the children are not being protected in their home, but do it in a non-judgmental way. The feelings are intense for everyone that is involved. Individuals who work with these families need to respect them and provide a safe environment in which they can explore their feelings about what has been happening to them.

A powerful support for children and their mothers happens in the group setting. Children meet other children who have been in violent homes. They hear their experiences, realize that they are not alone in what has happened to them, and discover that others understand their feelings. These children may have difficulty understanding their father's behavior, the events that follow that behavior, and the litigation requiring a continued relationship with him. Hopefully, the support they receive can help them come to terms with their feelings.

CONCLUSION

More and more children are in danger of becoming victims of violence. Some grow up to become violent themselves, thus passing the behavior on to another generation. It is important to listen to them and to believe what they say is happening in their homes.

The events that happen to children in homes where domestic violence is present result in numerous losses. The "voices" of advocacy for them are not always heard because children are not seen as a politically strong constituency. The issue of domestic violence has become a more frequently studied field in the last ten to fifteen years, and therefore, there is increasing awareness of the impact on children and their subsequent losses.

REFERENCES

1. National Coalition Against Domestic Violence, P.O. Box 15127, Washington, D.C., 20003, (1-800-333-SAFE).
2. U.S. Department of Health and Human Services, Clearinghouse on Child Abuse and Neglect and Family Violence Information, P.O. Box 1182, Washington, D.C. 20013, pp. 4, 5, 18-19, 1991.
3. R. J. Gelles and M. A. Straus, *Intimate Violence*, Simon and Schuster, New York, 1988.
4. L. E. Walker, *The Battered Woman*, Harper & Row, New York, 1979.
5. L. V. Davis and B. E. Carlson, Observation of Spouse Abuse. What Happens to the Children?, *Journal of Interpersonal Violence,* 2:3, pp. 278-291, 1987.
6. S. Prescott and C. Letko, Battered Women: A Social Psychological Perspective, in *Battered Women: A Psychosociological Study of Domestic Violence*, M. Roy (ed.), Van Nostrand and Reinhold, New York, 1977.
7. P. G. Jaffee, D. A. Wolfe, and S. K. Wilson, *Children of Battered Women*, Sage Publications, Newbury Park, California, 1990.
8. G. Margolin, L.G. Sibner, and L. Glerberman, Wife Battering, in *Handbook of Family Therapy*, V. B. Van Hasselt (ed.), Plenum Press, New York, 1987.
9. E. Hilberman and K. Munson, Sixty Battered Women, *Victimology, 2,* pp. 460-470, 1977-1978.
10. T. Moore, D. Pepler, B. Weinberg, L. Hammond, J. Waddell, and L. Weiser, Research on Children from Violent Families, *Canada's Mental Health, 38*:2-3, pp. 19-23, June/September 1990.

11. M. B. Levine, Interpersonal Violence and its Effects on Children: A Study of 50 Families in General Practice, *Medicine, Science, and the Law, 15*, pp. 172-176, 1975.
12. E. Stark and A. Flitcraft, Violence Among Intimates; An Epidemiological Review, in *Handbook of Family Violence*, V. B. Van Hasselt (ed.), Plenum Press, New York, 1987.
13. K. H. Coleman, Conjugal Violence: What 33 Men Report, *Journal of Marital and Family Therapy, 6*, pp. 207-213, 1980.
14. S. Cushing, Violence at Home. What Have We Come To?, *View*, pp. 9-13, August/September 1981.
15. L. E. Walker, *The Battered Woman Syndrome*, Springer, New York, 1984.

CHAPTER 9

What Do We Do with the Empty Desk?*

Margaret M. Metzgar

It is one thing to live in the
structured, concrete, logical
world of adults.
It's another to live in the evolving world of
fears, facts, and fantasies, as experienced by a child.
Children challenge us . . .
They call on our adult ability and creativity to bridge those
worlds,
providing protection, direction and answers [1].

There is no more challenging time than when we are called on to explain the death of a child to other children. As much as we want to believe that it does not happen, in 1990, 45,169 children between the ages of five and twenty-four died across the United States [2]. That equals approximately 124 child deaths a day or six children dying every hour of the day, twenty-four hours a day. Each death leaves another school questioning: How will we explain this death to the rest of the school? *What do we do with the empty desk?*

It is especially difficult if it is a sudden and/or traumatic death or if the person who caused the death is also a student at your school. This is not an impossibility; it could result from an accident, or even a homicide involving another student. According to the 1991 Uniform

---

*The information contained in this chapter is condensed from portions of the booklet, *But What Do We Do With The Empty Desk?* [1].

Crime Report, 3,787 children under the age of nineteen died as a result of homicide, 2,702 between the ages of fifteen to nineteen [3]. Out of those, where the age of both the victim and offender could be determined, both victim and offender were under the age of nineteen, in 295 cases [3].

Being confronted with the death of an innocent child, a child who as recently as yesterday was a shining face in your classroom, is one of the world's harshest realities. Frequently, there is little or no advanced notice. Often you are notified about an emergency staff meeting, walk in the door and are given the details with only a few precious moments to plan your response. Now you must find a way to convey that information to the rest of the children in your classroom. Graduate school seldom prepares teachers for this moment. You will have to immediately confront your own reactions, your own pain, and your own questions. Then, without any time to spare, you will have to face the already circulating rumors, fears, hysteria, pain, and the questions from the students. On some occasions you may also find yourself staring into a television camera being asked questions from the press, or needing to respond to the concerns of anxious parents.

It is time for all educators, professionals, parents, and schools of education to stop pretending "it will never happen here." It is time to say "YES" it does happen, children do die, and we must be ready for the time it *will* happen here. The following pages are for teachers, principals, nurses, school psychologists, parents, and any of the other interdisciplinary team members that will be available to respond in such a time of crisis.

The two primary focuses of this chapter are first, how do you say "dead." What are the specific important steps in telling children that one of their classmates is dead? Second, to explore ways of promoting healthy healing following the death of a classmate. This will include facilitating goodbye rituals, and delineating between a ritual of goodbye, a commemoration of the life lost, and a memorialization. Each of these have unique purposes and at times need to be handled differently. Suggestions and examples will be given, as well as identifying some of the common potential pitfalls.

Dealing with the death of a child in a classroom is not simply a matter of removing excess furniture. However, historically, many schools have responded in just that way. When a child died, the desk was removed. Frequently, it was put out in the hall to be stored until it was needed again. Talk of the absence was minimal, if any. Often the tragedy was compounded with a lie like "he moved," or "she is just not coming back." Or, by searching for gentle ways to soften the reality of death that completely avoid using the word "dead." These behaviors were supported by the misconceptions that children did not understand death, that they did not mourn and that they must be protected from this harsh reality. In recent years it has been increasingly more common for school officials, parents groups (such as The Eagle Forum), and newspaper or magazine articles to express the unsubstantiated fear that, in the case of a death by suicide, talking about the suicide would give children ideas that may promote additional deaths.

It is a known and universally accepted fact that children grieve. They do mourn and they do understand death. Their level of understanding is dependent upon their age and stage of development (a concept originally developed and studied by Maria H. Nagy, 1948) [4]. Yet, even the youngest child is able to comprehend that something major has happened in his or her world. When faced with the death of a classmate, children need our honesty, our stability, and our guidance instead of our denial or our feeble attempts at protection. They need, as the opening poem states, our ability and creativity to help them bridge their fears and fantasies with facts. This requires the ability to say "dead."

HOW DO YOU SAY "DEAD?" [5, 6]

There is not one right or easy way to say "dead." A "cheat sheet" of the right phrases is not available. Every situation will vary depending upon the type of death, the age of the children, and the availability of support. However, the following suggestions are the important steps to consider when sharing the news of the death of a friend with a child or group of children.

1. Stop . . . Breathe . . . Calm Yourself

In a time of crisis children need your stability. Yet, in order to provide that, you need to take a moment to come to terms with this painful reality yourself. First you must get yourself grounded or it will be easy to get caught up in the children's panic, pain, and confusion. This means acknowledging and respecting your own pain. This is not to be confused with putting on the "tough guy" armor, or being "strong" while denying your own emotions.

When working with young teachers I am always amazed at how frightened many of them are of "falling apart" or "crying" in front of a classroom, as if it were a sign of failure. Instead, I view the experience as an opportunity for students to be able to witness the process of "falling apart" and the strength to be able to pull oneself back together. This is better than verbally telling children "it's okay to cry" yet hiding your tears, only to shed them in hidden places. What kind of coping does this teach? Children need you to provide an honest role model when coping with tragedy. Many adults and children fear that if they "fall apart" they will never be able to get themselves back together again. Do not cheat them out of this process. Let them see your pain, your tears, your struggles, and your healing.

2. Think About What You Want to Say

Words are important and so is consistency. Thinking about what you want to say must include ensuring that all students are receiving the same information and that the information is accurate. Whenever possible, the facts, in the form of an actual written script, should be given to all the teachers to read in their classrooms. This will insure that all students receive the same information and will help avert rumors or misinformation. Be concrete, specific and avoid overloading children with unnecessary information. What children need to be told is the truth, the facts as they are known. They also need to be given information on grief. What they might expect to feel and what they might do to help themselves feel better. For example, it is important for children to know that they should expect to feel a mix of emotion including sadness, anger, confusion, guilt, and relief. They need to know that they are not alone, that there are people they can talk to that understand, and where they can find those people. If possible these facts and information should also be sent home to parents.

3. Think About How Children May Hear Your Explanation

What you say and what is heard is not always the same, especially when you take into account young children's concrete nature of understanding. It is important to know children's level of understanding when you are trying to determine how they will *hear* what you say. It may be helpful to actually preview how what you are planning to say might be heard. Here is an example of a child's misinterpretation. I was called in to work with a child following a homicide/suicide. A man had killed his wife in the presence of their child and then left the house and killed himself. The caretaker wanted to protect the child from the additional reality that Daddy had taken his own life. She felt that the child had been hurt enough and such information would serve no purpose. So when trying to explain the father's death to the child, she said, "Your Daddy felt so bad about what happened he died too." From this information the child assumed that she should prepare for her death and told everyone not to feel bad when she was gone. This was based on what she understood of the caretaker's response which was an attempt to soften the reality of her father's death. What she heard was, "when you feel so bad you die."

Our culture frequently uses cliches and euphemisms as a way to try to soften the reality of death. However, be cautious because they can easily fuel children's fears and fantasies. For example, I have worked with many children who have experienced sleep disturbances as a result of associations made between sleep and death. Or, they may fear that God will take them away too when God has been used as an explanation for the cause of death.

4. Use the Word "Dead" and Define It

Following a house fire in which a family was killed, one of the school children asked, "I know Suzie and John were burned up in the fire. I know God built a house for them in heaven and took them home. But do you know—are they still burned and hurting in heaven?"

When explaining "dead" to children it is important not to just use the word dead but to explain and define it. *Dead means the body does not work any more. When you are dead you do not breathe, your heart does not beat, you do not hurt or get cold, you do not laugh or play, and you do not eat or pee.* (In my experience, for some reason, the last item is very important for six- to eight-year-old little boys.) *"Dead" is not a place we can visit and you do not come back from being dead.*

This definition is not meant to preclude or replace religious or philosophical explanations but rather compliment them. Religious explanations which stand alone can cause confusion in a child's mind about what actually happens to the physical body. What is a child to think when he has been told that Todd has gone to heaven but he is standing there looking at Todd's body in the casket?

When you are in doubt about what a child understands or has heard, ask him to explain to you what he thinks has happened.

5. Use Short Sentences and Vocabulary that are Age Appropriate

In times of crisis, the content of long sentences will be lost in a child's mind. Personally, I recommend using sentences that are no longer than approximately fifteen to twenty words. Long, involved and complicated sentences are too much for children to understand when they are frightened or hurting. Yet, being verbose is one of the most common mistakes adults make when attempting to explain death. If the sentences are long, when you review your planned explanation, stop and start over again. Re-consider your explanation, and use a different approach.

It is also crucial that the information be age-appropriate. You would not say to a five- or six-year-old child, "Well, you know Sarah had a cardiac arrest. They tried to resuscitate her. They took her to the hospital and put her on the respirator in the intensive care unit. Then she had another arrest and they couldn't revive her." That explanation would mean nothing to a child of that age. Nor would you explain a death to a teenager using language appropriate for a four year-old.

It may help to see this task as three-fold: *educate, communicate, and validate* [5, 6]. *Educate* as to what is the normal grief response. Help children understand the grief process. We need to provide the road map. Explain what some of the experiences might be, what feelings might be experienced. We need to help children normalize their experience by using phrases and language they know and understand. *Communicate* means keeping the lines of communication open both ways. Do not just talk to children but listen to them. Let them provide the direction. The biggest mistake we can make is to try to dictate their process. In this context *validate* simply means letting the children know that you hear and understand what they are saying to you about how they feel and that you are there with them.

6. Do Not Promise Anything You Cannot Provide

Many times, when confronted by children's questions, we find ourselves wanting to say anything that might make them feel better. Our automatic reflex is to try to protect the child from more pain. Following a death, an example of a child's fear may be voiced by asking questions such as, "Are you going to die too?" and/or "Am I going to die?" It is difficult to answer "yes" to that question, but to say "no" would be a lie, it would be a promise you could not keep. There are ways to answer that question that can acknowledge the truth yet still provide a comforting response. One reply might be, "Yes, everybody dies someday. Nobody knows when they will die, but we are going to do everything in our power to stay healthy and live a very long time." This validates the child's feelings and fears yet, it also empowers them by giving them something you can do together at a time when we all feel so alone and helpless. Empowerment, especially when grieving, is a very difficult yet important task that, in children, can be supported by helping them to master appropriate developmental tasks.

7. Encourage Expression of Feelings

The previous suggestions have dealt primarily with how, as an educator, you might relate death information to children. Now, we need to shift our focus to helping children handle what they hear. Unless a child has been raised to fear or restrain their emotions it is common to see a brief, yet intense emotional response to loss. This is both normal and healthy. In order to help children cope and heal through loss we must honor, acknowledge, and encourage that expression of emotion. This should include the full range of emotion all the way from numbness, to sadness, to rage.

Many educators find it is easier to encourage sadness and tears than to help children find a safe way to express their anger. However, anger is a natural and healthy response to death. Anger may be expressed at the person who died, at God for letting it happen, or at the person who caused the death. Anger in children may also be expressed as violent play not directed at any specific person or thing.

There are many safe ways of promoting the expression of anger. All of them include acknowledging the anger, recognizing it as a normal part of the grieving process, and re-directing it into a constructive rather than destructive activity. For example, when working with teenagers, following a death by suicide, I frequently encourage them to write a letter to the student who died. Before the letter is ever written we discuss and decide what will happen to the letters at the end of the exercise. I give them permission to include anything in this letter. Most frequently those letters are filled with the "why" questions and the rage at their friend for "copping out." It is important to follow this kind of intense written exercise with time for discussion.

8. Listen to the Questions

Children are filled with questions following a death. Both the content and purpose of the questions will vary with age. The young child will ask questions like, "Am I going to die?" or "Why did their mommy and daddy not take better care of them." These questions are asking more for reassurance than for specific information and may be repeated often, to make sure that the answer has not changed. An older child's questions will be directed more toward requests for specific details "I know they are dead but, how did they die?" "How long did it take?" "Did it hurt?"

9. Include Children/Help Provide Closure

Following any death, we all need the opportunity to confront the reality of the death, share our sadness, and say goodbye. Funeral rituals are designed specifically to meet those needs. Yet, frequently children are excluded from the funeral or the funeral is designed primarily for adult participation. Children need to be included. The challenge is to help children find their own ways of saying goodbye rather than expecting them to copy adults' behavior. Letters, written by students following the suicide of a classmate, such as those described previously in the seventh guideline, are an example of helping to provide closure. Facilitating goodbye rituals will be examined in the following section.

10. Remember Grief is Process: It is Not Time Limited

Because the first few days following any major trauma in a school are the most intense, little structured school work will be accomplished. There are no three day "quick fixes." Still, it is not uncommon to hear "Okay, it's been three days. When are we going to get back to normal?" Grief takes time and children will wander in and out of their grief process. In children, behavior changes may be observed for months or years following a death.

Weeks or even years later children may ask more questions and explore their feelings about the death. As a child grows through their developmental stages their concepts and understandings of death mature and new questions arise. This is a process that I refer to as *regrieving*. It is not an indication of incomplete or unhealthy grieving but a normal, natural part of development and the grieving process.

HOW DO YOU HELP STUDENTS SAY "GOODBYE?"

Healing after a death has an immediate and long term component. As stated in the previous section, we all need the opportunity to: confront the reality of the death, share our sadness, and say goodbye. We also need to put this death into perspective within our own world. A ritual of goodbye affords us the opportunity to deal with the immediate pain of the grief and say goodbye. In addition, commemoration and memorialization provide us with the opportunity to deal with the long term aspects of the death, its impact on our world, and our memories.

WHAT IS A RITUAL OF GOODBYE?

A ritual of goodbye is an actual ceremony or exercise used to say goodbye. When working with children, it is important to help them by facilitating this process using age-appropriate actions and language. This requires helping them explore, create and develop their own children's way of sharing goodbyes. Sadly and all too often, children are asked or forced to adapt to adult goodbyes instead of being encouraged to create their own. The key is to facilitate this process, helping them find a way to share their goodbyes. This section will give you some ideas and samples of children's goodbyes that I have shared [5, 6].

A funeral is generally an adult ritual of goodbye. However, children should be included whenever possible. All children should be given detailed, specific, age appropriate information about what will happen at the funeral. Then, they should be given the choice to go and participate in the funeral, or to stay with friends or relatives, as an alternative. No child should ever be forced to go the funeral of a loved one.

Depending on the family's wishes there are even some occasions, following the death of a child, when the child's friends might be invited to actively participate in the planning of a funeral. One such situation continues to be the most moving experience that I have ever had attending a funeral. It was a funeral for a family (a mother and 2 children, a 10-year-old girl and a 7-year-old boy) that had been killed in a car accident. When the students in the older child's class heard of their classmate's death they recalled a comment that she had made only months before, following her aunt's funeral. She had said, "When I die, will you make sure that somebody puts blue and white stripes on my box. I don't want one of those boring dirty wooden boxes." Based on that request her classmates got permission to put the colored stripes on her "box." It was their way of both honoring her wishes and saying their goodbye. Through that activity (ritual) they confronted the death and shared their sadness while saying goodbye. The classmates of the younger child put together a memory table for the vestibule of the church. It included cards that they had made as well as memorabilia from his life—his skates, his old arm cast that he had saved and treasured, his soccer shorts, his report cards, and many other personal treasures. Everyone at the funeral was moved and all of the children benefited from their participation in this ritual.

In many school situations it may not be possible, or appropriate, to allow all of the children to participate in the funeral. However, funerals are not the only ritual of goodbye. With assistance, any classroom in any school can design a ritual that will fit their particular needs and situation.

Cards and flowers are the next most common ritual. Young children are frequently quick to get out their crayons and create great works of art that express their feelings and send their love. A group of middle school students taught me about candy cards. Their way of sending sympathy to a surviving sibling was to say it with candy. They took a large piece of butcher paper and glued candy bars on it letting the candy bar names express their message. An example might be—Dear Tom, We are so sorry that this is such a *ROCKY ROAD* for you right now. We send you *MOUNDS* of good thoughts and *KISSES*. Older students may choose to write letters rather than draw cards or use candy cards.

Some children may want to send flowers to the family. Others may want to put flowers on the desk of the student that died. Some may suggest planting a bush or tree. However, I caution you about plantings. Each time I think about planting a tree I remember walking into an elementary school and having a young child run up to me and ask, "Do you know where Mrs. Finkelstein is?" I said, "No, should I?" Her response was, "Well everybody knows where she is. She's out under the tree." Mrs. Finkelstein was a teacher who died, and the school had planted a tree in her honor. This child's fantasy was that they put her under the tree. This is only one of the many possible pitfalls to planting a tree, others will be discussed under memorials.

In recent years, helium balloons are used more frequently. Many schools had students tie messages onto the balloon strings. Then the balloons were released in a ceremony, sending their messages into the sky. This was a creative ritual that met many of the objectives of a goodbye ritual. (There is one problem with balloons that may need to be considered, most balloons are not environmentally safe and the ones that are tend to be very expensive.)

Sometimes, the season can influence the style of goodbye. Earlier in this chapter I mentioned two children that were killed in a house fire. That fire occurred just before Christmas. Christmas could not be ignored as we tried to help the children's friends decide how they wanted to say goodbye. The students were very sad that their two friends were going to miss the Christmas Pageant, so that is where we started. They finally decided that each of them would make a Christmas ornament in memory of their friends and hang them on the tree. After the Christmas pageant was over they took all of the ornaments and gave them to the surviving family members.

Given the chance children, of all ages, will decide what will work best for them. For example, let us consider pinwheels. One elementary class decided that their friend's favorite thing would be to see pinwheels in the wind. The way they decided to remember him was to decorate the entire tree just outside the window of their classroom with pinwheels. It was a wonderful sight and a very special goodbye.

WHAT ARE COMMEMORATION AND MEMORIALIZATION?

Following a death, I see commemoration as the act of calling to mind the life of a person that is no longer a part of our world. It includes finding ways of honoring and celebrating their life, while acknowledging our strength and need to go on. Whereas, when I refer to memorialization or a memorial I am generally referring to something tangible used to preserve the memory of a life, or person, that will last on into time.

Commemoration and memorialization go hand in hand. They are similar, yet, slightly different from each other and from the ritual of goodbye. It is possible, however, that they may all take place simultaneously. For example, students may decide to have a tree planting as their goodbye (a ritual of goodbye). At that tree planting special stories may be shared to honor the life lost, the current struggles, and the need to go on (commemoration). The tree then also becomes the tangible reminder of that person and their place in our life and our memory (a memorial). Again, as in planning the goodbyes, the task of the educator is to help the students find the ways they want to commemorate and memorialize their friend.

Memorials come in all shapes and sizes. The students may choose to, as stated before, plant a tree or a memorial garden. Perhaps their idea would be to have a memorial plaque made, or to devote a special section in the yearbook. Scholarships and trophies are common memorials. One high school class chose to write a play in honor of two students killed in a cross country track accident. Anything that serves as a reminder of that person can be a memorial.

However, in helping students decide on a memorial there are three important factors that we must keep in mind in order to avoid the common disasters and pitfalls:

1. What are we commemorating? Will this memorial commemorate the life of the person who has died or are we setting up a memorial to commemorate the death of that person?
2. What will be the immediate and long range impact of the planned memorial?
3. What are the possible pitfalls or repercussions of this plan?

Possible Pitfalls

The pitfalls of commemoration and memorialization usually have to do with poor planning, especially planning for the future. For example, if your school chooses tree planting as a memorial that may be right for one death, or two, but over the history of the school you may need to be aware of space considerations. What happens if the tree gets too large? I recently spoke with a man that had just returned from his twentieth class reunion. He was clearly distressed. While he was in school a dear friend had died and his class had decided to plant a tree. When he returned for his reunion he discovered that the tree had been cut down because it had grown too big for its space. He felt as if his friend had been killed all over again.

Planting trees or memorial flower beds also create other potential difficulties such as what happens if the plantings die or fail to grow? Whose responsibility is it to maintain them? What happens to them if the school closes or relocates?

Another example of poor future planning is the school that chiseled the names of the students who died on a huge boulder on the school grounds. When the school closed the boulder could not be moved. The school property was sold, and houses were built. Now, someone has a house complete with a boulder containing the names and dates of children who died. You can see from these examples that long range planning is important.

Difficult Deaths

Suicides and deaths resulting from drunk driving are two types of deaths that schools find the hardest to acknowledge and memorialize in healthy ways. Care must be taken not to romanticize the death or shower the dead student with the attention in death that he or she was reaching out for in life. By doing that you would be inviting other desperate students to kill themselves. Yet, you also do not want to ignore a life that was here yesterday and gone today. So what do you do? These deaths cannot be ignored. We cannot just pretend that the student went away. We must commemorate the life yet, not condone the means of the death.

It is crucial to honestly confront these deaths and the poor choices that were made. This can be done in many ways. Use these deaths as educational opportunities to teach students how precious life is and how to ask for help if they doubt the purpose of life. In this type of death we are not just mourning the death of a friend, but also their intentional choice to leave our lives. Do not be afraid to say, "He killed himself" or "She took her own life." It is important to acknowledge the pain and isolation that they must have felt in order to make that choice. Yet, it is also crucial to point out that death is a permanent solution to a temporary problem. Any commemoration or memorial following a suicide or a drunk driving death must include this message.

Ideally, as a result of this honest response, both the short and long term impacts will impress upon students that death is not an easy out or a way to get attention. Hopefully, they will consider the responsibility that they have for their lives and the choices they make. Dialogue and follow up can give meaning to these deaths. It was just such a death that started SADD (Students against Drunk Drivers) groups or youth suicide prevention groups, in many schools across the nation. Those groups have become a living commemoration and memorial to students whose deaths have resulted from drunk driving or suicide.

CONCLUSION

Death in childhood does happen. Schools and classmates are affected. There is no three day "quick fix" for the pain of grief. As educators, children look to you for the answers. They need your honesty, direction, and guidance during this difficult time. You are challenged to be prepared at all times for these realities. The information contained in this chapter was designed to help you with that challenge. Hopefully, you will read it before you are faced with a death in your classroom. However, even if you are not reading it before the last death, you are reading it before the next one. Death will touch your life as an educator, possibly many times. You can never be too prepared. Being prepared will not make death happen, it will however help you to reach out to your students to educate, communicate, and validate the crisis that the death of a classmate creates in their world.

REFERENCES

1. M. A. Metzgar, *Little Ears Big Issues Children and Loss*, Transition and Loss Center, Seattle, Washington, 1991.
2. National Center for Health Statistics, *Advance Report of Final Mortality Statistics*, 1990.
3. United States Department of Justice, *Crime United States 1991 Uniform Crime Report*, 1991.
4. M. H. Nagy, The Child's View of Death, *Journal of Genetic Psychology, 73*, pp. 3-27, 1948.
5. M. A. Metzgar, *But What Do We Do With The Empty Desk?* Transition and Loss Center, Seattle, Washington, 1993.

6. M. A. Metzgar, *The A. B. C.'s of Telling Children About Death*, Lecture, Seattle, Washington, 1987.

BIBLIOGRAPHY

Maurer, A., Maturation of Concepts of Death, *British Journal of Medicine and Psychology, 39*, pp. 35-41, 1966.

CHAPTER 10

Grief Responses and Group Treatment Interventions for Five- to Eight-Year-Old Children

Eileen Ormond and Heather Charbonneau

INTRODUCTION

The Grief Support Program for Children and Adolescents is a community outreach initiative of the Notre Dame of St. Agatha Children's Mental Health Centre. It began four years ago following a community needs survey conducted in the metropolitan area of Kitchener-Waterloo, Ontario, Canada. This survey reflected a lack of responsiveness to the needs of bereaved children. It also showed that adult bereavement groups were sporadically available and childhood groups were non-existent. In addition, hospitals were offering only limited support to children and families anticipating a death. Individual play therapy for young children to help them deal with an impending loss or following a death was largely inaccessible to middle and lower income families due to the costs involved.

In the field of death studies, there is a considerable body of literature focusing on adult and childhood bereavement, but very little information is based on research that focuses specifically on young children. Perhaps this is because young children are difficult to study, especially when we want them to tell us what they are thinking, feeling, and experiencing. We do know, however, that when children are able to show us what they think and feel, they provide us with useful information to help them. Our experience has demonstrated that groups for bereaved children can be of value because children process their grief most effectively through experiential and imaginative activities, discussion, and sharing.

Our group program for bereaved children, ages five to eight years, is designed to assist them in safely exploring their feelings and the meaning of loss through art work, imaginative play, music, and ritual expression. This chapter describes concerns presented by children at the time of referral and examines treatment issues and group interventions. Two case examples, as well as an analysis of our pre- and post-group evaluations, verify our position that group treatment with young bereaved children can be effective.

It is acknowledged within the field of death education that young children do grieve and that they should not be shielded from experiencing the reality of death. Educators agree that children grieve in accordance with their cognitive and emotional development, as well as their family's response to a death. When a loved one dies, children's needs to process their grief are frequently overlooked or dismissed because parents are preoccupied with their own grief. Current research findings indicate that loss in childhood significantly affects later psychological adjustment and interpersonal relationships [1]. Although the trauma of the immediate loss may not necessarily overwhelm children at the time of a death, subsequent minor losses or stressful life events may reactivate intense unresolved feelings which may then be overwhelming. Children may need help to work through their grief so that they can deal with future life transitions [2]. Due to developmental limitations, grief may require recycling several times as children mature [3]. Our groups are structured to provide the necessary guidance and experience to help children successfully cope with current grief issues and those they will encounter at future stages of development.

LITERATURE REVIEW

Early Childhood–Ages Four to Six Years

Young children under five years of age perceive death as reversible and believe that the dead are functioning somewhere else, far away from them. Children may often ask questions about where dead people have gone, how they will breathe under the ground, whether they are lonely, and when they will return. A four-year-old told us, "My father died and I may not see him until I am twenty-one." Of greatest significance is the fact that young children are separated from someone they love and depend upon. In Maier, Piaget places the cognitive development of four- to six-year-olds in the intuitive thought phase [4]. In this phase, as egocentricity is reduced and social participation increases, children progressively become aware of the meaning and importance of relationships. When death takes a loved one away during this phase, the resulting loneliness may be devastating.

Lonetto explains that young children understand life and death as a circle or unity in which one cannot exist without the other. Birth flows into death and death into birth [3]. Children do not usually have the capacity to separate, classify, and organize parts of their world into a larger whole. Vogel explains that young children's views of death are not logical. This means that factual, rational responses to their questions will likely prove ineffective [5].

Nugent and Offord point out that young children in distress act out their anger, sadness, confusion, and loneliness through reactions that are adaptive [6]. Their behaviors are immediate, concrete expressions that provide them with a way to work out their grief without the more sophisticated cognitive functions of older children or adults. In addition, children's verbal skills are often not adequately developed to express the intensity and complexity of their grief. Zambelli and her associates advocate that the use of creative arts therapy in work with young children is most appropriate as it provides them with opportunities for non-verbal expression of feelings [7]. When they are grieving, the use of memory objects and participation in dramatic role play, music-making, and ritual are creative, concrete forms of expression that can help children to process their grief.

The Middle Years–Ages Six to Eight

During the middle years from ages six through eight, children begin to conceptualize their world in a more linear fashion. Cognitive functions advance so that children understand cause and effect relationships. They become less egocentric and experience a world containing forces beyond their control [3]. Magical components are still part of their thinking and they will often personify death as a powerful monster who threatens to take their loved ones away [3,6]. At this time, mutilation anxiety, the fear of bodily injury, may become prominent [8,9]. Children gradually develop an understanding that death is irreversible and unavoidable.

In the same manner as younger children, six- to eight-year-olds think concretely and frequently have difficulty verbally expressing their thoughts and feelings. Their grief work also requires the use of creative concrete forms of expression. McIntyre states that in the use of art, healing comes about through the creative transformation of pain and conflict during the process. The creative transformation is also expressed in the artist's interpretation of the product. One of the benefits of using art is that it allows for the expression of multiple feelings in a single image [10]. Through well-placed creative opportunities, we can help young children to tell us about their grief.

FAMILY DYNAMICS

Parents may find it difficult to assist their children in the grieving process, particularly if their own grieving skills are maladaptive. Wessel explains that parents may be reminded of unresolved early losses in their own lives and have difficulty watching their children grieve. They may also struggle with the fantasy of the devastating impact that their own death might have on their children [11].

Parents often assume that their children are too young to understand death and therefore are not capable of grief. The death of a parent, in particular, challenges young children's natural dependency needs. They require a great deal of reassurance that they will continue to be cared for by significant others. Wessel suggests that children cope with their loss much more successfully when the supervising adults are consistently available to recognize children's needs, help them discuss their thoughts and feelings, and encourage expression of grief [11].

Although young children may become anxious when they observe their parent's sadness and tears, adult modeling of normal grief reactions permits children to express their own grief. Webber explains that it is necessary to assess whether parents are able to remain physically and psychologically available to their children [12]. If parents are able to manage their own grief and provide emotional support, children will likely be able to begin to mourn. Children at risk often have parents who are preoccupied with their own grief and unable to help their children, leaving them emotionally isolated. In addition, it is important to examine previous losses in children's lives as they frequently demonstrate areas of strength and vulnerability [12]. The roles children play in the family system, as well as their unique relationship to the deceased, may also yield valuable information about how a death may affect them.

PROGRAM DESIGN

In the Notre Dame of St. Agatha program, referrals are received from parents, teachers, or other professionals already involved with the child or family. Three times a year, our groups are offered free of charge to the community. Initially, we prefer to gather basic intake information by telephone directly from parents. If our service appears to be suitable, a home visit for the purpose of assessment is scheduled, ideally to include all family members. In our assessment, we compile a family history and examine previous losses experienced by all family members. We assess family members' grieving patterns in order to determine whether or not individuals within the family are expressing their grief in adaptive or maladaptive ways and the impact this is having on the child. The suitability of the group for children is determined by the assessment information and our interaction with them during the home visit.

In preparing children for the group, we describe some of the group activities and explain why they will be attending. We also encourage them to tell us about some aspect of their grief, either by sharing a memory, a picture of the deceased, or a drawing.

A referral is considered appropriate if the following criteria are met:

- the death must be of a significant person
- the death has already occurred
- the child will be five years of age or older when the group commences
- the child can tolerate a group setting with a ratio of two co-leaders to eight children
- the child is not overwhelmed by previous and/or additional difficulties (i.e., social, emotional, or behavioral problems) that would impede his or her ability to tolerate group interaction.

At the time of intake or during our assessment period, an alternate referral is made if our services are deemed inappropriate. Family therapy or individual play therapy may also be recommended prior to children's attendance in our program, concurrently, or at time of discharge. From the beginning, we advise parents that due to limited resources, we can only offer short-term support.

Following the home visit, children are placed on a waiting list for the next available group. These are offered for one and one-half hours once per week, in the fall, winter, and spring. In the ninth and final session, after the children's groups have concluded, the leaders meet with parents. In a group setting, they are invited to share their observations of their children during the previous weeks and discuss effective strategies they have used to cope with their own grief while supporting their children. In addition, parents spend time in private consultation with a leader to review progress and share recommendations for follow-up support.

In three months, following the completion of the group, parents are contacted to discuss their children's current level of adjustment. We offer to provide any additional support they may require, including the exploration of referrals to other resources if needed. The children and parents are also asked to complete and return post-measurement questionnaires.

Continued assistance is offered at an annual reunion of all "grief group graduates" where the children and families have an opportunity to meet again and remember that they are not alone in their grief.

GRIEF RESPONSES IN YOUNG CHILDREN

Young children in our group program are challenged by the grieving process and exhibit a number of symptomatic reactions and associated difficulties that are manifested in their behavior, verbalized thoughts, and imaginative exploration. These are discussed in greater detail in the paragraphs that follow.

Cognitive Challenges

Cognitively, these children have difficulty grasping the complex concept of finality and irreversibility. Young children integrate the reality of death by asking many questions about the deceased and the circumstances surrounding the death. They understand their immediate world through concrete description. Their drawings frequently depict the actual death as they understand it or contain concrete symbols such as caskets and gravestones.

Memory Recall

Many young children have trouble recalling life with the deceased either because they were too young to retain memories or because the shock of the loss drove the memories and accompanying pain underground. Without memories, children feel cheated, angry, regretful, sad, and confused. When a close family member dies, they may feel disoriented and experience a loss of identity.

Emotional Intensity

Young children may be overwhelmed by the intensity of their feelings. In many cases, they are experiencing powerful and painful grief for the first time. Their ego development is not sufficient to manage frightening emotions. Recurring nightmares and trouble settling down to sleep at night are common complaints. Their fears are often intensified and many believe that bad things will continue to happen to them. Many children also lack the verbal skills to articulate their pain. Due to the emotional intensity, it is common for children to grieve in a stop-and-start pattern or to delay their grieving. Some children in our groups appear "frozen" with fear claiming they feel "nothing" or feel "normal" when asked to verbalize their feelings. They may run and hide under furniture, signaling clearly that they are not ready to process their grief. Others will smile when expressing feelings of anger and sadness about the death as if to mask or hide their true feelings from the world. Although ambivalent feelings toward the death are a natural component of mourning, they can be very confusing and overwhelming for young children (e.g., they may feel angry that the parent or sibling abandoned them and sad that the deceased is gone). By the end of the group, most of the children are able to identify their ambivalent feelings toward the death.

Alienation

Grieving young children often say that they feel weird, lonely, and out of step with their peers. Commonly, their peers have not experienced a death of a loved one and can hardly begin to comprehend the reality of grief. Many of the children in our groups talk about being teased about the death by peers. One boy, whose family members had died in a fire, was chased on the playground at school by children yelling "Fire." Children often express appreciation toward group participants for listening attentively, empathizing, and sharing their grief experiences.

Behavior

A number of grieving children referred to our program exhibit behavior difficulties at home and/or at school. The inner turmoil created by their grief may challenge the ego beyond the functioning capacity of young children. In this case, anxiety is externalized in non-compliant and aggressive behaviors which may become chronic if the children do not receive support for their grief. In our group, we observe that many of these children have difficulty waiting their turn, attending to group activities, and listening to others. They tend to express their anxiety with high levels of physical activity, short attention spans, and disruptive behavior. Additional emotional support and group interaction often helps them to gradually acquire the skills to participate more constructively.

We are intrigued by the feedback from parents and teachers indicating that approximately mid-way through our program, young children frequently exhibit increased non-compliant and aggressive behaviors. However, by the end of eight sessions, they report that these same children have stabilized significantly. Non-compliance and aggression usually decrease, as do parental concerns about other problems reported at the time of referral.

Fears of Abandonment

Young children will often interpret a parent's death as abandonment, causing them to be fearful and anxious. Children under the age of five years may exhibit regressive behaviors that include clinging to the surviving parent, having temper tantrums, and wetting the bed. Children over the age of five may become preoccupied with the safety of the surviving parent and frequently express fear that this parent will also abandon them. These children may perceive the world around them as frightening, chaotic, and beyond their control. They frequently express a longing for the nurturing previously provided by the deceased parent.

Family Reactions

Young children process their grief in the larger context of a family system. Their grief response will, in many ways, reflect their parent's coping responses. Children may also experience alienation within the family structure due to the added stress of grief on all family members. If a long illness precedes the death, young children may struggle with additional issues. They may feel deserted or neglected by one or both parents when family members are preoccupied with providing care for the dying person. They may also be angry and express feelings of resentment toward the ill person for depriving them of the attention that they usually receive from the family. When children feel alienated, feelings of sadness, loneliness, fear, anger, and guilt will often follow.

In addition, we have observed that when a parent is having difficulty moving beyond feelings of denial, children typically experience the same reaction. Similarly, when parents try to "protect" children by masking their own grief reactions, children are often reluctant to express feelings and talk about the death.

When the same sex parent dies, an only child or the eldest child in the family tends to assume too much responsibility. Some children idealize and attempt to emulate the qualities and perform the roles of the deceased parent. Girls will often become "little mothers" and boys, the "man of the house."

We have observed that when a parent is reaching out for support, children are comfortable expressing the same need. Also, when a parent is feeling well supported by other adults, children appear more confident and secure.

INTERVENTIONS

Group activities are designed to help children experience and come to terms with their thoughts and feelings about the death. Creative arts, ritual, and storytelling engage them in individual, as well as small and large group activities. When they work alone, they are encouraged to share their achievements and interpret their work within the group. Our group activities are thematically designed to assist young children to understand the permanence of death and to express their confusion or denial concerning the irreversibility of death.

Within the group, we encourage children to work with their memories through storytelling, drawing, and sharing of tangible memory items. We listen to and respond to their stories. Each story is explored through discussion with the leaders and the group members with a focus on clear, true facts concerning death itself. The children are curious to hear their peers' "death stories" and have an opportunity to grapple with the reality of death with each new story. Children decorate treasure boxes to hold their memory items and they share them enthusiastically with the group. They also draw happy and sad memories and share photographs of the deceased. Children who lack a clear recollection of their loved one are encouraged to explore feelings associated with the deceased and talk about "shattered dreams and wishes" of times they could have shared. One young boy whose father died, said that the hardest time for him was going to baseball practices without his dad.

At all times, children's questions and feelings concerning death are listened to carefully and validated by the leaders. Confusion is normalized and children are assured that continued longing and wishing for the return of the deceased is a normal grief response.

The memorial service is designed to honor the memory of the deceased. The children are invited to create and participate in a ritual that involves lighting a candle and making a drawing for the deceased, reading their own special biography of the deceased, saying prayers, reading poems, and playing music. At the end of the service, children are assisted to blow out their candles and to say "goodbye" to the dead person.

Ritual is set apart from the everyday world and can effectively create a safe "container" for intense emotion. The ritual components of the group are designed to create a special place where children can safely share their grief. The opening and closing rituals at the beginning and end of each session help to clearly define the nature of the grief group "container." A special table with a colorful cloth, a heart, and two candles serves as a focal point to honor the memory of the deceased and to validate feelings. To open, the candles are lit and participants respond with the phrase, "All of our thoughts and feelings are okay." The children place their memory items, photographs, and work completed that day on the special table. Each session also includes a "feelings check-in" at the beginning and a "sharing from the heart" exercise when we close. At the end of the session, the candles are blown out by a group member. This signals the transition back to daily activities.

In our groups, we encourage the children to tell us what they require to help them deal with their grief. We also respect their need to limit what they say or do. They are allowed to refuse to participate in an activity at any time. Our policy is not to push children when strong resistance is evident. We firmly believe that sometimes denial and withdrawal may serve as valuable ego defense mechanisms that can protect them from encountering or being overwhelmed by strong emotions. In a safe, nurturing environment, we encourage them to gently "open the door" to their feelings. We allow them to be our teachers and follow their lead. Group rules are outlined simply through discussion in order to provide a clear, predictable structure. The children are also told, in language that they understand, that their confidentiality will be respected.

With this age group, we are challenged to provide a nurturing environment that works for children while still maintaining gentle but firm direction for those presenting non-compliant and aggressive behaviors. In group discussions, we interpret such behavior as being symptomatic of grief and point out the importance of the underlying feelings (i.e., fear, anxiety, anger, and resentment). We also give children additional one-on-one assistance and encourage more appropriate ways of expressing their difficult feelings and receiving recognition and support.

In addition, we are aware that many children in the group exhibit high levels of anxiety that may be intensified with the recall of memories of the death or time spent with the deceased. This may make normally short attention spans even shorter and may accelerate already high activity levels to a point where some children are difficult to manage. Consequently, play that provides physical outlets and a variety of creative activities are needed to engage them in a non-threatening way. In some instances, we will take a break to exercise and "let off steam." One boy found running around the room helpful and regularly returned to this activity until he was ready to participate with the others again. Also, animal play, in which children act out the behaviors of various animals, allows them to release physical energy and experience their emotions through dramatic expression.

The atmosphere of peer support in the group reduces children's feelings of isolation. The leader helps to maintain this atmosphere by frequently asking if children share similar feelings and inviting them to discuss them with the group. Participants are not permitted to be disrespectful or to make fun of others. Children often say that they "feel safe" to cry and talk about their feelings. Issues of peer and sibling conflict are addressed through storytelling, drawing, problem-solving, and role playing.

From experience, we have learned that young children can face the reality of death best when we use a gentle and cautious approach that does not overwhelm them. During the first session, we only examine general loss through role playing and discussion. Activities are designed to allow children to express their emotions through play and physical expression (i.e., punching a "feelings pillow," banging on a drum, or acting out the behavior of a ferocious animal). Non-verbal expression helps children connect with feelings that may have been repressed or were too overwhelming to confront directly.

The children are also encouraged to verbally interpret their work for the group. As they assign meaning to their grief experiences, a new understanding of the process, as well as a greater sense of mastery, is achieved. This also helps to normalize the grief process and reassure them that the overwhelming emotions they are experiencing are not "crazy."

In our contact with parents, we emphasize that family support is the most important factor in assisting children to deal with grief. One of our group activities helps children examine their support structure. We read *The Fall of Freddie the Leaf* by Leo Bascaglia [13] and the children draw a tree of life, labeling each leaf with the name of a loved one who helped them cope with their grief. Most of the children express uncertainty about their world and fear that their caregivers will also die. Bonds are severed with significant others at a time when their needs for nurturing and permanence figure prominently. Through discussion and creative experiences, the children are encouraged to explore their fears concerning abandonment and their lives in general. We reassure children that being frightened is part of a normal reaction to grief. We assure them that we will work with them and their families to insure that they feel supported. When their support systems are inadequate, we usually make additional referrals as needed.

Helping these children requires a nurturing and guiding approach. The leaders must be willing to experience and understand their own responses to loss. Children's mourning may be inhibited if they sense that the leaders are reluctant to share their feelings. In reality, we revisit our own losses and our own grief may re-surface as we discuss the experiences of the children. Our modeling must include a willingness, when appropriate, to honestly share our own thoughts and feelings as well as what we have learned about ourselves prior to and during the group process. Through their interaction with us, children learn that strong feelings are manageable within a safe supportive framework and gain courage to face their own reactions.

We believe that it is important for the leaders to support each other. Outside of the group, we assist one another to debrief and process our personal reactions to what has transpired. Clinical guidance is also received from our external consultant and the Clinical Supervisor at Notre Dame of St. Agatha.

Case Study: Mark

Mark was referred at five years of age by his father. When he was two years old, Mark's mother died in a car accident. His father considered him to be too young to attend the funeral. When Mark's father contacted us, he was concerned that his son was having difficulty adjusting to kindergarten. Mark was exhibiting high activity levels, low frustration tolerance, irritability, and aggressiveness. His father and his teachers both complained that he was defiant and non-compliant. In addition, Mark was asking many questions about his mother's death.

During the home interview, Mark became increasingly anxious and actually ran out of the room when the discussion turned to the family's response to the death. When he eventually returned to the room, he had calmed down and was curious about the upcoming group.

In the group setting, Mark's high activity levels and general anxiety made it difficult for him to pay attention to group activities. Throughout the first four sessions, he was disruptive and easily distracted. He had difficulty listening to others and required almost constant one-on-one support and redirection. He seemed confused and "out of sorts." He truly looked lost. In the group, Mark was quite verbal (often inappropriately), inquisitive, and enjoyed taking his turns. His verbal abilities and curiosity served him well, as we were able to draw out his thoughts and feelings.

The key treatment concerns for Mark were:

- cognitive difficulty grasping the concept of death
- overwhelming intensity of emotions
- difficulty recalling memories
- sadness about never having said "good-bye" to his mother.

Effective strategies for Mark involved supporting him both emotionally and behaviorally. In order to minimize group disruption, it was essential to set firm, consistent, yet flexible limits. Mark was redirected each time he disrupted the group and when necessary, withdrawn briefly with support until he was ready to return. He was always invited to come back and try again.

Due to the intensity of his emotions, Mark expressed himself best through non-verbal activities. The most effective interventions for Mark were:

- physical expression and release through the use of the "feelings pillow"
- the "animal exercise" and movement breaks
- playing musical (percussion) instruments
- expressing a variety of feelings (sadness, anger, fear) about his mother's death
- sharing memory items with the group
- saying "goodbye" to his mother at the memorial service.

In the fifth session, a dramatic improvement was noted. He appeared more relaxed and his non-compliance and aggression virtually ceased. He began asking many specific questions of group members concerning the details of their losses and how they felt. Mark's behavior stabilized throughout the remaining sessions and he frequently expressed anger and sadness.

During the memorial service, Mark was focused and very involved in the process of saying "goodbye" to his mother. He was also able to praise another boy in the group for expressing anger. He coped well with the ending of the group and was able to say a meaningful "goodbye" to group members.

In the follow-up parent interview, his father noted that he had seen considerable improvement in Mark's behavior. Mark's teacher also observed improvement, stating that he "seemed like a different child." Coinciding with our assessment, Mark's father noted that "a remarkable change" in his behavior had occurred following the fifth session. Mark was now able to pay attention in class and play consistently for age-appropriate intervals. A follow-up telephone call three months after the group ended confirmed that Mark's progress had continued at both home and school.

Case Study: Sarah

Sarah was referred by her father when she was eight years of age. When Sarah was six, her mother had died of lung cancer after one year of illness. During this period, Sarah's mother remained at home and openly acknowledged to her family that she was dying.

Before her death at home, Sarah's mother expressed concern that her daughter was having difficulty facing and expressing her feelings about the inevitable death. Sarah's father explained that when her mother spoke of her illness, Sarah would sometimes run out of the room. Sarah cried a lot on the day of her mother's death and returned to school, on her own volition, the next day. She had difficulty sleeping for several months and exhibited no other apparent grief reactions in the nine months following the death.

When her first Christmas without her mother arrived, Sarah became increasingly non-compliant at home and school. She was physically aggressive with her younger sibling and showed anger toward her peers. For the first time, she began saying that she missed her mother. She also became lethargic and cried frequently.

In the group, Sarah was uncomfortable and anxious when she talked about her mother's death. She participated minimally in all of the activities, covering up her tears with a sweet smile. When encouraged to describe what was "behind" her smile, she would withdraw, become anxious, and hold back tears.

The key treatment issues for Sarah were:

- her delayed grief reaction (nine months) resulting in her fortified defense mechanism of smiling and optimism;
- her cognitive difficulty in grasping the concept of death. At age five, she had been neither cognitively nor emotionally equipped to understand and mourn the reality of her mother's death. Like many young children, Sarah "dealt" with her grief by proceeding as if nothing in her life had changed;
- overwhelming feelings of loneliness and despair without her mother.

Interventions with Sarah involved the provision of guidelines and encouragement within a nurturing environment to allow her grief to surface. In the sixth session, Sarah shared with the group that her mother had left wrapped Christmas presents for her family before her death and they appeared under the tree on Christmas morning.

The next week, Sarah brought a cuddly stuffed animal to the memorial service. It was the Christmas present her mother had left for her. While sharing her animal with the group, she began to cry and was unable to speak. She welcomed a hug from the leader and sobbed in her arms for one hour. At the end of the group, Sarah recovered and told us that she was lonely without her mother.

In the three month follow-up interview, her father reported that Sarah was talking openly at home about her mother and asking many questions about her death. She was exhibiting less non-compliance at home and school and her physical aggression had ceased.

METHODOLOGY

Data Collection

Our study sample consisted of thirty girls and boys between five and eight years of age and their parents. These children participated in bereavement groups from September 1990 to March 1992. Children in our sample group were referred by parents, teachers, doctors, and mental health professionals.

Our measurement devices consisted of two questionnaires received from the St. Mary's Grief Support Center in Duluth, Minnesota. These were: "The Childhood Depression Inventory" (C.D.I.) administered to each child, and "Behavioral Manifestations of Childhood Grief" administered to each parent(s)/guardian. Both were given prior to the beginning of the group and three months following its completion.

The C.D.I. is an ordinal measurement developed by M. Kovacs at the University of Pittsburgh School of Medicine. This instrument requires children to choose one out of three possible answers to twenty-seven questions. Responses are ranked from 0-2; a non-depressive response is indicated by 0, a depressive response indicated by 1, and a strong depressive response by 2.

The Childhood Depression Inventory provides a general picture of how the child is thinking and feeling and includes grief symptoms commonly evident in young children. A choice of answers is offered for each question ranging from a negative image of the world and one's self to a reasonably optimistic image. For example:

- I am bad all the time
- I am bad many times
- I am bad once in awhile.

The Behavioral Manifestations of Childhood Grief questionnaire is an ordinal measurement requiring parents to choose one out of four possible responses to seventeen questions categorized in terms of emotional, physical, and social manifestations of childhood grief. Based on the child's recent behavior, responses are ranked as either: N/A (not applicable); 0 (unchanged); -1 (decreased symptomatology); and +1 (increased symptomatology).

This device measures either an increase or decrease in emotional, physical, and social manifestations of childhood grief such as:

- depression (sadness, crying spells, listlessness)
- irritability (anger, impatience)
- death anxiety (nervous about death of self or others)
- denial of loss
- physical symptoms
- sleep disturbance (nightmares, insomnia)
- increased dependency
- social withdrawal
- acting-out behavior.

Additional measurement devices include separate Child and Parent Written Evaluations completed at the end of the group. These elicit subjective responses and most are open-ended (i.e., "How did you feel about the death before coming to the group?" and "What changes do you see in your child that you attribute to the group?").

Data Analysis

Eighty percent of the group participants completed and returned the pre- and post-Child Depression Inventory questionnaires. The most predominant symptoms expressed in the pre-group measures included:

- sadness, most or all of the time
- fear that bad or terrible things will happen to the child
- low self-esteem (i.e., "I am bad most or all of the time," "I do not like myself," and "I can never be as good as other kids.")
- alienation and isolation (i.e., "I do not like being with people many times" and "I feel alone many times.")

The post-group responses indicated a general decrease in all of the above symptoms. Post-group overall scores were lower for nineteen of the twenty-four respondents, indicating a reduction of grief-related symptoms. The remaining five respondents revealed a slight increase. In some cases, the group process will intensify symptoms, particularly in those children who, at the time of referral, exhibit signs of arrested grief or denial of loss.

In the pre-group data gathered from the Behavioral Manifestations of Childhood Grief questionnaire completed by parents, the following grief symptoms were cited as having increased most often: irritability, depression, death anxiety, nervousness, denial of loss, acting-out behavior, and problems in school.

The post-group measurement data on the same questionnaire revealed a decrease in all of the above symptoms since the pre-group testing as shown in Table 1.

The Child Written Evaluations revealed some of the children's perceptions of their grief at the end of the group. In response to the question "How did you feel about the death in your family before coming to the group?", 79 percent answered "sad." Other responses included "angry," "scared," and "alone." In response to the question "How do you feel now?", 64 percent noted improvement (i.e., "a lot better than I used to" or "a little more happy than sad"). Thirty-eight percent responded with "sad."

When asked "What did you like about the group?", most respondents listed several activities. Of eighty activities mentioned, 66 percent expressed a preference for imaginative or ritual activities (i.e., animal exercises, drawing, playing musical instruments, candle lighting, and "sharing from the heart"). Their preference supports our claims that creative activities help children to express their grief.

When they began attending the group, many of the children were unable to identify any grief-related feelings. When the group ended, all of the children were able to verbalize these feelings. The majority of the children reported one or more improvements in their lives or increased well-being at the end of the group. However, we must note that improvement does not necessarily indicate an absence of grief, but perhaps a better understanding of it (i.e., "a little more happy than sad, but still a little sad").

The Parent Written Evaluation was completed during the final parent session. We asked, "What changes do you see in your child that you attribute to the group?" Ninety-four percent reported one or more improvements, i.e., "knows she's not alone," "more affectionate,"

Table 1. Decreases in Grief Symptoms

Grief Symptoms	Percentage of Decrease
Irritability	63.0
Depression	62.5
Death anxiety	62.5
Nervousness	80.0
Denial of loss	64.0
Problems in school	100.0

"improved behavior and concentration." Sixty-one percent reported "greater awareness of feelings."

When asked "Were there any particular aspects of the group that you or you child liked?", 33 percent described creative/ritual activities and 37 percent highlighted working with feelings. Some parents appreciated that their children did not feel alone, they felt accepted and supported, or they "could talk openly about the death."

In response to the question, "Were there any aspects of the group that you would like to change?", 78 percent requested that parents have increased involvement with their child's experiences while in the group. In response to this request, we now send home weekly group process notes including suggested family follow-up activities. We have yet to receive feedback from parents, but hope that this will promote increased communication and support within the family. In addition, many parents asked why similar groups were not available for adults in the community.

When asked "Would you recommend this group to others in similar circumstances?", all respondents answered "yes." The parents' responses indicated general satisfaction with the group process. The majority of parents noted that their children had achieved a greater awareness of feelings, accompanied by less anxiety. They thought that our work with the expression of feelings through creative and ritual activities were effective.

In discussions with parents and teachers at the end of the group, incidents of positive change included the following examples:

- began to grieve several years following a death
- had her anger about not attending the funeral of a family member validated, resulting in improved parent-child communication
- became less angry and aggressive
- began to ask many questions about the deceased person and wanted to visit the cemetery
- was able to sleep better
- understood the permanency of death
- stopped setting fires as soon as the group began
- experienced fewer incidents of enuresis and became less clinging
- found it easier to concentrate in school.

Parents' observations generally reflected that their children had acquired a greater ability to experience and express their grief in appropriate ways.

The data collected at the three month follow-up telephone contact with parents indicated that with family support, children were able to maintain and generalize gains made while attending the group. Parents generally noted that:

- aggression had decreased (i.e., improved frustration tolerance)
- children were continuing to talk about the deceased
- teachers reported improvements
- communication skills had increased
- children were now able to cry.

Parents sometimes tell us that the openness of their children's expression of grief has become a catalyst for their families to share and support one another through grief. This is in keeping with our goal to better equip children and families to grieve and heal together.

A more precise study of bereaved children and families would include a larger sample measured against a comparative control group that would consist of families that choose not to seek professional assistance. However, the overwhelming positive changes observed in our clients strongly suggest that group treatment and family support may lessen the burden of grief. This serves as a stimulus for continuing our program.

CONCLUSION

Our research and observations support the growing recognition that children grieve in accordance with their cognitive and emotional development and the family's response to death. In our clinical experiences, we have seen the loss of a loved one shatter the foundations of the worlds of many children. Our work is based on the conviction that if grieving children do not receive adequate support to build a new functional view of their world, they will remain vulnerable to long-term social, emotional, and somatic difficulties. Grief is a powerful journey through pain and healing for both children and adults. When children are allowed to experience normal grief reactions, a healing process unfolds. Our group setting provides children with peer and adult support to put this in motion.

When children experience the healing power of a supportive group process, their burden of grief is significantly lifted. As much as possible we follow their lead, validate their concerns, and guide them through their feelings. The safety of the group is reinforced by a regular format, consistent expectations, nurturing leadership, and creative activities that engage children at their developmental levels. For many children, the group "container" represents an invitation to "try out" their grief responses until they feel safe enough to share them with family members. At all times, we encourage parents to cultivate a safe place within the family for children to express their grief.

The family is the nucleus of a young child's world. The family's grieving pattern influences how well young children manage their grief. Our goal is to empower both children and parents to cope with their grief. We fortify parents to attend more effectively to their own, as well as their children's needs. In the parent session, we explain that their children will likely revisit their grief throughout the developmental process and suggest family work and resources to equip them for the future. Our task is to set the stage for the real drama to unfold within the family.

Future plans for the growth of our program include additional family involvement prior to and during the children's attendance at the group, as well as increased follow-up support. Concurrent family groups have been proposed in order to help parents deal with their grief and understand their children's needs. We hope to implement these in the near future in collaboration with community agencies. We have also been approached by an increasing number of professionals (i.e., therapists, social workers, clergy, and teachers) requesting consultation and additional services for bereaved families and children who require individual play therapy. Additional crisis support available at the time of death is a needed resource in our community as well. With increased staff and resources, we hope to eventually provide crisis support to families prior to and following the death, and offer individual play therapy for children when required. We also envision the creation of a bereavement resource and training center for community professionals.

Our research component has grown with the recent implementation of three month, six month, and yearly follow-up studies utilizing pre- and post-measurement devices (C.D.I. and Behavioral Manifestations of Childhood Grief). Three and five year follow-up studies have also been proposed to measure longitudinal factors in childhood grief and the long-term efficacy of our treatment.

We face some of our deepest vulnerabilities in our personal response to loss. When we share these fragile and authentic moments of grief with a child, a mutual healing takes place. In our work, the healing power of the grief journey is affirmed in the group setting as we witness bereaved children developing new strengths and startling insights into the nature of life.

REFERENCES

1. P. R. Silverman and J. W. Worden, Detachment Revisited, *American Journal of Orthopsychiatry, 62*:4, pp. 494-503, 1992.
2. A. Wolfelt, *Children at Risk Because of Death*, Lecture, King's College, London, Ontario, May 1992.
3. R. Lonetto, Children's Concepts of Death, in *Children and Death*, J. D. Morgan (ed.), King's College, London, Ontario, 1985.
4. H. Maier, *Three Theories of Child Development*, Harper and Row, New York, 1969.
5. L. Vogel, *Helping a Child Understand Death*, Fortress Press, Philadelphia, 1975.
6. K. Nugent and D. Offord, *Bereavement in Childhood: Impact and Preventive Strategies*, McMaster University, Hamilton, Ontario, unpublished manuscript.
7. G. C. Zambelli, E. Johns Clark, L. Barile, and A. F. de Jong, An Inter-Disciplinary Approach to Grace: Clinical Intervention for Childhood Bereavement, *Death Studies, 12*, pp. 41-50, 1988.
8. A. Dyregrov, *Grief in Children: A Handbook for Adults*, Jessica Kingsley Publications, London, 1990.
9. T. Huntley, *Helping Children Grieve*, Augseberg, Minneapolis, Minnesota, 1991.
10. B. McIntyre, Art Therapy with Bereaved Youth, *Journal of Palliative Care, 6*:1, pp. 16-25, 1990.
11. M. Wessel, *Children, When Parents Die*, Lecture, Second World Congress on Terminal Care, Montreal, Quebec, October 1978.
12. C. Webber, Diagnostic Interventions with Children at Risk, in *Childhood Bereavement and Its Aftermath*, S. Altschul (ed.), International University Press, Madison, Connecticut, 1988.
13. L. Bascaglia, *The Fall of Freddie the Leaf: A Story for All Ages*, Slack Incorporated, Thorofare, New Jersey, 1982.

BIBLIOGRAPHY

Bowlby, J., Childhood Mourning and Its Implication For Psychiatry, *American Journal of Psychiatry, 118*, pp. 481-498, December 1961.
Elkind, D., *Children and Adolescents*, Oxford University Press, New York, 1981.
Grollman, E. A., Explaining Death To Children, *The Journal of School Health*, pp. 336-339, June 1977.
Grollman, E. A., The Child and Death, *Canadian Funeral Director*, pp. 17-19, April 1978.
Kastenbaun, R., The Child's Understanding of Death: How Does it Develop? in *Explaining Death To Children*, E. A. Grollman (ed.), Beacon Press, Boston, 1967.

Morgan, J. D. (ed.), *Young People and Death*, The Charles Press, Philadelphia, 1991.

Wolfelt, A., *Helping Children Cope With Grief*, Accelerated Development Inc., Muncie, Indiana, 1983.

Wolfelt, A., Ten Common Myths about Children and Grief—Part I, *Bereavement Magazine*, pp. 38-40, January 1992.

Wolfelt, A., Ten Common Myths about Children and Grief—Part II, *Bereavement Magazine*, pp. 38-40, February 1992.

CHAPTER 11

Interventions with Bereaved Children Nine to Thirteen Years of Age: From a Medical Center-Based Young Person's Grief Support Program

Ben S. Wolfe and Linda M. Senta

We have learned much throughout the eleven years of facilitating bereavement groups for children and adolescents at St. Mary's Medical Center. During this time over 600 youngsters have participated in the Young Person's Grief Support Program (YPGSP). As each group begins we remind ourselves of the need to be flexible, and to help children to develop coping skills to deal with both the short-term concerns identified upon entry and long-term needs for positive coping patterns. We strongly believe that bereavement support groups for youngsters facilitate children's healthy adjustment to the death of a parent, sibling, grandparent, relative, or friend. We also recognize that not all youngsters and their family members benefit from groups. Our role as facilitators is to help children and their families make informed decisions about how to cope and to empower these youngsters to integrate a death into their lives, move on, and feel better after leaving the group than when they entered.

As adults we need to look at grief from a child's perspective. Grief is not something that gets "fixed" in a few weeks by attending a support group. Grief is an ongoing process which will reappear at different times in the youngster's life and will be viewed differently at each new "reappearance."

Questions from parents, relatives, friends, teachers, clergy, funeral personnel, health care professionals, and therapists related to impending death and bereavement issues are directed to us continuously. Some of these are: "Do you have groups for young people?" "When can my youngster start the group, his father just died one week ago?" "Should they go to their sister's funeral . . . it might be too hard on them?" "Is it okay if they really want to go back to school tomorrow, only one day after the death?" "Is there something wrong with my daughter? It's been three years and now she is starting to grieve?" "Since his grandparent's death he will not let us out of his sight." "After her brother's death she seems to be moving right along as if nothing happened. Does this mean it hasn't affected her?"

As an umbrella for various programs and services, St. Mary's Grief Support Center (GSC) in Duluth, Minnesota, was developed in 1985 as an extension of St. Mary's Medical Center and is located within the Social Services Department. The GSC provides a comprehensive program of counseling, support, advocacy, education, and research for individuals who are dealing with, or affected by, an impending death or who are bereaved. Programs and services are available to individuals and families within St. Mary's and throughout the region, as well as people in health and educational institutions, members of the community, and specialized groups in northern sections of Minnesota, Wisconsin, and Michigan.

Bereavement program consultation is also provided to churches, hospitals, hospice programs, physicians, funeral directors, first responders, community groups and agencies, schools and universities, and private industry throughout the United States, Canada, and overseas. The GSC's Young Person's Grief Support Program, originally developed in 1983, has been replicated in numerous locations in the United States, Canada, Great Britain, and Australia.

The goal of this chapter is to share what we have found useful when working with nine- to thirteen-year-old youngsters in bereavement support groups. It is important to recognize that there is a fine line between support groups and therapy groups. We believe that the children who participate in bereavement groups, and the persons who refer them, are seeking emotional and social **support** due to the death, not therapy. The youngsters are not directly trying to change their behavior, nor are they trying to analyze what happened by exposure to people who confront them about their actions and interpersonal conflicts. In addition, most bereaved children do not enter the group because they are clinically depressed or suicidal. Instead, they want to learn how to cope with the internal and external changes that death brings. Although grief is personal, most young people experience common feelings when coping with a death. Our job is to help them share these feelings and experiences, advocate on their behalf in the adult world, and provide assistance to their parents and guardians as needed.

Some Parents Comments on Why their Children have been Referred to the Young Person's Grief Support Program

One mother of an eleven-year-old girl said her daughter's behavior led to her participation in the group. She stated:

> She couldn't get along with friends, and this led to fights. She didn't want to go to school and her grades dropped. After group finished she started to relax and not keep things to herself. She started to realize a lot of her problems had been brought on by herself. She started to leave her own little world and be with others.

The mother of a thirteen-year-old boy who was ordered by the court to attend the group recounted how the group had influenced his behavior:

> After the sessions were finished he wasn't mad any more. He didn't blame himself for his dad's death, his grades improved, his truancy improved and he got better at listening, minding, and accepting responsibility.

When an eleven-year-old girl became anxiety-ridden, her mother enrolled her in the group. She stated:

> She was afraid I was going to die. She was afraid to go to sleep at night. She wouldn't go to school as she was afraid to leave me and wouldn't spend nights away from home. I had to make her take showers where before she would do it on her own on a daily basis. After group she was more relaxed, back to "normal," and started to go to school again. She is even staying at friends' houses again now, which she couldn't do one year ago.

In another situation, the mother of a nine-year-old girl described how her daughter's emotions and school performance changed after her grandmother's death, resulting in referral to the group. She said:

> Her grades went down and she was not as cheerful, she was sad. She wouldn't want to be away from me and was mad at her dad. She started to steal, and said she always thought about Nana and

then she would steal. It hasn't happened since group finished. She's a lot more confident now and knows her feelings are real and okay. She's started to lighten up. Compared to one year ago, she is 100 percent better.

CHILDREN AND GRIEF: AN OVERVIEW

Furman viewed the death of a significant person as a serious stressor for children that may lead to the adaptive process of mourning and successful coping with the loss or to an inability to mourn, with the loss remaining an unmastered burden [1]. She identified a number of factors that interact to assist or hinder mourning. These include: 1) individual characteristics of the children; 2) their relationship with the deceased; 3) life stressors preceding and following the death; and 4) the emotional support provided by parents and others.

Other factors which may also affect children's mourning include: the cause of the person's death—expected, unexpected, or violent; the age of the person who died; the age and developmental level of bereaved children; their past experiences with death, loss, and other crises; their level of cognitive functioning; where they lived at the time of the death; their cultural, spiritual, or religious backgrounds; their financial status and personal health; and the structure of their families.

Like adults, children are concerned about dying and death. Grief is often more traumatic and severe for a child than for an adult. The outcome of their grief is less predictable and may be more emotionally crippling because children are building a foundation for growth and development [2]. Many youngsters, after the death of a family member or friend, have problems relating to peers, are unwilling to remain in school, and have learning deficiencies. Behavioral difficulties characterized by withdrawal, anger, depression, guilt, delinquency, alcohol and chemical use, inability to communicate, clinging to adults, nightmares, and aggressiveness may also be amplified [3-6]. Youngsters may lie, steal, destroy their own things, and develop somatic complaints such as stomach-aches, headaches, or insomnia. Problems with bladder and bowel control or regressive behavior such as kicking, biting, and temper tantrums are also possible.

Some children and adolescents who are grieving may experience emotional distress that is severe enough to impede their development and adjustment. Studies have shown that the death of a parent may delay grieving [7]. Apart from infants, children who are bereaved in early childhood are at the highest risk for developing emotional disturbances, but these may not surface until adolescence. On some occasions, individuals in our adult grief support groups have indicated that their problems stem from a death of a significant person in their childhood. Although there are conflicting research findings, the literature supports the fact that when children have not mourned successfully, they may encounter depression, gender identification difficulties, somatic complaints, and even psychosis in adulthood [8-9].

Foster said that when they are bereaved:

> Children should be encouraged to talk freely about being born and about dying and death. They need to express their fears and fantasies to someone who can listen. Parents may not always be able to do this after a death, because it appears that the behaviour of the parent is dictated by their own inner needs rather than by a realistic appreciation of their children's feelings [10, p. 541].

Parents or guardians may also feel so overwhelmed that they cannot talk with their children about the death. Families who do not converse about their loss are at greater risk for behavior problems in their offspring than families where discussion about the dead person and his or her importance in their lives is encouraged [11]. Evans, Rosen, and Rosenthal each reported that when this happens, problems such as developmental fixation, acting out behaviors, and psychological disturbances may result [12-14]. Demi and Gilbert suggest that there is a relationship between children's use of denial and avoidance and the intrusiveness of their parents' style of grieving [15]. Clearly, children are very prone to responding to their parents' mourning behavior. Samaniego, in studying children ages six to ten years whose parents had died, found that those who were poorly adjusted came from families that allowed only infrequent discussion and little expression of emotions concerning the deceased [16]. In contrast, parents of well-adjusted children cried in front of the children, encouraged talking about the deceased, and took the children on regular family visits to the grave. These children also experienced greater stability within their families. Wolff suggested that parents will only be able to adopt realistic and helpful attitudes toward their children when parents are helped to master feelings that become conflicted in the face of death [17].

FAMILIES AND CHANGING TIMES

When families experience the death of a family member, relative, or friend, how does the family react? Wolfe describes the family unit as a mobile, with the entire structure changing its shape while trying to maintain an equilibrium [18]. The "parts" are all interrelated and what affects one part of the mobile will affect the others. Each "part" will grieve in his or her own way. Sprenkle and Piercy provide a systems approach that recognizes the interrelated, interdependent nature of behavior among bereaved family members [19]. If the behavior of one family member changes the entire family may be affected.

When we discuss "families," many individuals still see images of the traditional family, with the father employed and the mother at home. Today, reality paints an entirely different picture. For example, in the United States there are many family configurations. Over the past twenty years, we have witnessed a steady increase in families without fathers, children without families, and families without homes [20]. Perhaps one of the most dominant changes in family structure has been the steady flow of mothers into the work force. Over 65 percent of women with children ages three to five years are employed, representing the fastest growing portion of the U.S. labor market. In 1989, 75 percent of all mothers with children ages six to eighteen years were in the labor force [21]. By 1995, it is predicted that nearly 65 percent of all preschool children and 80 percent of school-age children will have mothers in the work force [22]. In addition, the divorce rate has increased sharply, single parenthood continues to grow, and gay and lesbian relationships are increasing. Families now consist of larger numbers of step-parents, cohabitating couples, and teens who are having children. When we consider the impact of these changes on children, we must also recognize that Palombo reported that almost 6 percent of American children from birth to eighteen years are faced with the death of one or both parents [23]. When we add the potential deaths of other family members and losses faced by children, many may be in need of support from sources outside of their families.

HISTORY AND STRUCTURE OF THE MEDICAL CENTER-BASED YOUNG PERSON'S GRIEF SUPPORT PROGRAM

The YPGSP began in November 1983 and was originally designed for youngsters nine to thirteen years of age. Prior to the beginning of the program, a large number of requests from professionals, relatives, and organizations were received by the Medical Center requesting assistance for bereaved young persons [24].

In the summer of 1983, there were only two group programs for seriously ill or bereaved children in Minnesota. One was only for young cancer patients and their siblings, and the other for bereaved siblings whose brother or sister had died from any type of injury or illness.

Since Duluth lacked the large population of Minneapolis and St. Paul (where the existing groups were located), we decided to establish a program that would be suitable for all youngsters who were bereaved from any death that affected them. We also decided that we would not have any "absolute time rules" for entry into our program, but that it would likely be inappropriate to admit newly bereaved children. This criteria continues to work extremely well. During the eleven years the program has been operational, youngsters have joined groups in time spans ranging from one week to ten years following a death. Over the years we have had parents, due to the impending death of a family member or friend, put their child or children on the "next group list" in order to be certain that they would be accepted. Most youngsters have joined a group between two months and one year after the death. The groups are only for bereaved youngsters and we only allow their friends to come for "moral support" if they knew the person who died.

Originally, the YPGSP sessions for nine- to thirteen-year-olds were conducted weekly for seven weeks during the fall, winter, and spring. Six weeks were for the youngsters and the seventh week for their parents and/or guardians. As a result of parent contact in the fall of 1984, it was clear that groups were needed for children younger and older than ages nine to thirteen years. The program was revised in order to accommodate five- to nine-year-old and ten- to fifteen-year-old children.

For the past nine years, our groups have been offered for children ages five to eight, nine to thirteen, and fourteen to seventeen years. Youngsters participate for seven straight weeks with the eighth week involving their parents and/or guardians. Programs still operate during the fall, winter, and spring on separate days during the week. Each group meets at the Medical Center from 3:30 to 5:00 P.M. in a comfortably furnished room.

Groups are intended to consist of no more than eight, nor less than four participants. On only two of the eighty-six times we have offered the program have we had fewer than four participants. It has been more common to have more than eight youngsters per group. On average our groups have started with 7.4 youngsters; of those, an average of 6.2 youngsters per group (87%) have completed the sessions with minimal absenteeism. Of the 633 youngsters who have completed the programs, 56 percent were girls, and 44 percent were boys.

Although participants have sometimes complained that there were too few sessions, we believe that seven weeks is long enough to work through a sufficient number of issues.

We have excellent parent and guardian attendance at the group meeting in the eighth week. They share observations, evaluate the program, and learn ways to continue to help their children. In their confidential evaluations, parents continue to comment that the parent sessions are beneficial.

During the first three years, ongoing support groups were offered for those who "graduated" from the initial grief support program. Three months after their group was finished, and every six months thereafter, "program graduates," and their parents or guardians, came back to the Medical Center and met with their original facilitators and their groups in order to determine how well the youngsters were managing. An annual pot-luck barbecue and games afternoon was also held in August of each year for six years for "graduates," their families, and friends. Unfortunately, due to time constraints, we have been unable to continue these activities.

When we examine the success of our program, it is encouraging to note that many of the parents or guardians who took part in either home interviews or parent meetings have also attended the Grief Support Center for one of the following groups: the Adult Program, Parent(s) whose child died under five years of age, Parent(s) whose child died over five years, SIDS, or Suicide. Many of these parents or guardians have also sought individual counseling through the Center.

Each YPGSG has two professional facilitators. Our experience and bias is that a female and male are best. However, it is possible that the effectiveness of facilitation may depend more on the personalities of the facilitators and their ability to deal with young people than on gender. Our facilitators have included medical social workers, bereavement counselors, and university students in medicine, psychology, or social work.

The major component of the program, which we have included from the beginning and feel strongly about, is the need to interview each child and at least one parent or guardian in their own home before group participation begins. The home visit is not a screening process. Instead, it is a way of getting to know the youngsters, understand their roles in the family, talk with them in their home environment, and give them the opportunity to meet informally with the facilitators. Parents have indicated on their evaluations that the home visits are appreciated with remarks such as: "Excellent idea." "Great, she felt more comfortable in familiar surroundings and not walking in without knowing anyone." "I liked the idea very much—it was good for my son to meet you and get an idea of what was going to happen in class."

Due to problems with time and distance, home interviews are not feasible for children who live beyond twenty-five miles from the Medical Center. Consequently, we meet these children in our offices prior to the first session. When possible, both group facilitators try to participate in all interviews but this has become more difficult in recent years due to workload. This has not been a problem as youngsters are familiar with at least one person when they arrive for the first group session.

Before we conduct our initial interviews, registrations for the program are received by phone and are only accepted from parents or guardians. At the time of registration, information about the youngsters are recorded, including whether or not they will be able to accurately "tell the story" of how the person(s) died and remember who gave them the information. This is particularly important because on numerous occasions, we have experienced situations where parents have finally "told the truth" about how the person died on the day before participants attended their first session. These parents thought that it would be too painful for the youngsters to know the truth before the sessions began. We believe that children need to know the truth directly from their parent(s) or guardian(s). It is **not** the role of the facilitators to tell "the story." However, facilitators can often help parents by providing possible approaches to consider when providing detailed information to their youngsters or correcting what was once considered to be the "truth."

As mentioned previously, the home visit is essential. We are convinced that personal contact with potential participants in **their own environment** makes a tremendous difference in facilitating group interaction and saving time on the first day. Over the years, parents have commented that their youngsters probably would not have participated in the program if we had not met them on their "own turf." We do not make phone calls to others about the program unless the referring professional, friend, or relative has advised these people that they were calling on their behalf and granted us permission to call them. We do not solicit our services.

WHAT IS MEANT BY
"TASKS FOR BEREAVED CHILDREN?"

More than fifty studies have examined children's understanding of death. This research has demonstrated that the concept of death is made up of several components. Three of the most widely studied are: 1) universality, the understanding that all living things die; 2) irreversibility, the recognition that once a living thing dies its physical body cannot be made alive again; and 3) nonfunctionality, the knowledge that all life-defining functions cease at death [25]. Speece and Brent note that the literature suggests that most children achieve a mature understanding of death somewhere between five and twelve years of age [25].

It is also important to recognize that there are the "psychological tasks" that must be undertaken by bereaved children. *"Tasks"* of grief have been used by Furman, and others in more recent conceptualizations of bereavement [1, 26-28]. *Early tasks* begin as soon as the child learns of the death. They involve gaining an understanding of what has happened, while employing self-protective mechanisms to guard against the full emotional impact of the loss. *Middle-phase tasks* include accepting and reworking the loss, and bearing the accompanying intense psychological pain. *Late tasks* include the consolidation of the child's identity and a resumption of progress on age-appropriate developmental issues. Baker, Sedney, and Gross state that in the present models these tasks are seen as time-specific, but remind us that they change over time [29]. In our work, these "tasks" are extremely important. We will revisit them in the detailed review of what happens in the support group sessions.

HOW DO WE HELP BEREAVED
NINE- TO THIRTEEN-YEAR-OLDS?

The following section describes each session of our eight week YPGSP and demonstrates how various techniques, as they relate to children's "tasks of grief," have been helpful for youngsters nine to thirteen years of age. These same techniques, with some modifications, can also be extremely helpful for younger and older children.

YPGSP–Session One

The first session is the most important and must connect youngsters to the group, allow them to feel safe and secure, and help them recognize the importance of what will happen in group interaction. This session should provide the "glue" that will keep them wanting to return for session two and beyond. As facilitators, we have learned that if we can encourage children to return for session number two, they will likely attend all of the sessions. During this first session, we explain the history of the YPGSP and review the "rules" of the group. There are only two "rules." These pertain to confidentiality and mandatory reporting by the facilitators of any concerns about the safety of the participants. We explain to the participants that after talking with them, we will contact their parents or guardians if we are concerned about their safety. We inform them that this is their group and that members are not only valued, but encouraged to participate to the extent that they feel comfortable. We also inform them there will be no grades given and not much homework. We encourage the youngsters to share whatever they wish about the group with their parents or guardians.

After the facilitators introduce themselves and "model" what is being expected, group members introduce themselves. This helps them to gain information about each other and "loosen up." It is not until later in the session that the youngsters describe, in detail, who died and the circumstances surrounding the death(s). During the group sessions, it is important for facilitators to be aware that their own memories of previous deaths and grieving experiences may return quietly and unexpectedly. Disclosure by facilitators of their thoughts and feelings, if used appropriately, may serve as a model for the participants and add to the group process.

In this first session, youngsters learn to appreciate that other group members are experiencing similar feelings and concerns. They are given the opportunity to share their personal "stories" about each death. Although it is never our goal to upset youngsters, this first session can be very emotional and tearful. Facial tissues are always available but facilitators do not hand them to participants. It is acceptable, however, for the youngster to take a tissue, or to have another group member pass the box to them.

From our experiences we have learned that humor is as important as tears. The group sessions need to be as "light" as they are emotional. This first session is no exception. A balance is needed to avoid overwhelming a youngster who is not used to sharing intimate stories. Participants may ask themselves, "If session number one was this heavy, do I really want to come back for more?" We certainly do not want to challenge fragile youngsters. We would like them to appreciate us as guides who help them explore their thoughts and feelings, learn new information, determine what choices are available, and empower them to work through their grief. Youngsters who feel defensive will not come back!

Early tasks begin as soon as the child learns of the death. They involve gaining an understanding of what has happened, while employing self-protective mechanisms to guard against the full emotional impact of the loss. Telling their "story" about the death means that participants have received the details from their parent or guardian. This is, as Furman noted, an indispensable first step in mourning [1]. Children need to be given general information about death and specific information about the death that affects them directly, in language that is appropriate for their level of development and understanding. It is important to remember that bereaved children often learn as much from adults by what is not said, as they do from what is said. To hide information or keep secrets from a pre-adolescent is only asking for trouble. Later, as part of their natural development in adolescence they will treat adults with negativism. Any "false information" given now may only add to their mistrust in the future. As facilitators, we must be sensitive to each youngster, but we must also ask probing questions and seek out information that may not have been shared with others prior to attending the group.

Case Example: Bob

Bob was twelve years old when his mother told him he had to stay at home with his younger sister while his older brother and mother would be flying to be with his injured father. He had just been severely burned in an accident on a ship where he was working. His burns were so severe and extensive that when Bob's brother and mother entered the hospital they were told, "It's going to shock you, he has almost doubled in size due to liquid retention." In their presence, his father died hours later in a Burn Unit located in a large city hospital.

Bob was informed of the death by a minister in his home community. He was angry because he was not able to see his father or be there when he died. He was concerned that some information may have been kept from him, and upset because he was not treated with the same respect as his seventeen-year-old brother. Prior to attending the group, a few months after his father's death, Bob had been treated in an adolescent mental health unit due to his comments about potentially harming himself. He was also seen by one of the group facilitators in family counseling sessions a few weeks before the bereavement group started.

One of the major issues identified in family counseling, was Bob's concern about his father's appearance. He wondered, "What did my father really look like after the fire?" It was apparent he was not going to "let go" of this concern. Consequently, one family session focused on whether Bob should have been allowed to see what had taken place. His mother said that a videotape had been shown on the local television station in the community where her husband died. It was decided that the videotape would help Bob learn about what had happened and see how his father looked directly after the fire when he was being transported to an ambulance. The youngster was pleased with the opportunity, and prior to group saw the tape, over and over again. At first, Bob's mother had been concerned about telling Bob everything, but it was obvious her concerns were short-lived. Bob needed to know what happened.

During the first session of the YPGSP, Bob cried openly and freely while he told the story of his father trying to save others and discussed his feelings about not being there when his father died. He acknowledged that it was important to have all of the information about the accident available, including the details of what took place in the Burn Unit, the death, and what happened to his father's body after he died. Bob told the group that he now felt that all of the information had been shared with him.

Case Example: Joanne

Joanne was thirteen years old when she attended the group. She was only recently informed that her mother had committed suicide thirteen years ago, one month after Joanne was born. Joanne only knew that her mother had died shortly after her birth. Her mother's death was the "family secret" and even her step-mother felt the need to maintain it. When she learned the truth, Joanne was upset and directed her anger at her father, step-mother, and step-sister. She was jealous of her step-sister, and her step-sister's birth raised questions about her own mother. Her anger created problems at home and school. The only way that she received any positive attention was through her participation in sports, where she excelled.

In the first session, Joanne discussed her knowledge of her mother's death and the group talked about postpartum depression. It was agreed that Joanne would learn more about the death for the next session. When asked how she would gather this information, she said that she would approach her grandparents, including her mother's biological parents and her father's parents.

In the following session, Joanne openly shared what had happened and described what her grandparents were feeling as a result of Joanne's need to raise the topic thirteen years after her mother's death.

Throughout the remaining sessions, Joanne participated freely and openly. She sought new insights into her feelings and behavior from the facilitators and other group members, and developed new friendships. Some of her new friends also had a family member who had committed suicide. Despite her positive adaptation to the group, Joanne continued to have difficulties at home. Months after the group was completed, she moved in with her paternal grandparents.

Activity: Journal Keeping

In this first session, we help youngsters to use journaling. We teach them that journals are personal and useful when ideas, feelings, or thoughts surface and they feel comfortable jotting them down. We stress that grammar and sentence structure are not important and that journal entries can often be just words or thoughts. Journals can be kept in a notebook, on blank pages, or in a "special blank pages book" given to each youngster. We believe that the journal should not be a diary, should not be time-consuming, or take the place of "listening ears." Journaling provides an opportunity for personal awareness and a way to explore how grief is experienced and internalized. Journals are private and may be shared with the group, the facilitators, or no one.

The following is an example of excerpts from a youngster's journal:

Wednesday: Nobody knows how it feels when a parent dies unless you've gone through it. I mean people say I know how it is my grandma died. That's different. When someone says their grandparents died, you'll probably believe it. But parents, no way. They just don't. I remember the feelings I had before mom died, they were, "I wish mom would just hurry up and die," it's hard waiting, hoping and knowing what's going to happen. I felt kind of guilty today for feeling that way. I'm not sure if I should feel that way or not. Sometimes, I can't believe mom is really gone, and sometimes I'll come home and shout out . . . mom . . . I hear dead silence. That hurts.

Sunday: My family went out to the cabin today. This is the first time since mother's death. It was hard. Something was missing. Her pep, her love, her caring . . . everything our family used to do . . . singing together by the fire in our yard. Mom would play the guitar. We didn't do that this time . . . something was missing.

Sunday (same day but later in the afternoon): I was baby-sitting today and a little boy asked me where my mother was buried. I know before I started this class two weeks ago, I probably would have started to cry, but instead I told him, without feeling any hurt. I think I'm dealing with it, or at least starting to.

During this first session we start to "terminate the group" by informing participants that the group is only seven sessions long and their attendance each week is important.

YPGSP–Session Two

*Activity: What Words Come to Your Mind When You
Hear the Word "Death?"*

At the beginning of this session each youngster is asked to write at least four words that come to mind when they hear the word "death." They can extend their list if they wish. Some youngsters struggle to find four words, while others record far more than requested. Once completed, each youngster is asked to share their words with the group, to select the one word that has the most significance to them, and talk about it. The larger the group, the quicker this exercise needs to be completed. Despite the fact that many of the words are similar, participants are still asked to tell the group why they selected their words.

Brainstorming Activity: What is Grief?

After the previous activity is completed, the concept of grief is discussed, along with how youngsters and their families have changed since the person(s) died. A flip chart or white board is used for this exercise, followed by a brainstorming process. This focuses on the variety of thoughts, feelings, physical symptoms, and behaviors that took place shortly after the death and may be continuing. After this is completed, participants identify areas in which they have been affected most. As an extension of this exercise, the youngsters are asked to identify the reactions of their parents and/or guardians and how these may be affecting them. During this process, they are reminded that bereavement should be seen as a period of crisis or life transition.

In his work, Gustafson emphasizes that grief is a complex experience consisting of the well-founded belief that a major loss has occurred, the desire that it had not occurred, and the feelings of pain and anguish over the impossibility of fulfilling that desire [30]. Attig states that grief needs to be seen as an **active** rather than a passive process. He suggests that:

> Conceiving the grieving process as active is preferable because (a) it is descriptively more accurate and encompasses more of the complexity of the experience of bereavement, (b) it is powerful in promoting self-understanding, and (c) it provides better direction for those who would help the bereaved [31, p. 39].

In the middle psychological task of mourning, bereaved youngsters must work their way through the emotional turmoil rather than avoiding, circumventing, or repressing it. *Middle-phase tasks* include accepting and reworking the loss and bearing the intense psychological pain involved. It is reassuring for youngsters to visualize on a flip chart and discuss their own experiences and those of other participants. As facilitators, one of our roles is to constantly summarize what we are hearing and try to connect the contributions of group members. We try to normalize the grief process as much as we can, indicating that each person will grieve differently for different periods and be influenced by cultural considerations and other factors. We remind the group that grief is an ongoing process, and throughout their lives there will be different "windows of grief" that may open, requiring each youngster to revisit the death and their relationship with the dead person. We continue to remind them that they are, as Attig states, participating in an active process by attending the group.

In their studies of attachment, Shuchter [26] as well as Glick, Weiss, and Parkes [33], found that bereaved individuals continue to show signs of internal attachment long after the death. They concluded that the ability to maintain an internal attachment to the person who has died may be a sign of healthy recovery, not of pathology. We believe that as facilitators it is our role to help the youngsters develop "a new relationship with the person who has died," help them hold onto the emotional connection with that person, and integrate the loss into their lives. Throughout the sessions, we also remind the group that grief is not "fixed" in a seven week YPGSP, but the program can provide an extremely healthy start to regaining control of their lives.

At the end of this session, youngsters are asked to prepare for the next session by bringing photos of the person(s) who died, and writing a short biography about this person on paper provided.

YPGSP–Session Three

Activity: Biography of The Person Who Died

A biography of each person who died is often read, just prior to the circulation of photographs to members of the group. One thirteen-year-old participant's biography of the person who died read as follows:

> My mom was born on January 12, 1942 in Minnesota. She had a brother who was eleven years younger than her and she had a mother and father. Some of her many hobbies were cooking, sewing, gardening, skiing, bike riding, and singing. She was always an optimist and all her friends say she changed their lives because after all her illnesses she still had a positive attitude. Her motto in life was "live each day to the fullest and let tomorrow take care of

itself." She had few dislikes but some of them were camping, cabbage, and complainers. Of all the people my mother knew, I have never known one who didn't like her. She was married in 1965. She then had two children.

In 1981, my mom found out she had a brain tumor. She then got spinal meningitis and was in a coma for three weeks. She then was blind, but overcame blindness in a few months. One year later she was diagnosed with breast cancer. She had a mastectomy. She had chemotherapy for about one year. Then she had uterine cancer and had her uterus removed. Then she was diagnosed with lung cancer. She tried to hold on, but she was so sick. She went around in a wheelchair and was in and out of the hospital for weeks. But she got worse. On September 21, 1984, my mom died. I think that everyone who knew her will never forget her.

Activity: Sharing Photos of Those Who Have Died

Each person shares photos of those who have died with the group and describes when the photos were taken and their significance.

Activity: List the Things You Liked About the
Person Who Died

Each group member is given a sheet of paper and asked to identify at least four things they liked about the person who died. The members usually find this easy to do and list many more than four items. We then discuss these "likes." Sometimes it is difficult for the participants to find positive things to say about the deceased person and this is also discussed. An example appears in the case below.

Case Example: Joe

Joe was ten years old when he entered the group, two months after his step-father had shot himself in the alley behind their home. Joe, his two sisters, and his mother all witnessed the death. Joe was not close to his step-father and would continually find negative things to say about him during the group. He could not find anything positive to recount when this activity began. By the conclusion of the activity, he was able to identify a few positive things that his step-father had done or said. This was helpful to Joe. When Joe could not find positive things to say, it was interesting to observe the other youngsters in the group who began to place more value on the "little things" in their own relationships with the person who died. These had not really been perceived as being important or meaningful prior to Joe's comments. Although Joe's relationship with his step-father was not what he had hoped it would be, he was not glad his step-father was dead. However, at this phase in Joe's life, it was easier for him not to have his step-father in the home.

Activity: List the Things You Disliked About the Person Who Died

Each group member, in a process similar to the previous activity, is given a sheet of paper and asked to identify at least four things they disliked about the person who died. The members find this much more difficult than listing four things they liked. We discuss these "dislikes" and why it is difficult to share them with others. Youngsters frequently grapple with the question of "loyalty to the dead."

From our perspective, this activity is important as it allows youngsters to openly discuss why it is acceptable and important to have a "total view" of the person who died and not just a view of a "perfect person." When participants are attending because of a baby's death, the "dislikes" may be harder to find until issues such as "more time was spent with the baby," or "everyone was asking about the baby and not about me," start to surface in the discussion.

Activity: "Quality of the Relationship"

Each group member is given more paper and asked to mark down the numbers one to five in sequence. They are then asked to write the name of the person who has died next to number one, followed by instructions to "list the four most important people in your entire world" next to the remaining four numbers, with only one name on each line. Some youngsters can do this quickly, while others find it hard to list even two people who are close or important. It is interesting that when they do their list some children exclude their parents' names.

At this stage of the group process, participants draw a circle and are asked to think of it as a pie. Using the five names they have listed they are then asked to cut the pie into pieces based on "how important these people are to you." After the pieces are cut and a percentage is given to each person, the facilitators discuss what makes people important in our lives and what happens to us when that piece representing the person who died is not there.

The various activities completed during this session continue to help the youngsters appreciate the changes death brings and examine the ***middle-phase tasks*** of experiencing the pain of grief. Exploring the relationship with the person who died brings with it memories of all the gratifying, ambivalent, and disappointing aspects of that relationship. This session also focuses on the ***late tasks*** which include reorganizing the children's sense of identity and reviewing the significant relationships that now exist in their lives.

As the session closes, participants are asked to bring a material possession that belonged to the person who died to the next session.

YPGSP–Session Four

Activity: Sharing and Discussing Material
Possessions of the Person Who Died

Material possessions that once belonged to the people who died are shared with group members. Participants discuss how they received their possessions and what makes them important. One of the group facilitators, at any given point in the "possession sharing time," interrupts the discussion and offers to buy for $5, $10, or even $20, the possession that is being shared. The facilitator tries to "buy" the item by stating, "It really isn't worth very much financially, so why not sell it and make some money on the deal." Some group members agree to the offer, take the money, and hand over the possession. **Soon after** these same people **always** say they want the possession back and will return the money. The facilitator says, "A deal is a deal," and argues about buying it "fair and square." This **always** produces great discussion about the "value" of a possession. The "relationship to the possession" and the meaning behind having something that belonged to the dead person is then discussed further.

Case Example: Joe

Joe, who was mentioned previously, brought his step-father's expensive leather cowboy hat to the group for the sharing of material possessions. When the facilitator pulled out a twenty dollar bill and offered to buy the hat, Joe jumped at the deal. His twelve-year-old sister who was also in the group hollered out, "Mom will kill you if she ever finds out you sold dad's hat!" Joe appeared not to care and was really excited to have the twenty dollars. The rest of the young people in the group wondered how he could sell the hat, but also saw that twenty dollars was a lot of money.

After a lively discussion, the group finished for the day, and Joe wanted to get his step-father's hat back in exchange for the twenty dollars. The facilitator, who had now been wearing the hat for the past hour, continued to give reasons why "a deal is a deal" and why Joe should have thought about its value when he first sold the hat. All the other group members were wondering what would happen if he did not get the hat back. Would his mother really kill him as his sister indicated previously? As the discussion ended, the facilitator returned the hat and Joe returned the twenty dollars.

Additional questions discussed during this session include:

1. How did the school personnel respond after the death? What should they have done, or could still do differently to support you?
2. How have your friends and other support systems helped, or have they abandoned you after the death?
3. What changes have happened at home since the person died? How have grandparents and other relatives dealt with the death?
4. What new roles or expectations now exist? (If other siblings are in the same group this question usually stimulates a lively discussion!)
5. Should your parent date or remarry, or enter into a new relationship?
6. Who would you live with if something happened to your parent(s), or if your surviving parent died?
7. Where does religion or spirituality fit into your grief process?
8. What do you think that developing a new relationship with the person who has died means?

YPGSP–Session Five

This session is intended to review what happened to the body after the death. It focuses on any involvement the youngsters had in decisions related to: organ or tissue donation; embalming, burying or cremating the body; preparing the body or helping with dressing or fixing the hair of the deceased; being part of the visitation or wake and the casket or urn selection; participating in the funeral or memorial service; assisting with poster displays, music, flowers, and arranging of objects for the service itself; being present at the cemetery for internment after the service; lowering of the casket at the cemetery; placing or throwing objects into the grave; and the time after the cemetery— did they go back to a special place for something to eat? Additional questions deal with whether or not the people that the youngsters wanted around them during those first few days were present or not and whether the church/synagogue provided them with what they had hoped would be "a meaningful service for the person who died?"

This session concludes with other questions or concerns regarding the funeral/memorial service and questions that participants may want answered the following week when the group goes on a field trip to a local funeral home.

YPGSP–Session Six

Activity: Funeral Home Visit

When we conduct home interviews and our initial assessments, we inform the adults and youngsters that we will be going on a "field trip" to a local funeral home. The purpose of this one-hour visit is to allow participants to question a funeral director and explore the funeral home at a time when they are not emotionally involved. They **do not** see a dead body. We invite parents to join the group on the tour if they wish.

In the first fifteen minutes after our arrival at the funeral home, we usually discuss the role and functions of funeral directors, and answer the youngsters' questions. We then go into a casket room where group members may look, touch, and ask questions about caskets that are not just for adults, but for infants and children as well. The youngsters are able to look inside the caskets with the mattresses lifted up, to hold different types of urns, and examine full-size vaults in which caskets may be placed. For many years, we would then visit the preparation room to see the embalming table and tank, and other equipment, but recently due to government safety regulations, this is no longer permitted. Instead, we use slides and discuss what takes place in the preparation room. The use of cosmetics is then demonstrated, and if we have time we close by inspecting the limousines and hearses. After the tour we return to the Medical Center for refreshments. We discuss the tour, and answer any additional questions raised by the children or their parents.

YPGSP–Session Seven

In this final session we focus on the *later tasks* of grief. These include how group members: develop "a new relationship" with the deceased, integrate the death into their daily lives, appreciate that the grief process is ongoing, and reorganize their lives including investing in new relationships.

To start the session, we discuss issues that the group may still need to explore along with various rituals that may be considered for anniversary dates, such as holidays or birthdays.

Case Example: Diane

Diane was ten years old when she entered the group. Almost one year before, her fifteen-year-old brother had shot himself. He did it in the house, while the entire family was at home. Diane was the first one to find her brother. When the planning for the visitation and funeral was in process, Diane was invited, but not encouraged, to participate in all of the events. In a group session, Diane shared how angry she was that her older sister, a high school student, had received all of the attention from their friends after the death and was allowed to deliver a short reading at the funeral. Diane thought that now she also wanted to do something, even though it was almost a year since her brother's death.

The approaching anniversary of the death helped her realize that she could still do something meaningful which would help her in her grief work. She told the group that she would write a short poem and read it at his grave when her family and friends went there on the anniversary.

In the group session that followed the anniversary, she talked openly about how she read her poem at the grave site and felt better for being treated as an equal to her sister.

During this session, we also ask participants to remember the concerns of their parents, guardians, or themselves seven weeks ago when they entered the group and discuss their opinions about how they have progressed.

This session allows the youngsters the opportunity to share what they have learned in the group and discuss how they can help others.

The following comments were made by four ten-year-old participants after they had completed the program:

- "It was like after the group I could start a new life."
- "Group helped me learn that other people had the same problems I did and that they grieve too."
- "I still miss my dad, but after sharing with other kids a weight has been lifted off me."
- "It's different now because now I can go away from home and not be scared."

We also explore what the participants liked and disliked about the group and what would they like us to discuss with their parents and/or guardians the following week at the parent meeting. We remind them of our need to protect their confidentiality and assure them that we are not going to tell their parents or guardians "all the secrets."

Various activities over the years have been used to close the program, at which time certificates are distributed as well as names, addresses, and telephone numbers of each group member and both facilitators.

YPGSP–Session Eight

During this session, parents and guardians are asked to introduce themselves and share information about their children who were enrolled in the group. We ask them to describe why they wanted their youngster to participate and the changes they have seen over the seven weeks. Since one of the YPGSP "rules" is to maintain confidentiality, we remind the parents that this will not be a "tell everything about the youngsters" meeting.

Parents, like their children, have been positive about meeting at the Medical Center and made the following comments about interacting with other parents as part of the program:

- "Was good as we had a chance to ask questions about unsettled questions."
- "Was good to hear other parents talk about their relationship with their kids."
- "Most beneficial as we found out the kids reactions and they were most enlightening."
- "It also helps the affected parent realize the problems are not only theirs, but many are shared by others. It also gives one ideas about how to cope with their problems."

CONCLUSION

The death of a loved one is a transition point that begins an ongoing grief process. When death affects a family member, close relative, or friend, we will be changed forever. Youngsters are no exception. It is unrealistic to expect youngsters to be unchanged by the death, and not to feel different. When nine- to thirteen-year-olds struggle with their changing bodies, thoughts and feelings, and encounter a death, everything can seem to be out of control and overwhelming. As facilitators, we know that we can help youngsters to cope with their grief in group settings and take advantage of the support of bereaved peers who are struggling with similar thoughts and feelings. At the same time, we are constantly reminding ourselves that youngsters are also part of a larger family unit. It is **not** our function to fulfill or take over the supportive role of parents or guardians, but rather to support them in every way possible.

It is our hope that this chapter will provide a map to guide you in your work with bereaved nine- to thirteen-year-olds. Through the years, we have learned much from those who are bereaved and have written this chapter from our perspective of what has and has not worked. We thank the youngsters and their families for the privilege of allowing us to enter their lives and share their stories.

REFERENCES

1. E. Furman, *A Child's Parent Dies: Studies in Childhood Bereavement*, Yale University Press, New Haven, Connecticut, 1974.
2. H. Finkelstein, The Long-term Effects of Early Parent Death: A Review, *Journal of Clinical Psychology, 44*, pp. 3-9, 1988.
3. B. Siegal, Helping Children Cope With Death, *American Family Physician, 31*, pp. 175-180, 1985.
4. J. Gyulay, The Forgotten Grievers, *American Journal of Nursing, 75*, pp. 1476-1479, 1975.
5. B. Zelauskas, Siblings: The Forgotten Grievers, *Comprehensive Pediatric Nursing, 5*, pp. 45-52, 1981.
6. D. McCown and C. Pratt, Impact of Sibling Death on Children's Behaviour, *Death Studies, 9*, pp. 323-335, 1985.
7. C. Norris-Shortle, P. Young, and M. Williams, Understanding Death and Grief for Children Three and Younger, *Social Work 38*:6, pp. 736-742, 1993.
8. E. Gelcer, Mourning Is a Family Affair, *Family Process, 22*, pp. 501-515, 1983.
9. G. Parker and V. Manicavasagar, Childhood Bereavement Circumstances Associated With Adult Depression, *British Journal of Medical Psychology, 59*, pp. 387-391, 1986.
10. S. Foster, Explaining Death To Children, *British Medical Journal, 282*, pp. 540-542, 1981.
11. D. Black and M. A. Urbanowitz, Family Intervention with Bereaved Children, *Journal of Child Psychology and Psychiatry, 28*, pp. 467-476, 1987.
12. N. Evans, Mourning as a Family Secret, *Journal of American Academy of Child Psychiatry, 15*, pp. 502-509, 1976.
13. H. Rosen, Prohibitions Against Mourning in Childhood Sibling Loss, *Omega, 15*, pp. 307-316, 1984.
14. P. A. Rosenthal, Short-term Family Therapy and Pathological Grief Resolution with Children and Adolescents, *Family Process, 19*, pp. 151-159, 1980.
15. A. Demi and C. Gilbert, Relationship of Parental Grief to Sibling Grief, *Archives of Psychiatric Nursing, 1*, pp. 385-391, 1987.
16. L. Samaniego, Parent-loss in Childhood: Ego Functions Death and Mourning, *Dissertation Abstracts International, 38*, 5593B (University Microfilms No. 78-01328), 1978.
17. S. Wolff, *Children Under Stress*, Allen Lane, London, 1969.
18. B. Wolfe, Grief and the Family Mobile, *Minnesota Sudden Infant Death Center Newsletter*, September 1992.

19. D. H. Sprenkle and F. P. Piercy, A Family Therapy Informed View of the Current State of the Family in the United States, *Family Relations, 41*, pp. 404-408, 1992.

20. National Conference of State Legislatures, *Family Policy: Recommendations for State Action*, Denver, Colorado, 1989.

21. M. Gnezda and S. Smith, *Child Care and Early Childhood Education Policy: A Legislator's Guide*, National Conference of State Legislatures, Denver, Colorado, 1989.

22. Children's Defense Fund, *FY 1989: An Analysis of our Nation's Investment in Children*, Washington, D.C., 1989.

23. J. Palombo, Parent Loss and Childhood Bereavement: Some Theoretical Considerations, *Clinical Social Work, 9*, pp. 3-33, 1981.

24. B. Wolfe, Children Grieve Too: A Four Year Hospital-Based Young Person's Grief Support Program, in *Bereavement: Helping the Survivors*, J. Morgan (ed.), King's College, London, Ontario, pp. 89-104, 1987.

25. M. W. Speece and S. B. Brent, The Acquisition of a Mature Understanding of Three Components of the Concept of Death, *Death Studies, 16*, pp. 211-229, 1992.

26. S. R. Shuchter, *Dimensions of Grief: Adjusting to the Death of a Spouse*, Jossey-Bass, San Francisco, 1986.

27. J. W. Worden, *Grief Counseling and Grief Therapy: A Handbook for the Mental Health Practitioner*, Springer, New York, 1982.

28. S. Fox, Helping Child Deal with Death Teaches Valuable Skills, *The Psychiatric Times*, pp. 10-11, August 1988.

29. J. E. Baker, M. A. Sedney, and E. Gross, Psychological Tasks for Bereaved Children, *American Journal of Orthopsychiatry, 61*, pp. 105-116, 1992.

30. D. Gustafson, Grief, *Nous, 23*, pp. 457-479, 1989.

31. T. Attig, The Importance of Conceiving of Grief as an Active Process, *Death Studies, 15*, pp. 385-393, 1991.

32. I. O. Glick, R. S. Weiss, and M. Parkes, *The First Year of Bereavement*, Wiley-Interscience, New York, 1974.

CHAPTER 12

Adolescent Grief Support Groups

Catherine Johnson

Adolescence, the transition from childhood to adulthood, is characterized as a time of increasing changes and focuses on the need for
independence [1-3]. According to Fleming and Adolf, adolescents ages
fourteen to seventeen years, "may perceive their residual dependence
on their parents as a threat to their desire for autonomy" [4, p. 103]. In
spite of this desire for autonomy, adolescents still want support. Peer
support decreases the need for teens to directly seek help from adults,
for "to do so suggests weaknesses that the adolescent wishes to deny"
[5, p. 162]. This need for independence emerges at a time when adolescents are confronted with a myriad of changes that require adaptation—socially, psychologically, cognitively, and vocationally. Unlike
normal developmental changes, however, the death of a parent creates
a separation that is sometimes sudden and unexpected, but always
final and irreversible [6].

Support groups for grieving teenagers are a way for young people to
seek care and nurturing without the threat of becoming as dependent
on adults as they were at an earlier age. There is neither the accompanying stigma of seeing a professional individually ("There must be
something wrong with me."), nor the dreaded fear of immature dependence on the family. As Corey and Corey have observed:

> . . . for most people adolescence is a difficult period, characterized
> by paradoxes: they strive for closeness, yet they also fear intimacy
> and often avoid it; . . . they are not given complete autonomy, yet
> they are often expected to act as though they were mature
> adults; . . . they are asked to face and accept reality, and at the
> same time they are tempted by many avenues of escape; they are
> exhorted to think of the future, yet they have strong urges to live

for the moment and enjoy life. With all these polarities it is easy to understand that adolescence is typically a turbulent and fast-moving time, one that can accentuate loneliness and isolation. Group experiences can be very useful in dealing with these feelings of isolation and making constructive choices for a satisfying life [7, p. 283].

Further, Gordon has noted that "nothing in previous experience has prepared the youth for the feelings of rage, loneliness, guilt, and disbelief that accompany a personal loss" [8, p. 22]. Support groups can create a forum in which teens learn to cope with those feelings. They can provide the secure relationships that Rando believes are necessary to facilitate successful adolescent mourning [9].

GUIDELINES FOR ESTABLISHING A GROUP

Although there are many deaths that may significantly impact on an adolescent, such as the death of a grandparent, cousin, or friend, my experience has led me to limit group membership to those who have encountered the death of a parent or sibling. Occasionally, following the death of a peer, I have initiated an additional group to deal specifically with that loss. Although correlations can be found in the grief experiences of the two groups, the nature of the two relationships is perceived differently and the pain of grief on separation is experienced differently. These differences can create major obstacles in the development of empathy and trust, vital components within a group.

A second guideline in establishing a group is associated with the recruitment of new members. As Fleming and Adolf pointed out:

Adolescents frequently exhibit great resistance both to professional intervention, for example individual, group, or family therapy, and to involvement with mutual or self-help groups . . . [4, p. 110].

How, then, can teenagers be encouraged to attend a support group? As a facilitator, I have found two options to be successful. The first involves a short visit with prospective members during which I relate how I received the referral (e.g., school counselor, funeral director, or others), describe the purpose and functioning of the group, and share the different topics that are discussed in the group. I also provide an opportunity for them to share their personal story, including as much or as little as is comfortable. Without asking for a definite commitment, I share information regarding the day and time of the next meeting and invite the teen to attend on a trial basis. Just prior to the meeting, I send a reminder note of welcome. The majority of young people respond favorably and do attend.

It is important to remember that just as groups are not suitable for all adults, neither are they suitable for all adolescents. For some, the pain is too fresh and is only augmented by listening to the pain of others. Some people, because of their personality or cultural conditioning, are very private and would never consider speaking in a group. Therefore, being sensitive to and respecting the needs of individuals is important so that they do not feel pressured.

The second option is to have group members invite their peers. It is not unusual for a friend or an acquaintance to know of the death of a peer's parent or sibling when many adults, including teachers and school counselors, do not. The advantage of teens inviting one another is that they can allay many fears that elude the notice of adults ("No, we don't just sit around and cry all the time . . ."). They can elaborate on the personal benefits experienced as a result of group attendance. Such testimonials can be powerful in attracting shy, reluctant, or fiercely independent teens. Even those who do not join a group can offer testimonials, as evidenced by the following letter received from a seventeen-year-old girl:

> When my father died a year ago, I was invited to go to a support group. The whole idea made me uneasy and I dismissed it immediately, maybe because if I went it would be acknowledging the fact of my dad's death. There's also the social taboo on crying in public, especially in front of strangers. I felt very uncomfortable with the whole idea.
>
> So I guess I just went along the next few months not dealing with anything. I didn't want to act upset around my friends because I thought they wouldn't know how to deal with it. But I wasn't thinking about myself and dealing with my problems. My mom's friends and my relatives all told me I had to be strong for my mom. I really resent that now because I had guilt feelings if I broke down in front of my family. But I didn't have anyone else to break down in front of, so I kept everything to myself. This is where the support group would have been really helpful.
>
> Later, most people thought I was over my grief, but the truth was, I hadn't even begun. I had been too busy covering everything up. By then it was more painful to work through my grief (or at least start) because I also had to work through the walls I'd built up to keep all my feelings out.
>
> Still, it doesn't seem real to me now. Whenever I get a chance to talk about it, I usually seem to talk forever—it's very therapeutic. If I had gone to the support group, I'm sure I would be in much better shape now.

A final suggestion for the initial formation of a teen group is to eliminate any arbitrary, pre-conceived number of members necessary to have a group. A few participants, especially at first, may not be an indication of failure or lack of need. If attending the group is a positive experience, those first two or three teens may become the most vocal advertisement for additional members.

GUIDELINES FOR CONDUCTING A GROUP

Teenagers tend to feel bombarded when initially handed a list of rules and expectations. Therefore, I keep formal rules to a minimum and discuss these when new members enter the group.

I consider two guidelines to be basic and essential: confidentiality and voluntary participation. Assurance of confidentiality is paramount to adolescents who value privacy and are seeking independence. Further, because peer relationships are so important, teens need reassurance that reputations outside the group will not be marred by gossip generated from information shared within the group. As a facilitator, however, it is important to be honest at the outset regarding the legal limits of confidentiality—in our state this includes issues of abuse and self-harm. Therefore, if there is a need to disclose information, group members will not feel deceived or betrayed.

The second guideline, voluntary participation, removes the pressure to share when the individual may not be ready. It reassures members that their level of involvement in the group is within their control. Thus, this guideline validates the need for participants to recognize their own needs and to take care of themselves. Sometimes this means talking and asking questions; at times it means listening and reinforcing nonverbally; from time to time it means quietly letting the tears flow; and at other times it means simply sitting quietly until an unexpected, intense pain subsides.

Any additional rules and guidelines can be addressed informally as they emerge. Most will probably be simple reminders about courtesy, such as the use of appropriate language or not monopolizing the discussion.

COMMON ISSUES FOR BEREAVED ADOLESCENTS

The ultimate goal of the adolescent grief support group is to provide an appropriate format and safe environment in which to work through the six major mourning processes described by Rando. These include:

1) recognizing the loss; 2) reacting to the separation; 3) recollection; 4) relinquishing old attachments; 5) readjusting; and 6) reinvesting [10, pp. 43-60]. In addition to these processes, there are issues specific to adolescent development that frequently need to be addressed.

Bereaved adolescents often lack the social support given to younger children or adults. According to Adams and Deveau:

> Along with the expectation that behavior will be totally rational, is the assumption that adolescents are often capable of independent thought and action and less amenable to adult assistance and guidance. Such independence means that adolescents are expected to require less emotional support than younger children. Since loss and grief are viewed as being very personal, leaving adolescents on their own to manage their thoughts and feelings fits in with the belief that their privacy should be respected and no one should intrude [11, p. 280].

Thus, acquiring needed support and understanding is a major issue dealt with in teen groups. Not only is there a deficit of support from adults, there is also a void in support from friends. Frequently, the bereaved adolescent's friends are inexperienced and feel vulnerable ("How would I feel if it were MY mother who died?"). As a result, they find it difficult to be supportive in a way that is needed by the grieving teen. Further, like adults, many friends simply do not know what to say, so they choose to say and do nothing.

Augmenting this issue is the need (or perceived need) to be the strong one in the family. As noted by Adams and Deveau, "adolescent(s) . . . may be expected to comfort and care for their parents and place everyone else's needs before their own" [11, p. 280]. Consequently, a major issue becomes the validation of teens' needs for support and legitimization of the right to have those needs met.

School, too, can be a major source of pressure for bereaved adolescents. Accustomed to feeling support from classmates and friends, school now becomes emotionally barren. Moreover, interactions with teachers can be fraught with tension. On the one hand, grieving teens fear being singled out as being different, and, on the other hand, they are angry that exceptions cannot be made on deadlines for assignments since they are unable to concentrate in class. The lessons that at one time may have been interesting, now seem irrelevant. Yet, students recognize the need to function, at least minimally, to avoid spending more than the required number of years in high school—the goal is to at least pass all courses. Therefore, making it through the emotionally difficult class hour, surviving the school day, and improving communication with teachers are frequent topics of discussion within the safety of the support group setting.

Another concern of adolescents emerges from unrealistic role expectations of others and the pressure to conform to society's ideal of wellness. According to Fleming and Adolf, much of the literature and advice directed to mourners "cruelly encourage(s) unrealistic expectations of early recovery from the very normal pain of grief" [4, p. 113]. They go on to note, "The bereaved need support and encouragement in their struggle to recognize and curtail the disruptive influence of existing 'shoulds'" [4, p. 113]. The group, then, can become a forum to gather more accurate information and develop resistance to others' expectations.

Finally, bereaved adolescents struggle with major philosophical issues as a result of the death. As Balk has observed:

> The bereaved teenager is faced with perplexities that confound all reflecting adults. Questions about the nature of life and death, about good and evil, and about the meaning of life become personal; the death . . . has shattered trust in a benign, innocent universe [12, p. 14].

Unanswered and unanswerable questions abound: "Why did my sister have to die?" "Exactly where is my father?" "Is my mother excluded from heaven because she committed suicide?"

Several of these issues that confront grieving adolescents can be noted in the following case examples:

> Carol entered the group at age fifteen, four months after the death of her father. He had died three days after a job-related accident. Over the course of the next eight months, the majority of Carol's concerns centered around school and family. Although she worked hard to maintain good grades, she had one teacher who particularly lacked either understanding or compassion, and allowed no "excuses" for lapses of attention in class. At home, Carol was coping with her mother's new social life. Although understanding her mother's need for adult companionship, she felt somewhat neglected as she and her sister were left to themselves. Carol said that she had not cried at her father's funeral, so she was especially upset six months later when she cried at the death of her father's dog.
>
> Naturally shy, Carol was usually soft-spoken, hesitant, and brief during group interactions. A major turning point came for her

after another group member shared his reluctance to touch his father's dead body in the casket. At that point, Carol tearfully shared her greatest guilt—her refusal to see her father in the hospital during the last three days of his life. She now regretted her fear of seeing him hooked to tubes and machines and worried that he died thinking that she did not love him.

Greg, age sixteen, entered the group several months after the sudden death of his thirteen-year-old sister. An autopsy had revealed an undiagnosed cancerous tumor as the ultimate cause of death, although the technical terminology on the death certificate was confusing to Greg. All that most people knew was that his sister collapsed and died at school one day. The cause of death triggered memories of Greg's own bout with cancer when he was thirteen. Added to this stress, ten months after his sister's death, his mother was hospitalized for recurring breast cancer. At this point Greg experienced declining grades in school as well as deteriorating behavior which led to disciplinary action.

Greg was now the only child living at home. His father was preoccupied coping with his own grief as well as his wife's health problems. Much of Greg's out-of-school time was spent at a job. The support group became a forum for Greg to deal with his anger, fear, and confusion and to reconcile what had happened to his sister, as well as to face the vulnerable state of his mother's health.

Tina, age seventeen, joined the group three years after her father's sudden, accidental death. Within a year of the death her mother had remarried and the family moved to another state 1200 miles away. That move separated Tina from her grandparents, extended family, friends, familiar neighborhood, and school. She was thrust into a new environment with a stepfather she resented and step-siblings she disliked. Although she prospered in her new school, Tina's home situation deteriorated and her mother divorced the new family. Tina, her mother, and sister chose to stay in the new home since the girls were now attached to new friends and school. As her home life became more tranquil and as high school graduation approached, grief issues surfaced for Tina, renewing the pain of not having the father who was such a constant source of love and fun in her life. At this point, her grades plummeted and she displayed disciplinary problems at school. It was particularly difficult for Tina to feel supported in her journey through grief outside of the support group, for none of her current friends had known her father and most assumed that the death had occurred so long ago that she was surely over it by now.

ISSUES AND CHALLENGES FOR THE
GROUP FACILITATOR

In ideal circumstances, it would be advantageous to have separate teen support groups with membership based on cause of death (cancer, suicide, violence), relationship (grandparent, sibling, parent), or length of time since the death (1 to 12 months, 1 to 3 years, more than 3 years). Most facilitators do not have the luxury of such specialized groups for a variety of reasons. The majority of groups are diverse, which presents challenges for the facilitator. The issues being dealt with by someone whose father committed suicide are very different from those whose brother was a victim of a drunk driver. Thus, the facilitator needs to make an effort to engage all members and create the links between the diverse experiences.

There are two criteria in which the facilitator may exert more control in screening the teens for group membership: age and sex. When possible, I encourage the use of separate groups for younger and older teens. If the groups take place in the school setting, this occurs naturally by grade: grades seven to nine and grades ten to twelve. When teens, aged thirteen to eighteen, are placed together in the same group, the older teens (15 to 18 years) have a difficult time relating to those in the group who are less mature (13 to 14 years). Although grief experiences are similar, older teens perceive their maturity as a barrier. This prevents them from being able to identify with younger teens. Additionally, as Fleming and Adolf described, the developmental tasks and conflicts experienced by younger teens are very different than those encountered by older teens. This makes the issues of one group irrelevant for the other [4].

The gender of group members can also be a challenge for a facilitator. Engaging male members of a group is much easier when there are females in the group. As Staudacher observed:

> As compared to their female counterparts, boys . . . have more difficulty expressing sadness and longing because they are likely to associate yearning for a parent's presence with unmasculine behavior [13, p. 51].

When there are only male bereaved teens in the group, sharing feelings honestly is a much more difficult task. As one adolescent male said, "You know, it's a guy thing." The need to be seen by others as a strong male who is in control supersedes the need to unburden himself of his grief.

On the other hand, when there are females in the group who volunteer their feelings readily, this provides not only positive role modeling, but also the ideal confidant, one who is sympathetic and understanding. This is not to say that an all-male adolescent grief support group is impossible, for much depends on the personalities of the individuals in the group. However, the dynamics of a group with both sexes makes the job of facilitating much easier. The first time a female cries without embarrassment or apology, or the first time a male brashly brings up a "forbidden" topic, opportunities for growth for all members are created. Further, including both sexes creates a richer environment for feedback in a number of activities, such as role playing or brainstorming.

REWARDS AND MAJOR LESSONS

As a facilitator of adolescent grief support groups I have learned to disbelieve the "I'm together" facade that teens want others to see, and I have learned to expect the unexpected. Most of all, I have learned to trust a powerful process that I can neither see clearly nor understand totally. Sometimes, when I thought that there was no progress, others (parents, teachers) noticed great strides by an individual teen. More importantly, the teen believed that participation in the group was tremendously helpful.

One positive outcome of such groups has been noted by Gray who found that 76 percent of those who had participated in a peer support group, compared to 8 percent who did not participate in peer support groups, reported that peers understood them after their loss [14]. Given the importance of peers to this age group, this is no small victory.

Finally, though life crises can threaten adolescents' well-being, they can also provide opportunities for growth [15, 16]. With a sensitive, caring, and skilled facilitator, support groups can create opportunities for healing and growth. As one group member said, "Everyday I try to think of new ways to make the pain and anger go away, but they don't. Talking about it helps." According to another, "Everyone needs to find their own way to heal." Support groups can create the environment for young people to find those ways. Allen has observed:

> They (the adolescents) learn that they have strengths that they were not aware of having. As they discuss in group difficult individual situations, they learn coping skills and discover untapped strengths within themselves. They experience personal growth and healthy maturity [17, p. 39].

In the words of another teen, "I no longer think that the deaths ruined my life; instead, I think they've made me grow up—I've learned a lot from them."

CHALLENGES FOR RESEARCH

Obviously, I am a believer in support groups for bereaved adolescents and my experiences reinforce that commitment. However, there is no concrete support in the professional literature. Fleming and Adolf regard mutual help groups for bereaved adolescents as "an important option for assistance, though one whose effectiveness has not yet been demonstrated" [4, p. 111]. In a review of literature on bereavement follow-up, Osterweiss concluded that very little is actually known [18]. Yet, having a firm foundation in research would not only legitimize the work of current teen group facilitators, but also reassure them that their efforts will indeed augment healing for grieving young people. We may already know that in our hearts, but having empirical validation is valuable.

Until research findings are available, however, it is affirming to have testimonials from former members of adolescent support groups, such as the following experience related by Sara, now age twenty:

> I entered the group about six months after my brother died and I hadn't been able to find anyone in that time who knew my pain. As I sat in the group, everyone introduced themselves and told how their parent or sibling had died. I was so scared about telling my brother's story and tried to figure out beforehand what I would say. When my turn came, I began from the day before he died and retold the events that took place up to his traumatic death. The story that I told that night was not what I had rehearsed in my head. However, it was exactly the way I wanted it told. A tremendous burden was taken from me that night as I spoke. I had never been asked, nor told anyone for that matter, how he had died. Everyone I knew and everyone in my town had read their version of it in the newspapers or saw it on television. Those versions failed to include the guilt I felt for not being there, and my last yelling words to him. Those versions did not include how it felt to be on the beach with police, fireboats, helicopters, and flares without any answers.
>
> What helped me the most in the group was being able to share over and over, my feelings and thoughts. To be able to talk about whatever was on my mind with "permission" was incredible. Every time that I spoke about my brother there was an emotional and physical burden lifted. I would hear myself say things that would qualify why I was feeling a certain way. I knew that there was a real bond between the people in the group. We were all unfortunate

to know a kind of pain that unless you've lost someone that close, you would not know.

How fortunate we are as caregivers and support group facilitators to be in a position to generate this healing environment for bereaved adolescents.

REFERENCES

1. E. H. Erikson, *Childhood and Society*, W. W. Norton & Co., Inc., New York, 1950.
2. S. M. Valente and J. R. Sellers, Helping Adolescent Survivors of Suicide, in *Adolescence and Death*, C. Corr and J. McNeil (eds.), Springer Publishing Company, New York, 1986.
3. A. Wolfelt, Bereavement and Children, *Bereavement Magazine*, pp. 34-35, February 1990.
4. S. J. Fleming and R. Adolf, Helping Bereaved Adolescents: Needs and Responses, in *Adolescence and Death*, C. Corr and J. McNeil (eds.), Springer Publishing Company, New York, 1986.
5. B. Raphael, *The Anatomy of Bereavement*, Basic Books, Inc., New York, 1983.
6. P. A. Murphy, Parental Death in Childhood and Loneliness in Young Adults, *Omega*, *17*:3, pp. 219-228, 1986-87.
7. M. S. Corey and G. Corey, *Groups, Process and Practice*, Brooks/Cole Publishing Company, Monterey, California, 1987.
8. A. K. Gordon, The Tattered Cloak of Immortality, in *Adolescence and Death*, C. Corr and J. McNeil (eds.), Springer Publishing Company, New York, 1986.
9. T. A. Rando, *Grief, Dying and Death: Clinical Interventions for Caregivers*, Research Press, Champaign, Illinois, 1984.
10. T. A. Rando, *Treatment of Complicated Mourning*, Research Press, Champaign, Illinois, 1993.
11. D. W. Adams and E. J. Deveau, When a Brother or Sister Is Dying of Cancer: The Vulnerability of the Adolescent Sibling, *Death Studies*, *11*, pp. 279-295, 1987.
12. D. E. Balk, Sibling Death, Adolescent Bereavement, and Religion, *Death Studies*, *15*, pp. 1-20, 1991.
13. C. Staudacher, *Men and Grief: A Guide for Surviving the Death of a Loved One*, New Harbinger Publications, Inc., Oakland, California, 1991.
14. R. E. Gray, The Role of School Counselors with Bereaved Teenagers: With and Without Peer Support Groups, *School Counselor*, *35*, pp. 185-193, 1988.
15. R. J. Moos, *Coping with Life Crises: An Integrated Approach*, Plenum Press, New York, 1986.

16. B. Baldwin, A Paradigm for the Classification of Emotional Crisis: Implications for Crisis Intervention, *American Journal of Orthopsychiatry*, *48*, pp. 538-551, 1978.
17. L. Allen, Working with Bereaved Teenagers, in *The Dying and Bereaved Teenager*, J. Morgan (ed.), The Charles Press, Philadelphia, 1990.
18. M. Osterweiss, Perceptions Not Yet Matched by Research, *Journal of Palliative Care*, *4*, pp. 78-80, 1988.

About the Editors

David W. Adams, M.S.W., C.S.W. is a Professor, Department of Psychiatry, Faculty of Health Sciences, McMaster University and Executive Director, Greater Hamilton Employee Assistance Consortium. Over the past twenty-five years in his affiliation with Chedoke-McMaster Hospitals and McMaster University, he has concentrated much of clinical social work practice and teaching on life-threatening illness, dying, death and bereavement in childhood, and the impact on children and families. He is the author of *Childhood Malignancy: The Psychosocial Care of the Child and His Family* and *Parents of Children with Cancer Speak Out: Needs, Problems, and Sources of Help*. David is co-author with Ellie Deveau of *Coping with Childhood Cancer: Where Do We Go From Here?* He is a charter member of the board and Chair, Professional Advisors of the Candlelighters Childhood Cancer Foundation Canada, Chair of the International Work Group on Death, Dying and Bereavement and past Chair of the Psychosocial Services Committee of the Pediatric Oncology Group of Ontario. David is a certified death educator and grief counselor. He has contributed numerous chapters and articles and is internationally known as a speaker, program consultant, and workshop facilitator.

Eleanor (Ellie) J. Deveau, R.N., B.Sc.N. is coordinator of program evaluation in the Educational Center for Aging and Health, Faculty of Health Sciences, McMaster University, Hamilton, Ontario, Canada. She is bereavement consultant and advisor to Friends in Grief, Inc., Hamilton, Ontario and a founding member of their board of directors. Ellie is a certified death educator through the Association of Death Education and Counseling (USA) and a member of the International Work Group on Death, Dying and Bereavement. Many years of experience as a nurse practitioner in the pediatric hematology/oncology program at McMaster University Medical Center led to her co-authorship of the award-winning book, *Coping with Childhood Cancer: Where Do We Go From Here?* Ellie is a speaker and workshop facilitator and has contributed chapters and articles which focus on issues relating to children and adolescents' understanding of death, the impact of life-threatening illness and palliative care on children, siblings and parents, the pattern of grief in children and adolescents, and child and adult bereavement.

Contributors

THOMAS W. ATTIG, Ph.D., Professor of Philosophy, Bowling Green State University; President, Association for Death Education and Counseling, Bowling Green, Ohio, United States.

DAVID E. BALK, Ph.D., Associate Professor, Human Development and Family Studies, Kansas State University, Manhattan, Kansas, United States.

HEATHER CHARBONNEAU, M.S.W., C.S.W., Social Worker, Social Services Division, Regional Municipality of Waterloo; Grief Counsellor and Consultant, Waterloo, Ontario, Canada.

BETTY DAVIES, R.N., Ph.D., Professor, School of Nursing, University of British Columbia; Investigator, Research Division, British Columbia's Children's Hospital; Board of Directors, Canuck Place: A Hospice for Children, Vancouver, British Columbia, Canada.

SANDRA L. ELDER, B.A., B.Ed., M.Ed., Ph.D., Registered Grief Counsellor, Association for Death Education and Counseling; Program Coordinator, Living and Learning Through Loss, Victoria, British Columbia, Canada.

NANCY S. HOGAN, R.N., Ph.D., Associate Professor, School of Nursing, University of Miami, Miami, Florida, United States.

CATHERINE JOHNSON, B.A., M.A., Bereavement Services Coordinator, Weeks' Funeral Homes, Buckley, Washington, United States.

RUTH ROTHBART MAYER, M.S.W., C.S.W., Director, Mayer-Avedon Women's Support Group, New York, New York, United States.

MARGARET M. METZGAR, M.A., C.M.H.C., Psychotherapist and Certified Mental Health Counselor, Transitional Loss Center, Seattle, Washington, United States.

MARY ANDERSON MILLER, B.A., M.S.W., Director, Bereavement Program, Growth Opportunity Center, Huntingdon Valley, Pennsylvania, United States.

EILEEN ORMOND, M.A., Manager and Clinical Consultant, Grief Support Program, Notre Dame of St. Agatha, Children's Treatment Center, St. Agatha, Ontario, Canada.

THERESE A. RANDO, Ph.D., Clinical Director, Therese A. Rando Associates, Ltd.; Director, Institute for the Study and Treatment of Loss, Warwick, Rhode Island, United States.

LINDA M. SENTA, M.S.W., L.I.C.S.W., Medical Social Worker, St. Mary's Medical Center, Duluth, Minnesota, United States.

BEN S. WOLFE, M.Ed., L.I.C.S.W., Program Director, Therapist, Educator, and Consultant, St. Mary's Grief Support Center, St. Mary's Medical Center, Duluth, Minnesota, United States.

BARBARA C. ZICK, R.N., B.A., M.A., C.M.H.C., Psychotherapist and Group Support Leader, Redmond, Washington, United States.

Index

A

Abandonment
  bereaved adolescent's feelings of,
    48-49, 57, 58, 140
  bereaved child's feelings of, 48-49,
    57, 58, 140, 187, 188, 191, 222
  by God, 64, 68
Abuse (*see also* Abused/Battered
    adolescent and child; Alcohol
    and drug abuse; Domestic
    violence; Sexuality/Sexual
    activity)
  of authority and power, 53
Abused/Battered adolescent and
    child, 115, 153-164 (*see also*
    Domestic violence; Support
    group)
  behavior, 158, 164
  confusion, 158, 159, 161
  death of abusive parent, 139, 141
  feelings, 156-157, 159, 160, 161,
    162, 163-164
  impact of domestic violence on,
    156-161, 164
  lack of control, 156, 158
  losses, 3, 153, 157, 158, 160, 164
  physical problems, 158
  school problems, 158, 159, 160
  self-esteem, 55, 158, 159
  trust, 156, 159
Accidental death (*see* Death)
Adaptation (*see* Coping)

Adolescence/Adolescent (*see also*
    Bereaved adolescent; Support
    group; Suicide)
  aggressive/violent behavior, 139,
    147, 206
  alcohol and drug abuse, 125, 130,
    139, 146, 148, 206
  autonomy/independence, 1, 54, 57,
    58, 138, 139, 229, 232, 233
  choices, 1, 46, 48, 53, 58, 109, 178,
    213, 230
  delinquency/truancy, 139, 206
  dependency issues, 48, 53-55,
    229
  developmental tasks/phases, 1, 45,
    57, 66, 72-74, 101, 103, 107,
    108, 117, 110, 138, 139, 141,
    206, 214, 229, 230, 233, 236,
    237
  developmental transitions, 1, 101,
    102, 110, 229
  dying, 62
  risk-taking behavior, 148, 159
  understanding of death, 62,
    141-142
Adult (*see* Anticipatory grief;
    Bereaved family/family
    member; Bereavement; Parent;
    Family)
Advocacy, 16, 20, 36, 164, 204
Affective processes (*see* Anticipatory
    grief)
Afterlife, 46, 69, 138